More Advance Praise for *Better Results*

This book has the potential to change the field of psychotherapy in remarkable ways. The authors give us the tools needed to take the guesswork out of the complexity of mind care by providing a path to professional excellence that is both orderly and governed by a clear set of principles.

—*Dan Short, PhD, lead author of* Hope and Resiliency

In this empirically sound and remarkably engaging work, Miller, Hubble, and Chow remind us that psychotherapy is a cocreative process that is more effective when corrective feedback, individualized treatment strategies, and continuous refinement are applied. This work gives hope to those who have felt confined and limited by rigid adherence to theories and techniques and seek to move beyond outdated clinical orthodoxies. I highly recommend this book to all who practice the art and science of psychotherapy.

—*Paul J. Leslie, EdD, author of* The Art of Creating a Magical Session: Key Elements for Transformative Psychotherapy

Better Results provides clinicians practice-based guidance to help clients achieve the results they are hoping for in counseling and therapy. It also provides tangible strategies for improving one's own practice.

—*Robbie Babins-Wagner, PhD, RCSW, Chief Executive Officer, Calgary Counselling Centre, and Adjunct Professor & Sessional Instructor, Faculty of Social Work, University of Calgary, Calgary, Alberta, Canada*

BETTER RESULTS

BETTER RESULTS

Using Deliberate Practice to Improve Therapeutic Effectiveness

SCOTT D. MILLER   MARK A. HUBBLE

DARYL CHOW

 AMERICAN PSYCHOLOGICAL ASSOCIATION

Published by
American Psychological Association
750 First Street, NE
Washington, DC 20002
https://www.apa.org

Order Department
https://www.apa.org/pubs/books
order@apa.org

In the U.K., Europe, Africa, and the Middle East, copies may be ordered from Eurospan
https://www.eurospanbookstore.com/apa
info@eurospangroup.com

Typeset in Meridien and Ortodoxa by Circle Graphics, Inc., Reisterstown, MD

Printer: Sheridan Books, Chelsea, MI
Cover Designer: Blake Logan, New York, NY

Library of Congress Cataloging-in-Publication Data

Names: Miller, Scott D., author. | Hubble, Mark A., 1951- author. |
 Chow, Daryl, author. | American Psychological Association, issuing body.
Title: Better results : using deliberate practice to improve therapeutic effectiveness /
 by Scott D. Miller, Mark A. Hubble, and Daryl Chow.
Description: Washington, DC : American Psychological Association, [2020] |
 Includes bibliographical references and index.
Identifiers: LCCN 2019053164 (print) | LCCN 2019053165 (ebook) |
 ISBN 9781433831904 (paperback) | ISBN 9781433833441 (ebook)
Subjects: LCSH: Psychotherapy—Evaluation.
Classification: LCC RC480.5 M5355 2020 (print) | LCC RC480.5 (ebook) |
 DDC 616.89/14—dc23
LC record available at https://lccn.loc.gov/2019053164
LC ebook record available at https://lccn.loc.gov/2019053165

http://dx.doi.org/10.1037/0000191-000

Printed in the United States of America

10 9 8 7 6 5 4 3 2

The principle goal of education . . . should be creating [people] who are capable of doing new things, not simply repeating what other generations have done.

—JEAN PIAGET (DUCKWORTH, 1964, p. 499)

CONTENTS

FOREWORD

Most of us want to be actively engaged in our work and lives. Psychotherapists are uniquely prepared to help when psychological difficulties and personal issues interfere with that objective. All such practitioners undergo extensive training and engage in continuous professional development to maximize their ability to deliver the requisite expertise. *How* psychotherapists develop and *what* can they do to improve are the subjects of this book. Although specific to psychotherapy, the research and training methods described apply across many helping professions—medicine, counseling, and teaching—enabling those who use them to achieve *Better Results*.

Some of the material presented in this volume is based on research my colleagues and I conducted over the past 4 decades. We were particularly interested in understanding how elite musicians, chess masters, and Olympic-level athletes did what they did, reaching world-class performance levels and managing to continuously improve. For me, interest in the subject of expertise and expert performance started early. In high school, I wanted to become a nuclear physicist to solve the energy problems of the future. To accomplish my objective, I studied the biographies of famous scientists, thinking that if I learned what they did, it might help me succeed.

From my extensive reading, I concluded a key to success was finding a *Big Question*—one the answer to which would make a big difference. I also decided that whatever subject I chose to pursue, it would have to be something I was genuinely interested in; otherwise, it would not be possible to sustain the deep interest necessary to last a lifetime. Motivation, I came to understand, was critical as many well-known scientists encountered challenges, roadblocks, and long periods of failure before achieving success. This latter recognition ultimately caused me to abandon training as a nuclear physicist and pursue psychology instead.

Not surprisingly, perhaps, my initial research focused on understanding how people think when solving problems. I developed a scientific protocol, a method known as *think aloud,* whereby, as the name implies, subjects shared their thoughts openly as they engaged in different tasks. While my colleagues and I started with college students, in time, we turned our attention to expert performers. We were especially interested in highly motivated individuals— those who wanted to go beyond their current level of performance in their domain of expertise. Along the way, there have been starts and stops, reviews and revisions. At the same time, our understanding of the development of expertise and achievement of expert performance has increased dramatically (Ericsson, Hoffman, Kozbelt, & Williams, 2018).

In 2010, I was contacted by Scott Miller, who was organizing an international conference for psychotherapists. He wondered if I'd be willing to talk about how our research on chess masters, elite athletes, and outstanding musicians might apply to the professional development of psychotherapists. I agreed, knowing at that point that no direct research, and only one article written by him (Miller, Hubble, & Duncan, 2007), had been published on the subject in his field. When we met at the conference, I was immediately struck by his and the attendees' enthusiasm. *This was a group that wanted to improve.* I was also impressed by their willingness to do the hard work and research needed to translate our findings for psychotherapy.

Scott had already developed an empirically sound method for measuring therapists' clinical work (Miller, Duncan, Sorrell, & Brown, 2005). As seen in the pages of this volume, having valid and reliable tools for assessing performance is a critical first step in improving performance. Together with Daryl Chow, Scott was beginning to study clinicians with superior outcomes essential for understanding the specific variables associated with better results in any given performance domain. Everyone I met was deeply committed to helping students and experienced professionals alike improve their outcomes.

Ten years on, their work continues. Reading *Better Results,* I was amazed by the progress. You can feel the excitement in these pages. While reading, I was frequently reminded of the passion and sense of adventure I've experienced in my own research career.

One of the absolute high points, for example, occurred when I worked as a postdoctoral fellow with two famous cognitive psychologists, Herbert Simon and Bill Chase, at Carnegie Mellon University. The year was 1978. I was in San Antonio, Texas, with Bill for the annual meeting of the Psychonomic Society. He was at the front of the room, presenting findings of our research on training memory performance. At the time, the capacity of short-term memory was believed fixed. Presented with one digit at a time, it appeared most adults topped out at around seven random digits. The world record performance on this task was held by a mathematics professor who was able to repeat back 18 digits correctly.

Bill showed a graph of one of the participants in our research, a college student named Steve Faloon.[1] In the first trial, Steve, or SF as he was known in our published article in the prestigious journal *Science* (Ericsson, Chase, & Faloon, 1980), performed like most adults, recalling seven digits. Over a series of testing sessions, however, his performance improved, surpassing not only the assumed limit but the world record. As recounted in my coauthored book *Peak: Secrets From the New Science of Expertise* (Ericsson & Pool, 2016), with a few hundred hours of training, Steve was eventually able to recall sequences of more than 80 randomly presented digits! Other subjects followed, with one eventually managing to recall over 100 digits.

Most memorable to me were the surprise and excitement in the audience. To be sure, some doubted the findings. Others suggested we'd merely lucked out, recruiting a naturally "gifted" person. A few accepted the results but questioned their significance. I remember one well-known cognitive scientist asking, "Who cares about improving one's memory for random digits?"

Still, many were and have remained interested, in particular, about the changes in SF's thought processes that accompanied his progress. The most general insight emerging from this research was that ability could be significantly extended by presenting tasks just beyond an individual's performance level, giving immediate feedback, and then allowing time to reflect and problem solve before proceeding with further attempts to improve. In time, we would call this process *purposeful practice.* When a teacher and coach agreed to monitor and guide each individual trainee to engage in particular training tasks, the improvements were greater and more predictable. This type of training we termed *deliberate practice.*

Over the years, I've met people who think our research shows anyone can achieve anything. Even some researchers appear to believe this is our perspective (cf. Macnamara, Hambrick, & Oswald, 2014). Nothing could be further from the truth. What we actually found is scientific evidence about how *some* achieve amazing results: a map, so to speak, of the types of training activities and encoding (memory) methods that others can follow to obtain similar, specific exceptional performances. Of note is the word *specific* in the previous sentence: One critical finding from our studies is that expertise is domain specific. Participants in our digit span studies, for example, did not exhibit superior memories on other, seemingly related tasks, such as recalling letters and geometric symbols. Nonetheless, the general principle remains true: To improve, memory processes, mental representations, and expanded working memory have to be developed for *each* particular skill domain.

Decades later, numerous studies conducted by different researchers document that engagement in extended practice tailored to the specific task and individual learner can lead to improvement across a wide range of human activities, including music, ballet, gymnastics, chess, the word game Scrabble®,

---

[1]SF never hid his identity. After our article was published, he was interviewed several times on local and national television, and in newspapers, and he has encouraged us since to use his real name.

radiology, and education (Ericsson et al., 2018). To be sure, some remain skeptical. I've met experienced professionals from a variety of performance domains, for instance, who seriously doubt their ability to improve meaningfully beyond their present level. When asked, many say they have reached a limit determined by their unique inheritance of genes. It's a compelling notion, despite an overall lack of empirical support for such constraints on increases in expert performance (Ericsson, 2014). Indeed, recent studies of middle-aged identical twins provide compelling evidence of the diverse outcomes that can be achieved with an identical set of genes when the twins pursued dissimilar developmental paths and engaged in different amounts of practice (Bathgate et al., 2018).

Rather than engage in abstract arguments about the role genetics may or may not play in the development of expertise, what I've found most helpful in addressing skepticism is showing what the best performers in the same domain actually do to improve and excel. That's precisely the approach taken in *Better Results*. Its publication at this time heralds, I believe, a major change in the conception and implementation of training of beginning therapists, and, perhaps even more impactful, change in the methods used to ensure continued refinement of experienced therapists' performance throughout their entire careers. It clearly shows that a given clinician's performance is not the result of some inherent, immutable limit on their ability to succeed but is a function of the methods they use to train and develop. Most important of all, it provides therapists with the means for delivering more effective care.

—K. Anders Ericsson, PhD
Conradi Eminent Scholar and Professor of Psychology
Department of Psychology, Florida State University, Tallahassee

PREFACE: BETTER RESULTS ARE WITHIN REACH

There's two possible outcomes: If the result confirms the hypothesis, then you've made a discovery. If the result is contrary to the hypothesis, then you've made a discovery.
—ENRICO FERMI (QUOTED IN JEVREMOVIC, 2005, p. 490)

FIGURE 1. Changes in Client-Level Standardized Mean Differences in Pre- and Posttreatment Outcome Scores

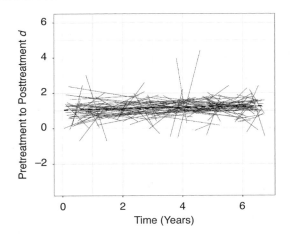

d = Cohen's d, which is a common measure of effect size that compares the difference between two means (i.e., pre- vs. posttreatment), divided by the sample's pretreatment standard deviation. From "Creating a Climate for Therapist Improvement: A Case Study of an Agency Focused on Outcomes and Deliberate Practice," by S. B. Goldberg, R. Babins-Wagner, T. Rousmaniere, S. Berzins, W. T. Hoyt, J. L. Whipple, S. D. Miller, and B. E. Wampold, 2016, *Psychotherapy, 53*, p. 372. Copyright 2016 by the American Psychological Association.

The promise of this book is captured in the data plot (see Figure 1). Along the horizontal axis is time in years. The impact of treatment is found on the vertical axis. Each thin black line depicts the outcomes of a single practitioner working in a large community mental health setting. Spanning the entire figure from left to right is a thick dashed line representing the effectiveness of the agency as a whole. And while it may be difficult to see amid the apparent chaos, the therapists in the study—153 in number—managed to do something never before recorded in the history of psychotherapy. Both as a group and individually, they improved their outcomes, steadily achieving better results year after year—for some, up to 7 years in a row (Ericsson, 1996; Goldberg, Babins-Wagner, et al., 2016).

The preceding summary of findings from our 2016 study (Goldberg, Babins-Wagner, et al., 2016) reflects the culmination of our more than 25-year effort directed at understanding how to improve the effectiveness of psychotherapy (Bertolino & Miller, 2012; Duncan, Hubble, & Miller, 1997; Duncan & Miller, 2000; Duncan, Miller, Wampold, & Hubble, 2010; Hubble, Duncan, & Miller, 1999; Miller, Duncan, & Hubble, 1995; Miller & Hubble, 2011; Miller, Hubble, & Duncan, 2007; Prescott, Maeschalck, & Miller, 2017). Along the way, we ended up in a number of theoretical cul de sacs, empirical blind alleys, and technical detours, returning in a few important ways to where we originally started. Although frustrating, in retrospect, each setback contributed to the development of the evidence-based approach responsible for the results obtained in the study and laid out in the pages of this book.

The process, known as *deliberate practice*, is not specific to any particular professional discipline. Clinical social workers, psychologists, marriage and family therapists, and counselors participated and saw their outcomes improve, as did students and licensed and provisional professionals. Moreover, its applicability is not limited to particular psychotherapeutic approaches or client populations. Both the clinicians and the people they treated were diverse, representing the demographics and services typically seen in a modern community mental health outpatient setting. The approach employed in the study offers a pathway to better results that is transtheoretical and transdiagnostic.

As the astute observer will likely have noticed, the increase in effectiveness documented in the study, while consistent and statistically significant, is not particularly dramatic. Indeed, it pales in comparison with the claims clinicians regularly encounter about treatments developed by "leading innovators" promising to "transform your effectiveness," and "overcome the most challenging clinical issues" (Miller, 2018a). And yet, a slow, gradual rate of improvement has the advantage of being consistent with the broader empirical literature regarding the development of expertise and expert performance reported in other fields, such as sports, medicine, arts, and the sciences (Ericsson, 1996; Ericsson, Hoffman, Kozbelt, & Williams, 2018). In addition, it highlights the potentially large cumulative effect of small changes accrued over time, offering practitioners the very real possibility of the continuous professional development that research shows is critical to their identity and survival in the field

(Orlinsky & Rønnestad, 2005; Rønnestad, Orlinsky, Schröder, Skovholt, & Willutzki, 2019).

With such positive results within reach, one might conceivably wonder about any potential shortcomings, drawbacks, or contraindications associated with getting started. With regard to the first concern, what can be said with certainty is that the instructions that follow do *not* constitute a method for doing psychotherapy. Although part of the process involves developing a detailed and explicit map of your performance, it's assumed you have, or are learning, a way of working, including a theoretical orientation and associated strategies and techniques. Stated more directly, this book does not teach you how to do therapy. Instead, it helps you, regardless of your preferences, improve your effectiveness as a therapist.

While not arranged in a typical workbook format, the entire volume is composed of short chapters designed to be readable in a single 15- to 20-minute sitting. Each ends with points to reflect on and tasks to complete. Although the information or activities are not difficult to comprehend or execute, they will take a fair bit of time and effort to bear fruit—a fact some may consider a drawback; but, as most readers know, change is not easy.

The book begins with two chapters describing what the field and therapists believe to be necessary for the conduct of effective psychotherapy and what research actually shows to be true. As the part title indicates, it is "The State of Our Art." The next part, "Expertise and Expert Performance: The Evidence Base," uses examples drawn from sports, medicine, and music to show that similar principles and practices lead to superior results across a wide range of human endeavors. In the third, "Getting Started: What To Do First To Achieve Better Results," we lay the foundation, introducing the tools and metrics critical to achieving better results. The fourth, "Moving Forward: Identifying What To Deliberately Practice," teaches you how to identity what *you* need to address to maximize your professional development efforts. As the final section title implies, the last chapters show you "How to Deliberately Practice." A set of appendices provides additional insights and supportive materials, including detailed explanations of certain topics, statistical formulas, deliberate practice tools, and troubleshooting tips.

We recommend starting at the beginning. Use the volume as though you are learning to play a much-loved musical instrument rather than listening to a favorite song. In other words, don't read the book from start to finish in one sitting. Take each chapter in turn, completing the exercises before proceeding. Doing otherwise, we have found, is likely to trigger the single greatest risk associated with implementing deliberate practice, namely, quitting.

Reading the "fine print" of the study by Goldberg, Babins-Wagner, et al. (2016), cited at the outset of the Preface, reveals a fairly high percentage of practitioners gave up early on in the study, choosing to leave the agency rather than employ the strategies described in this volume. While distressing, such a finding is also consistent with the broader expert and expertise literature, documenting that most who achieve a satisfactory level of skill within a particular performance domain—be it driving, cooking, writing, or their job—stop doing what's necessary to improve (Ericsson & Pool, 2016). Thankfully, evidence-based steps, and realistic, realizable time frames have now been identified that improve the odds of successful implementation (Bertolino & Miller, 2012; Brattland et al., 2018; Fixsen, Blase, Naoom, & Wallace, 2009; Nilsen, 2015). The order and content of what follows have been purposefully constructed with these findings in mind. If there's any advice we can offer at this point, it's "No need to rush. Take it one step at a time."

ACKNOWLEDGMENTS

We are deeply indebted to the hundreds of researchers in both psychotherapy and the field of expertise and expert performance without whom this book would not have been possible. We want to personally thank K. Anders Ericsson, the psychologist who originally coined the term *deliberate practice* and whose research and thinking provided the foundation for what you find in this book. He has also been a major source of support as we have worked to apply his findings to the field of psychotherapy, freely offering his time and expertise for more than a decade. Any misinterpretations or misapplications are entirely our own.

A big thanks as well to goes to our acquisitions editor, Susan Reynolds; Elise Frasier, director of editorial development; copyeditor Laurel Vincenty; and the American Psychological Association. All have followed us on our journey, providing guidance, skillful editing and feedback, and an outlet for our work as it has evolved. Gratitude also goes to our families, in particular, Karen Donahey, Michael Miller, Jean Hubble, and Tan Liqin, for their patience and steadfast support.

We also want to thank (presented alphabetically): Wendy Amey; Bill Andrews; Robbie Babins-Wagner; Susanne Bargmann; Bob Bertolino; Jeb Brown; Simon Goldberg; Rod Goodyear; Lynn D. Johnson; Michael Lambert; Gunnar Lindfeldt; Cynthia Maeschalck; Harold Miller, Jr.; Jesse Owen; Liz Pluut; David Prescott; Tony Rousmaniere; Eeuwe Schuckard; Jason Seidel; Liz Sheehan; Rich Simon; Birgit Valla; Niklas Waitong; Bruce Wampold; and Jeffrey Zeig. We are deeply indebted to these friends and colleagues around the world who have listened patiently; applied the ideas to their own lives and work; allowed us to study their work and data; given us feedback (at times, arguing passionately and persuasively); provided a public forum for sharing our findings; and, in some instances, written about and published with us. If history is the best predictor of the future, we're certain the research and our understanding will evolve and that we will need your help, support, and input in the future.

THE STATE OF OUR ART

1

What Therapists Will Say, Won't Say, and Can't Say

In theory, there is no difference between theory and practice. In practice, there is.
—WALTER J. SAVITCH (1984, p. 366)

At the beginning of our professional workshops, we pose a series of questions. The first is, "Does psychotherapy work?" The response of the audience is nearly always the same. By show of hands, 50% immediately vote, "Yes." Forty percent or so, "No." The rest either want to qualify their response—"If I'm understanding the question correctly . . ."—or refuse to participate. On occasion, someone quips half-jokingly, "Is this a trick?"

http://dx.doi.org/10.1037/0000191-001
Better Results: Using Deliberate Practice to Improve Therapeutic Effectiveness, by S. D. Miller, M. A. Hubble, and D. Chow

3

WHAT THERAPISTS *WILL* SAY

Our next question generally results in unanimous agreement: "Are you more effective now than when you first started?" The energy in the room changes: "Yes, we *are* better." Without any prompting, attendees begin to share stories of how awkward and uncomfortable they felt in their earliest sessions. Even the simplest of acts was the subject of intense and often critical scrutiny. "Where do I look and for how long?" "Should I lean forward or back in my chair, cross my legs, or keep my feet on the floor?" "How do I sound?"—not to mention, "What in the world do I say?"

A few brave souls take it even further, recalling moments that can only be described as "cringeworthy." One we will never forget. As a practicum student, this therapist-in-training was meeting with a person struggling with anxiety. About midway through the first appointment, the client leaned forward and quietly asked, "Can I tell you something in private?" "Yes, please," said the student, taking this as a sign of developing trust. Now, almost whispering, the man continued, "Sometimes, when I really get anxious, . . . I masturbate to relieve the tension." Caught up in a moment of heartfelt empathy, the trainee blurted out, "Oh, me, too."

When asked what eventually helped them overcome their initial anxieties and smooth out the rough edges, participants consistently cite a small number of activities. Supervision and mentoring top the list. They are followed by personal therapy. Last comes experience, with many expressing some variation of, "Clients are the best teachers."

No matter the specifics or the particular contribution emphasized, we are always struck by therapists' deep commitment to professional development. They truly want to learn and improve their effectiveness. Their love for the work always comes through. Clearly, it is not about the money. The feeling we get is that, for many, helping others is a calling.

At this point, we introduce our final question: "What percentage of your clients get better as a result of working with you?" Unlike before, this time, we instruct the audience to commit their answers to paper and cover them so their neighbors can't see. The rationale for the secrecy is to enable them to answer candidly. Once done, we tell them what polls reliably show: 80%. That is, most therapists believe they help 80% of their clients.

Judging from the group's reaction, it's clear attendees are not surprised by this figure. They look up, nod their heads, giving every appearance of feeling validated. No doubt, practitioners sincerely believe they help the majority of people they see. But is this accurate? As is true of life in general, no psychotherapist's career is all "moonlight and roses." In small group discussions and on breaks, the weight of responsibility that comes with the job is palpable. A majority report that the problems they encounter now are far worse than when they first entered the field. For ourselves, just when we think we've heard it all, someone will relate a story that would shake the confidence of even the world's most experienced therapist.

WHAT THERAPISTS *WON'T* SAY

What therapists won't say out loud at our presentations is just how uncertain many continue to feel about their work. We know this in part because we've "been there, done that." Whenever we disclose how frequently we still find ourselves "grasping at straws" or "flying by the seat of our pants," participants titter. Obviously, our admission hits home. If our own experience is any guide, other doubts and insecurities lie just below the surface:

- Am I doing the right thing?
- Why am I not helping this person?
- Whoa, I didn't see that coming!
- Why didn't my client come back?
- How effective am I, really?
- Why do I never seem as quick/clever/helpful as . . .
- What if I haven't improved over the years? And on and on.

However motivated we may be to address these unpleasant thoughts and feelings, our usual solutions not infrequently fall short. Although reading books, attending workshops, speaking with colleagues, or consulting senior practitioners may help, the relief never seems to last. When all else fails, one tried-and-true but short-lived solution, encouraged by the field's theories and traditions, is shifting responsibility for our reactions and experiences to the client. How many times have we heard, "If this person were not so . . . [insert dysfunctional, damaged, resistant, or unmotivated here], then therapy would be successful"? As tempting as it may be to attribute failure to our clients or their life circumstances, it is rarely satisfying. After all, therapists enter the field to help, not blame.

Midway through the morning, we take the first break of the day. Most times, there's a buzz in the air. The hesitancy typical at the outset of any workshop has given way to conversation and interaction. People mill about. The volume rises as they talk while helping themselves to food and beverages.

When they are back in their seats, we thank them for their candor and then ask them to bear with us. The information we are about to deliver will, in all likelihood, be unfamiliar, and more, challenge the way they see themselves and what they do.

"We'll start with the good news," one of us says, advancing the slides. And, this is what we tell them: Psychotherapy is effective! In fact, much better than many might believe based on their vote at the start of the day. Turning to the research, we review studies dating back 4 decades documenting the efficacy of clinical work (Duncan, Miller, Wampold, & Hubble, 2010; Hubble, Duncan, & Miller, 1999).

Participants are pleasantly surprised when we share that the field's outcomes are equivalent to coronary artery bypass surgery and 4 times greater than the use of fluoride in preventing tooth decay (Griffin, Regnier, Griffin, & Huntley, 2007; Lipsey & Wilson, 1993). The good news continues. Additional investigations show real-world practitioners achieve results matching those reported in tightly controlled, randomized trials (Minami et al., 2008; Saxon et al., 2017; Stiles, Barkham, Mellor-Clark, & Connell, 2008; Wampold & Brown, 2005). Such findings, we relate, are impressive because clinicians in research settings enjoy advantages seldom available to the rest of us (e.g., lower caseloads, secure income, an absence of the typical demands for productivity, a carefully screened clientele, ongoing training and consultation with the field's most prestigious and knowledgeable experts). It is here someone inevitably shouts out, "Where can I sign up?" Laughter ensues, although we know it will be short lived. We are about to drop the proverbial other shoe.

WHAT THERAPISTS *CAN'T* SAY

As the morning session of our workshop continues, we know the good times will soon end.

Here it is: Beyond personal impressions and informal feedback, the majority of therapists have no hard, verifiable evidence that *anything* they do makes a difference. Accordingly, they cannot possibly know if they are effective or getting better with time, experience, supervision, or training. Absent a valid and reliable assessment of their performance, it also stands to reason they cannot possibly know what kind of instruction or guidance would help them improve.

Given the field's emphasis on accountability and fiscal responsibility, it is ironic clinicians have nothing other than faith to justify the huge investment they make in professional preparation and development. How large is it? New graduates from doctoral training programs are entering the workforce, on average, $100,000 in debt (Winerman, 2016). Additionally, millions are spent annually on continuing education, including workshops, books, journals, instructional videos, and the like.

In all fairness, it's not that trainees or practicing clinicians are uninterested in their effectiveness. It is, rather, they already believe they know. Actually, they're *certain*! Not only do the results from our informal morning poll indicate as much, it is confirmed by research. In one large-scale survey, for example, mental health professionals reported helping 80% of the people they treated. Nearly a quarter were confident that 90% or more of their clients profited from their care, with few, if any, deteriorating (Walfish, McAlister, O'Donnell, & Lambert, 2012).

At the workshop, when we finally get around to pointing out that, without a formal measure of effectiveness, therapists can't possibly know how effective they are, much less what they need to target for improvement, stunned disbelief comes over the room. Of course, it is human nature to reject any doubt cast on the accuracy of personal perceptions. Looking across the audience, the skepticism shows on many faces. In short order, shock gives way to grudging acceptance. It is inescapable. Without data, how certain can or, more importantly, *should*, one really be?

It turns out the answer to this question initially proves quite discomforting. Fortunately, in the end, "the facts," as Carl Rogers once observed, "are always friendly" (Rogers, 1961, p. 25).

TO SUM UP

So, what is it therapists will say? As the old saying goes, "We are 'cooking with gas!'" We are effective, helping the majority of people we treat. What won't they say? While we become more confident about the work as experience grows, doing therapy remains fraught with a great deal of uncertainty and self-doubt. What can't they say? Beyond our own judgment, most of us lack any tangible proof—"real data"—about our actual effectiveness.

WHAT TO DO RIGHT NOW

It's unbelievable how much you don't know about the game you've been playing all your life.

—MICKEY MANTLE, NEW YORK YANKEES BASEBALL PLAYER
(MANTLE & CREAMER, 1999, p. 42)

The research evidence is clear: Psychotherapy works. Despite this fact, most of us have no actual data regarding our effectiveness. The truth is, we tend to rely on our memory and overall gut sense. So, how effective are you? Before reading any further, take a moment to reflect on the following questions. We're not looking for actual statistics here (unless you have them, of course; then by all means, list them); just your best guess. We return to these figures later.

1. Using a percentile (0–100), rate your current effectiveness as compared with your peers.

2. Next, use the same scale to rate your effectiveness during your first year of clinical practice.

3. On a scale from 1 (*not at all*) to 10 (*entirely*), rate how confident you are about your answers to the first two questions.

4. If your answer to Question 1 is higher than the percentage reported in Question 2, describe three factors that contributed to your improvement.

2

What Do We Really Know About Psychotherapy After All?

The truth will set you free, but first it will piss you off.

—JOE KLAAS (1982, p. 15)

Two weeks before his 30th birthday, Sigmund Freud placed an ad in *Neue Freie Presse* announcing the opening of his private practice in Vienna. Having just returned from studies in Paris and Berlin, he was offering himself as a specialist in the treatment of "nervous diseases." Within a decade, he began using the term *psychoanalysis* to describe his method.

Many trace the origin of modern psychotherapy to Freud's work (Zeig, 2017). In time, the "talking cure" left its obscure beginnings behind, not only becoming a part of, but also a major force in, shaping Western culture (Fancher, 1995; Lasch, 1979; Rieff, 1987). Nowadays, many consult a therapist or know someone who has. The practice is frequently depicted in television shows and the cinema. It is also the subject of more than 55,000 popular and professional books (Miller & Hubble, 2017).

THERAPY THEN AND NOW

In the ensuing 150 years, the number of therapy approaches has rocketed into the hundreds (Duncan, Miller, Wampold, & Hubble, 2010). Beginning in the mid-1970s, meta-analytic research provided the first robust evidence for

http://dx.doi.org/10.1037/0000191-002
Better Results: Using Deliberate Practice to Improve Therapeutic Effectiveness, by S. D. Miller, M. A. Hubble, and D. Chow
Copyright © 2020 by the American Psychological Association. All rights reserved.

the overall efficacy of psychologically informed interventions (Smith & Glass, 1977). Since that time, research studies—including clinical trials and meta-analyses—have exploded (Wampold & Imel, 2015). On PubMed, when the term *psychotherapy* is searched together with *clinical trial* and *meta-analysis*, an astonishing 800,000 plus citations are returned! From this burgeoning literature, the Society of Clinical Psychology has compiled a list of 80 empirically supported treatments for 27 of the 157 diagnoses cataloged in the latest edition of the *Diagnostic and Statistical Manual of Mental Disorders* (fifth ed. [*DSM–5*]; American Psychiatric Association, 2013).

If interest in, research about, or number of therapy approaches can be considered an accurate gauge of achievement, then only one conclusion exists: The field has made tremendous progress. Little wonder the job forecast for psychology and related careers is much better than average (Bureau of Labor Statistics, n.d.). And why not? Our discipline, it is commonly believed, can now identify and differentiate mental health problems with near pinpoint accuracy. Moreover, clinicians have at their disposal access to a systematic, well-researched psychological formulary of interventions (cf. Beutler & Harwood, 2000; Chambless & Hollon, 1998; Roth & Fonagy, 2013). Training is readily available, too. Any provider wishing to acquire the latest knowledge and skills can do so with ease. The public can also rest assured. Owing to the establishment of licensing and regulatory bodies, as well as strict practice guidelines (DeAngelis, 2017), access to the most competent generation of practitioners in history is guaranteed.

SAY IT ISN'T SO

Assuming the progress just described is true, one would expect an accompanying gain in overall clinical effectiveness. It would be both an obvious and natural conclusion. It is also patently false. As Shakespeare warned in *The Merchant of Venice*, "All that glisters is not gold." The apparent advances notwithstanding, the outcome of psychotherapy has not improved in more than 40 years (Prochaska, Norcross, & Saul, 2019; Thomas, 2013; Wampold & Imel, 2015).

The data are sobering. To illustrate, following a comprehensive review of the research literature, Wampold and Imel (2015) determined "from the various meta-analyses conducted over the years, the aggregate effect size related to absolute efficacy is remarkably consistent" (p. 94). Efforts aimed at boosting the effectiveness of psychotherapy via the development and dissemination of specific treatments for specific disorders have done nothing to alter this fact. Moreover, studies comparing one method with another reveal few, if any, meaningful differences (Wampold et al., 2017). Given such findings, it should come as no surprise that neither competence in conducting specific types of therapy nor adherence to their prescriptive protocols contributes anything to outcome (Webb, DeRubeis, & Barber, 2010; see Figure 2.1).

For many practitioners, the lack of evidence favoring any one therapy over others is welcome news. It helps confirm the concerns many have regarding

FIGURE 2.1. Relationship Between Growth in Treatment Approaches and Outcome

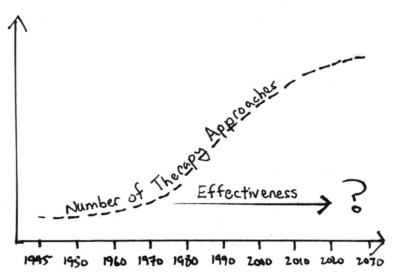

any encroachment on their professional judgment and freedom. Tailoring services to the client has long been the sine qua non of good clinical work (Norcross & Lambert, 2011; Norcross & Wampold, 2011b). It goes without saying, "one size does not fit all." No protocol imposed from above or afar can substitute for the mastery of a craft that can only come from years of formal education, supervision, and personal and professional experience.

What About Training?

As comforting as it may be to believe that professional training and time in the field count, it turns out they matter very little. One searches in vain for *any* evidence that courses attended, degrees earned, professional discipline, hours of continuing education (CE), certification, or licensure makes one a better therapist (Miller, Hubble, & Chow, 2017; Caldwell, 2015). Consider, for the moment, CE. Overall, clinicians report being very satisfied with postgraduate educational activities. Additionally, they *believe* their participation leads to more effective and ethical practice (Neimeyer, Taylor, & Wear, 2011). Although mandated by licensing and regulatory bodies worldwide, no evidence exists establishing a connection between the quality and outcome of professional services and participation in CE (Neimeyer, Taylor, & Wear, 2009; Rousmaniere, Goodyear, Miller, & Wampold, 2017).

And Supervision?

It fares no better. As noted earlier, supervision ranks highly among activities therapists cite as influential in their professional development. In fact, in a study of 5,000 clinicians conducted over a 15-year period, supervision was perceived to be second in impact to actual clinical work (Orlinsky & Rønnestad, 2005). Nevertheless, after reviewing literature and research spanning a century, Watkins (2011) wrote, "We do not seem any more able to say now (as opposed to 30 years ago) that psychotherapy supervision contributes to patient outcome" (p. 235).

More recently, Rousmaniere, Swift, Babins-Wagner, Whipple, and Berzins (2016) used a sophisticated statistical process (i.e., hierarchical linear modeling) to examine the effect of supervision on treatment results. The study is notable for its size and duration. Data were gathered for more than 5 years on 23 supervisors working in a real-world setting with 175 trainee therapists and 6,521 clients. They found supervision was only marginally related to clinician performance, accounting for less than 1% of the variance. What is more, in terms of outcome, the supervisors' experience level, discipline (e.g., social work versus psychology), and professional qualifications were inconsequential.

Should you find these results disconcerting, hang on. Later, we demonstrate how the information and strategies in this book can potentiate the impact of supervision on treatment outcomes.

Any Hope for Clinical Experience?

Research confirms therapists believe the most significant contributor to their skills and effectiveness is the amount of time spent in actual face-to-face meetings with clients (Orlinsky & Rønnestad, 2005). A cursory search of therapists' business websites shows it is not uncommon for practitioners to reference the number of years they have been in practice if not the actual number of hours spent with clients.

Here again, the evidence is hardly supportive; it even points in the opposite direction. Instead of improving over time, effectiveness plateaus early, then begins to decline at a rate much like a slow leak from an inflated balloon (Miller & Hubble, 2011). In the largest study to date, Goldberg and colleagues (Goldberg, Rousmaniere, et al., 2016) documented a steady diminution in performance over a 5-year period. Importantly, the deterioration was unrelated to several factors often advanced as moderating variables, including client severity, number of sessions, early termination, caseload size, or various therapist factors (e.g., age, years of experience, theoretical orientation; see Figure 2.2).

Of no small concern, other research documents it is *only* confidence that increases with experience (Chow et al., 2015; Walfish, McAlister, O'Donnell, & Lambert, 2012). The available evidence reveals clinicians routinely overestimate the number of people they help—on average, 65% more than they actually do (Chow et al., 2015; Walfish et al., 2012). In addition, when asked to rate themselves, the least effective believe they are as helpful as the best (Hiatt & Hargrave, 1995). Left unchecked, self-deception—no matter the form it takes—undermines performance and professional growth (see Figure 2.3).

FIGURE 2.2. Relationship Between Experience and Effectiveness

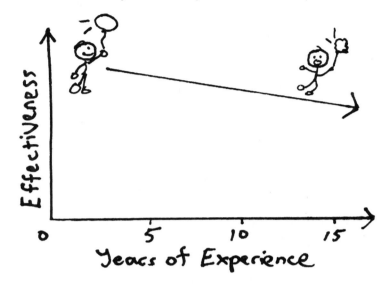

FIGURE 2.3. The Results of Experience on Confidence and Competence

Over time, clinicians' ability to deliver standardized treatments with fidelity increases, as does their confidence. Effectiveness remains flat.

IS IT TIME FOR THERAPY?

By now, if you're not confused, the foregoing revelations may give rise to denial, anger, and, ultimately, demoralization. Should you be tempted to enter therapy to help restore your faith and confidence in the field and, perhaps, yourself, think again. Depending on theoretical orientation, between 72% and 98% of practitioners turn to therapy for personal and professional growth (Bike, Norcross, & Schatz, 2009; Orlinsky & Rønnestad, 2005; Pope & Tabachnick, 1994). Malikiosi-Loizos (2013) reminds us that Freud strongly believed, "personal therapy is the deepest and most non-negotiable part of clinical education" (p. 33). In many countries, it is required for certification or licensure. For instance, the training standards for the European Federation of Psychologists' Associations requires psychologists specializing in psychotherapy to undergo the equivalent of 2 years of weekly sessions. Despite widespread and long-standing belief in and regulatory support for "therapy-for-the-therapist," the evidence is at best "mixed and inconclusive" (Geller, Norcross, & Orlinsky, 2005; Malikiosi-Loizos, 2013, p. 43; Miller et al., 2017).

Murphy and colleagues (Murphy, Irfan, Barnett, Castledine, & Enescu, 2018) published the first systematic review and metasynthesis of qualitative research findings in the area of mandatory personal therapy during a trainee's training period. The results are eye-opening. While half of the themes that emerged indicated a positive experience (e.g., development of the self, experiential form of learning, stress management), the remaining were anything but. Several trainees spoke about the stress and anguish the requirement caused in their personal lives. Mandatory therapy was also experienced as a financial and personal burden on top of the pressure of being assessed. Finally, trainees reported being forced to meet with therapists who were unprofessional in their conduct toward them. Such results are consistent with findings from other studies documenting a significant number of trainees, upwards of 24%, who found the experience "somewhat" to "exceptionally" harmful (Pope & Tabachnick, 1994)!

TO SUM UP

Turns out, after considering the evidence, virtually everything therapists believe, and the profession endorses, as the foundational basis for clinical effectiveness has no substantive empirical support. Mindful of these findings, Rogers's (1961) assertion (shared at the end of first chapter), "The facts are always friendly," would have to strike a reasonable person as patently absurd. Conventional wisdom and tradition, in the end, provide no real guidance to anyone hoping to improve their results. Nonetheless, knowing and accepting this reality frees the field to look elsewhere. In the lesser known half of his maxim about "the facts," Rogers (1961) continued, "Every bit of evidence one can acquire leads one that much closer to what is true" (p. 25).

Fortunately, research from outside the field provides direction for making the growth clinicians desire a reality. Drawn from decades of study on expertise, the findings to be reviewed next are less concerned with the particulars of a given performance domain (e.g., psychotherapy) than with how mastery of any human endeavor is achieved (Colvin, 2009; Ericsson, 2009; Ericsson, Charness, Feltovich, & Hoffman, 2006; Ericsson, Hoffman, Kozbelt, & Williams, 2018).

WHAT TO DO RIGHT NOW

Reality is that which, when you stop believing in it, doesn't go away.
—PHILIP K. DICK (1995, p. 261)

A large number of empirical findings have been reviewed in this chapter. Take a moment to reflect on and write your responses to the following questions. Now may be a good time to start a record of your experiences—a "professional development journal"—as you work your way through the rest of the book:

1. Which facts in particular stood out for you? Confirmed or contradicted your beliefs and experience?

2. What did you find motivating or discouraging? And which, if any, did you doubt, discount, or reject out of hand?

3. If training, supervision, credentials, or clinical experience are not valid indicators of expertise or effectiveness, what might be?

II

EXPERTISE AND EXPERT PERFORMANCE: THE EVIDENCE BASE

3

Learning From the Experts on Expertise

Odds are that few, if any, of the people around you are truly great at what they do—awesomely, amazingly, world-class excellent. But why aren't they?

—GEOFF COLVIN (2009, p. 2)

When asked to explain why so few are great at what they do—reach the top of their chosen trade, profession, or avocation—most people offer one of two explanations. The first is a lack of hard work, a willingness to settle for "good enough." The other is an absence of raw talent, the result of having little or no control over the circumstances of one's birth. Both possibilities, at first blush, not only seem reasonable but often line up with our personal experience and observations.

You don't have to look far for confirmation. Think of Olympic athletes. They devote their entire lives to practicing their chosen sport often to the exclusion of everything else. Even more, compared with most, they are blessed with bodies "made for success." The celebrated basketball player, Michael Jordan, could jump vertically 48 inches in the air—the average height of an 8-year-old child! How could other players, much less an ordinary person, ever hope to compete with such a gift?

Mozart is another example. No one would argue with his genius. His works are considered world treasures and remain among the most widely played pieces of music today, more than 200 years after his death. He was composing music at age 5, and playing the piano and violin in public performances by 8.

http://dx.doi.org/10.1037/0000191-003
Better Results: Using Deliberate Practice to Improve Therapeutic Effectiveness, by S. D. Miller, M. A. Hubble, and D. Chow

In the Oscar-winning film *Amadeus* (Zaentz & Forman, 1984), the Austrian-born musician doesn't compose so much as transfer scores of remarkable intricacy from head to paper without revision or error. Attributing such abilities to anything other than a "divine spark" seems woefully inadequate.

A HARD LOOK AT 'HARD WORK'

Together, Olympic athletes and Mozart are exemplars of our customary explanations for the origin of exceptionality. Enter K. Anders Ericsson, a psychologist whose interest just so happened to be the acquisition of expertise in sports and music. With his colleagues in 1993 (Ericsson, Krampe, & Tesch-Römer, 1993), he published what would prove to be a groundbreaking series of studies of violinists and pianists. Why, he wondered, did some, despite being matched with similar endowment and training, become virtuosos while others ended up playing in a local ensemble or not at all?

The team of researchers collected and analyzed detailed logs of how musicians at the Music Academy of West Berlin spent their time. How much was devoted to practice versus performing? What did they say about the relevance of their lessons and pleasure they experienced while learning? Did they rehearse alone or with others? How much effort and concentration were expended in service of improving? And what about rest, relaxation, and leisure time? Ericsson and colleagues left no stone unturned.

The subjects of the research were remarkably similar in background. All began their studies and decided to pursue music as a career at a similar age. Additionally, they had the same number of music teachers and played the same number of instruments prior to specializing in violin or piano. All spent at least 10 years practicing and devoted the same amount of time per week to "music-related activities" ($\bar{x}$ = 50–60 hours).

What then separated the best from the rest? Turns out, the top performers *were* hard workers. They both started earlier and allotted more time each day to solo practice—at least twice as much as others on average. Not ones for fooling around, they also spent less time engaged in leisure activities than their less capable counterparts and could recount with greater accuracy when they chose to set their instrument aside and "kick back."

So, given the foregoing, can we place a point in the "win" column for conventional wisdom? Is superior performance merely a matter of putting in the requisite number of hours? This was certainly the argument popularized by Malcolm Gladwell (2008) in his persuasive, bestselling book *Outliers*. "Ten thousand hours," he wrote, "is the *magic* number of greatness" (p. 41; italics added). Perhaps that is why the book sold so well. It confirmed what everyone believed anyway!

Unfortunately, like many popularizations of scientific work, Gladwell's (2008) turned out to be a gross simplification. "Paying your dues" is necessary, but the data show that *how much* is much less important than *how* top performers spend their practice time. As Apple founder Steve Jobs was fond of saying, "Quality is more important than quantity." To be effective, specific goals, full concentration, ongoing measurement and feedback, and access to expert coaches must be pulled together in a systematic effort to extend the current limits of performance.

Research shows the process taxes both mind and will, with those at the top spending more time *purposefully* resting. That's right, resting. For example, on average, the top violinists engaged in 5.4 hours more shut-eye than their less able counterparts, with the best resting 60 hours per week compared to 54.6 hours for average performers. Not only did the top violinists sleep more (8.6 versus 7.8 hours), they took more naps in the afternoon. One wonders why Gladwell and other popularizers did not talk about a "60-hour rule" for sleep instead (Chow, 2018c)!

To distinguish this highly specialized practice activity from mere repetition, Ericsson (1996) coined the term *deliberate practice* (DP). Much more than the presence of any innate ability, prolonged engagement in DP has proven central to the development of expert performance across a broad and diverse range of human endeavors, including chess (Charness, Krampe, & Mayr, 1996; Gobet & Charness, 2018), mathematics (Butterworth, 2018), business (Sonnentag & Kleine, 2000), computer programming (Sonnentag, Niessen, & Volmer, 2006), teaching (Stigler & Miller, 2018), medicine and surgery (Ericsson, 2007; Mamede, Schmidt, Rikers, Penaforte, & Coelho-Filho, 2007; Norman et al., 2018; Schmidt & Rikers, 2007)—and, yes, music and sports (Côté, Ericsson, & Law, 2005; Ericsson et al., 1993; Krampe & Ericsson, 1996; Lehmann, Gruber, & Kopiez, 2018; A. M. Williams, Ford, Hodges, & Ward, 2018).

Returning to the two examples cited earlier, almost all fans know that "His Airness," Michael Jordan, didn't make his varsity basketball team at Emsley A. Laney High in Wilmington, North Carolina. Although the precise reasons are a matter of some debate, what followed is not. According to *Forbes* contributor Susan Kalla (2012), Jordan stopped messing around, became "ultra determined," and devoted hours to practicing deliberately every day—a regimen he followed the rest of his career. Determined to perfect his game, he first visualized what he wanted to achieve, then set specific objectives, developed a plan, and sought and utilized feedback and coaching. He constantly monitored his progress, revising his plan, goals, and coaching needs along the way. When he finally retired for good in 2003, he'd scored 32,292 points, the fourth highest total in NBA history. In the end, he attributed his success to practicing at his edge. As he himself put it, "I've missed more than 9,000 shots . . . lost 300 games . . . been trusted to take the game winning shot and missed. . . . And that is why I succeed" (Goldman & Papson, 1998, p. 49).

The role DP played in the life and work of Mozart is equally evident. In direct counterpoint to the stories often told about him, the composer did not emerge from the womb quill and paper in hand, nor did his compositions emerge wholecloth without changes or additions. The Hollywood portrayal notwithstanding, historical records convincingly show Mozart was constantly revising and reworking his pieces, a process that sometimes lasted for years!

Additionally, like most elite performers, Mozart had access to the best teachers. The real story behind his success begins with his father, Leopold, who was a highly accomplished and popular music instructor. In his day, he wrote *the* book on the violin. He was also an established composer and virtuoso in his own right, one who began teaching his son to perform and compose when the boy was only 3 years old.

Mozart's tutelage did not end with his father. He traveled in elite circles, counting Johann Christian Bach and Joseph Haydn as friends and mentors. As Geoff Colvin (2009), author of *Talent Is Overrated*, observed, by the time the prodigy wrote what most consider his first masterpiece, Piano Concerto No. 9, he "had been through eighteen years of extremely hard, expert training" (p. 26).

So much for the "practice makes perfect" and "divine spark" theories of greatness. Graffiti scrawled across the doorway to excellence reads, "No Muse Here" and "Gladwell Got It Wrong." At the same time, the backstory does not detract from the remarkable accomplishments of either Jordan or Mozart. To the contrary, it makes their achievements all the more awe-inspiring and enviable.

For all that, old ideas die hard. Consider what happened when Cornell University's Herbert Gussman Professor of Music, Neal Zaslaw, dared to suggest that Mozart was more mortal than immortal—a "working stiff" who primarily wrote music for money, an artist whose compositions were not considered particularly special at the time. When he presumed to make these points at a conference sponsored by the Vienna Philharmonic Orchestra, Zaslaw was roundly denounced professionally and personally. How dare he question Mozart's gift? The session moderator and participants argued the composer's music "belonged only to the highest spheres of creativity," born "out of inner impulse" (Colvin, 2009, p. 31).

HOW MUCH DIFFERENCE DOES DELIBERATE PRACTICE MAKE?

Yes, I see. Scientific . . . but could you be a little more specific?
—Signor Garamond to Professor Bramani in Umberto Eco's (2007)
Foucault's Pendulum (p. 250)

As inspiring as the stories and research evidence may be, the role DP plays in the development of expertise has been challenged (K. N. Anderson, 2016; Gardner, 1995; Marcus, 2012; Sternberg & Lubart, 1996). In 2014, Macnamara, Hambrick, and Oswald went beyond scholarly reviews of the available literature, publishing the first meta-analysis examining its impact on a broad range of performance domains. Finding an overall aggregate correlation of .35, the researchers concluded, "Deliberate practice is important, but not as important as has been argued" (Macnamara et al., 2014, p. 1).

In a subsequent article, the team suggested an alternative explanation for the genesis of expertise, emphasizing the role of genetic factors, primarily intelligence (i.e., IQ), genotypic physical characteristics (especially for sports and certain musical performance), and personality traits such as grit and motivation (Ullén, Hambrick, & Mosing, 2016). Termed the *multifactorial gene-interaction model*, the theory focuses on "the potential importance of [a] more complex interplay between genes and environment" (p. 13). Proponents of the model argue their perspective is timely and necessary, asserting "deliberate practice theory is unable to account for major recent findings relating to expertise and expert performance" (p. 427).

As it is, the results reported by Macnamara et al. (2014) generated the same degree of public interest as Gladwell's (2008) earlier work extolling the virtues of DP. "New Study *Destroys* . . . [the] 10,000-Hour Rule," trumpeted the *Business Insider* (Baer, 2014; italics added). Others piled on. "Scientists debunk the myth" that practice makes one an expert (Ferro, 2014). In *Slate* magazine, the banner for an article by Hambrick, Ferreira, and Henderson (2014) even claimed the whole idea of DP "perpetuates a cruel myth" as it promotes the false belief "people can help themselves to the same degree if they just try hard enough."

So, what can be reliably said about the role and importance of DP? In truth, the question of whether it is the sole or primary contributor to the development of expertise is a matter of continuing debate (cf. Ericsson, 2014; Ullén et al., 2016). No doubt, environmental and genetic factors are important (Miller & Hubble, 2011). That said, putting the correlation reported by Macnamara et al. (2014) in the context of other well-known associations can be instructive.

Consider several examples. First, few doubt whether obesity, excessive drinking, or smoking are unhealthy behaviors. Second, people with cardiac and metabolic diseases, as a rule, believe that adhering to their physicians' recommendations to take certain medications extends life. Third, people who are more intelligent are thought to be more successful and earn more than

others. And, finally, major league baseball players with the best batting averages are paid more than average players.

What are the *actual* correlations for these common, and presumably evidence-based, beliefs? The data, as well as the proportions of variability in the criterion accounted for by each predictor, are presented in Table 3.1.

If the values reported in Table 3.1 can be considered "benchmarks," then the .35 correlation between practice and performance reported by Macnamara et al. (2014) must be considered substantial. After all, the .08 to .23 correlations

TABLE 3.1. Correlation Coefficients and Percentage of Variance Accounted and Unaccounted for Between Various Predictor and Criterion Variables

Predictor variable	Criterion variable	Correlation coefficient	Percent of variance accounted for by predictor	Percent of variance unaccounted for by predictor
Obesity[a]	Mortality	.08	< 1%	> 99%
Excessive drinking[a]	Mortality	.13	1.5%	98.5%
Smoking[a]	Mortality	.21	4%	96%
Intelligence[b]	Income	.21	4%	96%
Adherence to effective medication[c]	Mortality	.23	5%	95%
Amount of deliberate practice	Performance	.35	12%	88%
Batting average[d]	Major League salary	.43	18%	72%

Note. Associations that were reported as odds ratios (*OR*) or *ln*(*OR*) were converted to approximate Pearson product-moment correlations using methods described by Bonett (2007) and attributed to Pearson (1900). [a]Holt-Lunstad, Smith, Baker, Harris, & Stephenson (2015) and/or Luo, Hawkley, Waite, and Cacioppo (2012). [b]Strenze (2007). [c]Simpson et al. (2006). [d]Averbukh, Brown, and Chase (2015). From "To Be or Not to Be (an Expert)? Revisiting the Role of Deliberate Practice in Improving Performance," by S. D. Miller, D. Chow, B. E., Wampold, M. A. Hubble, A. C. Del Re, C. Maeschalck, and S. Bargmann, 2018, *High Ability Studies*, advance online publication, p. 4. Copyright 2018 by Taylor & Francis. Adapted with permission.

for the various predictors of mortality are large enough to justify the expenditure of massive amounts of time and money on public health policy and initiatives aimed at changing people's behavior. In the United States, for instance, health care costs associated with obesity—the smallest correlation reported—range from $147 to $210 billion dollars per year (Cawley & Meyerhoefer, 2012). An additional $60 billion is spent annually on weight loss products and programs (R. L. Williams, 2013). In sum, the size of the correlation between DP and performance is, compared to other predictor variables, sufficient to recommend its application.

Recent research not only affirms but also strengthens this conclusion. In 2018, Miller, Chow, Wampold, Hubble, Del Re, Maeschalck, and Bargmann reanalyzed the data set used in Macnamara et al. (2014). Concerned about the appropriateness of some of the studies included in their meta-analysis, Miller, Chow, et al. (2018) enlisted blind raters to select only those meeting a strict definition of DP. When studies were excluded for not meeting established criteria, the correlation coefficient for DP increased from .35 to .40.

So, what can be concluded? When it comes to accounting for any aspect of human behavior, the pendulum of popular opinion often swings from one extreme to the other. Are experts born or made? The answer is, "Yes and yes." Future research will undoubtedly sort the relative contribution of the various factors, but with what is known now, DP is the most effective, evidence-based method one can employ for improving performance (Miller, Hubble, & Chow, 2018).

THE BIGGER PICTURE

> None of us see the world as it is but as we are, as our frames of reference, or "maps," define the territory.
>
> —Stephen R. Covey (1990, p. 109)

With the empirical case for DP established, the question remains, How does it work? What changes take place when a person engages in a sustained and systematic effort to "push the envelope," to go beyond the limits of their current abilities? And how do these changes improve performance?

The short answer is: DP is transformational. Inch by inch, note by note, or step by step, it changes the physiologic and cognitive structures mediating performance (Ericsson, 1996, 2004). Studies of musicians, for example, have documented growth of specific regions of the brain (e.g., those associated with hearing tones and controlling finger movements) and quantity of myelin (the protective sheath around the axon of neurons that enables the rapid transmission of signals from one cell to the next) that are directly proportional to the amount of practice (Coyle, 2009; N. M. Hill & Schneider, 2006). In a prospective study of brain changes in individuals training to be London taxi drivers, neuroscientist Eleanor Maguire and colleagues (Maguire et al.,

2000; Maguire, Woollett, & Spiers, 2006; Woollett & Maguire, 2011) of University College found that the size of the posterior hippocampus—the part of the brain critical to memory—actually grew over time. Such changes were not seen in those who started but failed to complete the demanding licensing process or never underwent instruction.

At the cognitive level, studies of chess players link greater success to an individual's development of a more complex and well-organized mental representation of the game. As Ericsson and Pool (2016) observed, such "maps" are made up of "patterns of information—facts, rules, relationships, and so on—that . . . make it possible to process large amounts of information quickly . . ." (pp. 60–61). In short, the best literally see a bigger picture, a wider range of strategies for effective action and innovation not accessible to less capable performers (Feltovich, Prietula, & Ericsson, 2018). Turning the well-known Zen saying on its head, "In the expert's mind there are many possibilities, but in the beginner's, there are few."

Understanding *how* DP works is best illustrated by looking at our own personal experience when learning something new. Take, for instance, psychotherapy. At the outset, as shared in Chapter 1, it is not uncommon for therapists-in-training to feel awkward and overwhelmed. Imaging studies (functional magnetic resonance imaging) of novices in other performance domains confirm as much. Consider Figure 3.1, which shows the brains of music students at different levels of instruction. In the early stages, they are lit up like city lights in high-density urban areas at night. It is any wonder, really? The amount of information to be processed is literally mind-boggling—notes, fingering, timing, rhythm, and volume, to mention but a few.

FIGURE 3.1. Brain Changes in the Development of Expertise

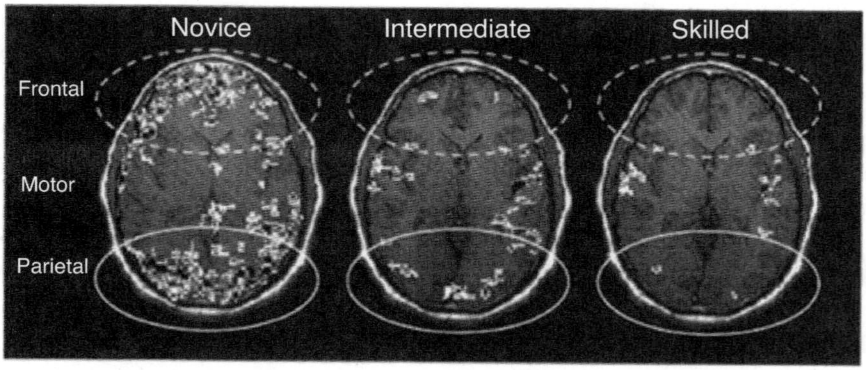

From "Brain Changes in the Development of Expertise: Neuroanatomical and Neurophysiological Evidence About Skill-Based Adaptations," by N. M. Hill and W. Schneider, in *The Cambridge Handbook of Expertise and Expert Performance* (p. 654), by K. A. Ericsson N. Charness, P. J. Feltovich, and R. R. Hoffman (Eds.), 2006, Cambridge, England: Cambridge University Press. Copyright 2006 by Cambridge University Press. Adapted with permission.

Beginning psychotherapists are no different. Trainees are filled to the brim with theories, diagnostic formulations, treatment models, techniques, supervisory advice, and admonitions—all of which have to be *consciously* sorted and properly applied in real time. More, as psychologist Derek Truscott (2010) observed in the opening pages of his book *Becoming an Effective Psychotherapist,* "To attempt to help another human being . . . is a tremendous responsibility" (p. xiii). Whether a rank beginner or an experienced clinician attempting to learn a new approach or technique, the pressure is intense. Wanting to get "it" right, not infrequently, makes everything seem wrong.

In time, with repetition and corrective feedback, the amount of mental exertion decreases. It's not that therapists stop processing information. They just do so differently. Returning to the brain images of musicians, we see the number of regions involved gradually drop out as the knowledge and skills required to act effectively are mastered and consolidated (Bilalić & Campitelli, 2018; N. M. Hill & Schneider, 2006). With regard to cognitive changes, the performer develops higher order units, or "chunks," for conceiving, understanding, and organizing their actions, enabling them to store and retrieve relevant information with greater ease, speed, and effect (Feltovich et al., 2018). On that score, studies of experienced counselors show they are better able to attend to factors most relevant for doing therapy; novices, by comparison, are more easily distracted by irrelevant or superficial details (Mayfield, Kardash, & Kivlighan, 1999).

In the end, what once required tremendous mental energy is done with barely a thought. Neuroscience research shows just how quickly this transformation takes place. N. M. Hill and Schneider (2006), for example, documented dramatic reductions (approximately 85%) in activation in the areas of the brain associated with task execution, attention, and memory following a single hour of focused practice on a novel task. Thus, clients are greeted, empathy is extended, and therapeutic actions are selected and carried out (including the coordinated use of eyes, hands, body language, and voice) with increasing efficiency and effectiveness. In fact, it is that precise experience—seamlessness, effortlessness, and being present in the moment—most associate with having "learned" to do something, whether it be tennis, playing the guitar, or doing psychotherapy.

Automaticity, as researchers refer to this stage in the development of expertise, is both good and bad (see Figure 3.2). On the positive side, a new, higher level of control over one's performance has been attained. The downside is this coincides with the time that improvement generally begins to stall and even deteriorate. "People," Ericsson (2006) pointed out, "lose conscious control-over the production of their actions and are no longer able to make specific intentional adjustments to them" (p. 694). Recall the study by Goldberg, Rousmaniere, et al. (2016) reported in the previous chapter documenting a steady diminution in effectiveness over time among practicing therapists—a tendency seen across a wide range of human endeavors (Ericsson & Pool, 2016).

FIGURE 3.2. Automaticity in Performance

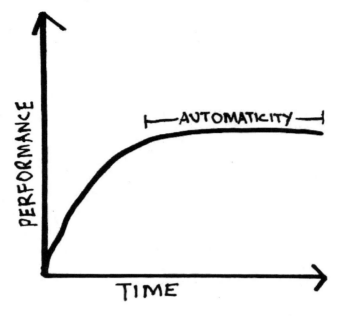

TO SUM UP

Purposefully counteracting the automaticity that accompanies the satisfactory execution of a new skill is at the heart of DP (see Figure 3.3). Simply put, it works by continuously and systematically pushing performers to reach for objectives just beyond their current abilities. As will be seen, not all practice is created equal—a fact that is painfully obvious considering the lack of improvement in psychotherapy outcomes over the past 40 years. In the next chapter, attention is turned to the elements of effective DP. Four characteristics are identified and illustrated that, when applied, result in better results.

FIGURE 3.3. Counteracting Automaticity in Performance

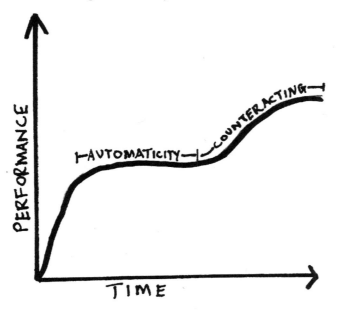

WHAT TO DO RIGHT NOW

Self-knowledge is the beginning of self-improvement.
—BALTASAR GRACIÁN (1653/1904, p. 40)

Take a moment to reflect on the concepts and ideas presented in this chapter, starting with your own beliefs regarding the nature of talent and development of expertise:

1. In what circumstances are you more inclined to attribute a particular skill or ability to genetic inheritance versus hard work? Why? What difference does it make in your efforts to improve?

2. Recalling the concept of automaticity, how might your "therapeutic reflexes" or habits get in the way of your attempts to achieve better results?

3. Imagine you need to describe how you conduct a typical therapy session to another practitioner. Now, create a schematic or blueprint for how you do therapy sufficiently detailed so another practitioner can replicate it. Heads up: You will be using what you create in future chapters, so take the time to complete it before proceeding.

4

What Is (and Is Not) Deliberate Practice?

A career is born in public—talent, in privacy.

—MARILYN MONROE (BERRINGTON, 2017)

One evening, virtuoso violinist Mischa Elman was walking back to his hotel following a rehearsal. Head down, face drawn, and exhausted, the session had not gone well. On turning a corner, he encountered two tourists. Spying his violin case, they asked, "Would you happen to know the way to Carnegie Hall?" According to the story, Elman replied without even bothering to raise his head. As he continued to walk, he muttered, "Practice, practice, practice."

It's an old joke. In fact, a number of variants with different protagonists have emerged over the past century. Some feature violinist Jascha Heifetz; others, pianist Arthur Rubinstein, an anonymous taxi driver, and an unknown beatnik poet ("The Joke," n.d.). In all, the point is the same. No shortcuts exist. To succeed, you have to pay your dues.

Devoting time to rehearsing what one wants to improve is hardly a novel idea. Any parent knows it to be true and has said as much to their children. References to enhancing one's skills or abilities through focused concentration and effort date back more than 2 millennia (Amirault & Branson, 2006; Ericsson, 2006). And yet, only recently—the past 25 years, to be precise—did serious scientific inquiry begin into *deliberate practice* (DP).

http://dx.doi.org/10.1037/0000191-004
Better Results: Using Deliberate Practice to Improve Therapeutic Effectiveness, by S. D. Miller, M. A. Hubble, and D. Chow

Early studies, beginning with those reviewed in the last chapter, confirmed the impact of DP on performance. In later studies, similar results were obtained across a wide range of endeavors. Surprisingly, regardless of its long-standing, intuitive appeal and growing empirical support, little consensus exists regarding the essential elements of effective practice. Is it just about putting in the time? Accumulating a certain number of hours? What about feedback? Is it important? If so, when and what kind? Can you practice effectively on your own or is a coach or teacher necessary?

Providing empirically supported answers to the questions just posed is not a trivial matter. In conducting their meta-analysis, for example, Miller, Chow, et al. (2018) found significant variability in how DP has been defined and operationalized in the scientific literature. To illustrate, in many investigations, researchers used "study time" and "attendance at lectures" as instances (Macnamara, Hambrick, & Oswald, 2014). But are they? Any college student who has, despite their best intentions, slept through an important class or spent study time chatting with friends knows otherwise. And indeed, when Miller, Chow, et al. (2018) eliminated such studies from their meta-analysis, they found the correlation between practice and performance was twice as large (viz. .40 vs. .21, $p < .001$)! Clearly, DP is more than showing up or expending time.

THE BUILDING BLOCKS OF DELIBERATE PRACTICE

> The whole structure of science gradually grows, but only as it is built upon a firm foundation. . . .
> —Owen Chamberlain ("Owen Chamberlain Banquet Speech," 1959),

What then are the ingredients of effective practice? In 1996, Ericsson and Lehmann proposed the following:

> . . . individualized training activities especially designed by a coach or teacher to improve specific aspects of an individual's performance through repetition and successive refinement. To receive maximal benefit from feedback, individuals have to monitor their training with full concentration, which is effortful and limits the duration of daily training. (pp. 278–279)

Based on this description and their own research, Miller, Chow, et al. (2018) suggested—in the interest of creating a shared understanding—that four specific criteria be met for any training activity to qualify as an instance of DP (see Figure 4.1). In the sections that follow, each is identified and explained. Care is taken to show what does and does not count as bona fide building blocks of effective practice.

Individualized Learning Objectives

Not surprisingly, effective DP starts with setting goals. To realize better results, performers must determine the *what* before the *how*. On this score, findings

FIGURE 4.1. The Structure of Deliberate Practice

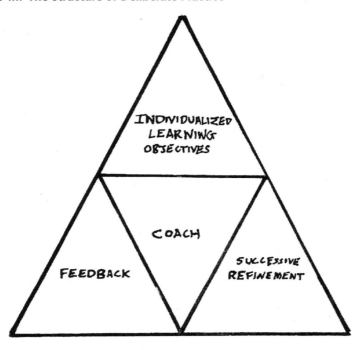

from the expertise literature show the poorest performers frequently avoid goal-setting, plodding along instead of planning. Those with average results, the majority, do set goals. Nevertheless, their objectives tend to be insufficiently specific and overly focused on the final outcome. The best performers are mindful of the outcome but direct most of their time, attention, and energy to the steps required for achieving what they desire (Ericsson, 2018; Zimmerman, 2006). Doing so, the evidence suggests, not only leads to better results in the end but higher levels of involvement and motivation along the way (S. Graham & Golan, 1991; Nolen, 1988).

Watching an accomplished guitarist practice reveals they spend a significant amount of their time rehearsing small, technical aspects of a composition they hope to master—the constituent parts, such as strumming, picking, chord progression, tempo, and dynamics (e.g., volume). Novices, on the other hand, are more inclined to "jump in with both feet," attempting to play a piece from start to finish.

In basketball, moreover, the most successful players focus on improving their dribbling, rebounds, passing, layups, and so on, as opposed to winning more games or sinking more shots. "I believe in the basics," celebrated UCLA basketball Coach John Wooden once observed. "Attention to, and perfection of, tiny details." He was famous for not allowing his players to scrimmage, choosing instead to focus on the fundamentals of the game. "They may seem trivial," he added, "even laughable to those who don't understand, but aren't. . . .

They are the difference between champions and near champions" (Wooden & Jamison, 1997, p. 60).

It is not enough for performers to be careful and compulsive in selecting their goals. The objectives they pursue must also be challenging. In the words of Ericsson (2009), learners must purposefully work to "go beyond their current level of reliable achievement" (p. 425), pushing into what pioneering psychologist Lev Vygotsky called the "zone of proximal development" (Vygotsky, 1978). Briefly, the *zone of proximal development* is the "sweet spot" between too easy and too difficult, what one already does well and what far exceeds current abilities or, as depicted in Figure 4.2, the zone between "comfort" and "panic."

It cannot be stressed enough: Learning goals are different from performance goals. The former relates to the skills, knowledge, or abilities one must master to succeed; the latter to the final result one hopes to achieve through DP. Naturally, every competitive sprinter wants to run faster, and many have a performance goal, such as medaling in their specific event. All but the least informed would consider buying a stopwatch a critical step in the process. Rather, using their current abilities as a starting point, they best focus their efforts on learning objectives such as improving the strength of their leg muscles, length and frequency of their stride, and economy of their running technique (Haley, 2014). As learning objectives just beyond an individual's ability are continuously set and reached, a greater degree of control over the elements related to performance is achieved.

FIGURE 4.2. Zones of Development

A Coach

It's no accident that those who reach the top—be it in sports, arts, music, in fact, most performance domains—work with a coach, mentor, or teacher throughout their careers (Ericsson, 2018; Hunt, 2006). Among chess players, for example, studies show having access to a coach results in half a standard deviation advantage on international rankings of skill level (Charness, Krampe, & Mayr, 1996). Ericsson (2016) reported a correlation of .9 between the amount of coach-led individual training and objective performance. In line with a focus on individualized learning objectives, most elite performers now work with a team of coaches, each specialized in one particular element essential to a successful performance (Starkes, Deakin, Allard, Hodges, & Hayes, 1996). To illustrate, in figure skating, the best have an instructor for equipment, and others for spinning, jumping, choreography, off-ice fitness, and physical strength.

The job of the coach/teacher is to see what the performer cannot see, such as a skater's elevation when attempting a triple axel or the head and elbow positions of a swimmer doing the forward crawl (Kostich, 2017). Particular attention is directed to isolating aspects of an individual's overall performance that consistently undermine or detract from success, and then designing practice activities to correct or enhance the learner's skills or abilities (Colvin, 2009). While any coach uses both praise and encouragement, the lion's share of their time is spent giving specific instruction on technique and execution. They are teachers first and cheerleaders second. Returning to UCLA Coach John Wooden, a study of his teaching style published in *Sport Psychologist* found slightly less than 7% of his time was spent dispensing compliments or disapproval (Gallimore & Tharp, 2004). Seventy-five percent comprised "discrete acts of teaching . . . pure information: what to do, how to do it, [and] when to intensify an activity" (Coyle, 2009, pp. 168–169).

Feedback

"We all need people who give us feedback," Bill Gates (2013) once said. "That's how we improve." Few would argue with the founder of the world's most dominant computer operating system. Like practice, feedback has become widely accepted as essential to personal and professional improvement efforts. Enter the phrase "importance of feedback" in Google, and 2.5 billion hits result!

Given its popularity, one might assume a universally accepted definition of the term exists. It does not. In fact, what it is, and how it works, remains a subject of continuing investigation and debate. And, as anyone who has been on the receiving end knows, not all feedback is created equal. In truth, the empirical literature shows it can either help or harm. While the weight of the evidence affirms a positive impact, a meta-analysis by Kluger and DeNisi (1996) found more than a third of feedback-related interventions were associated with *worse* performance.

Researchers have been sorting the evidence for decades to understand what needs to be in place for feedback to be beneficial. Certain characteristics stand out as key (Hysong, 2009; Ivers et al., 2012; Larson, Patel, Evans, & Saiman, 2013; Wiggins, 2012). To wit, feedback is more likely to be effective when it is

- timely,
- immediate,
- continuous,
- individualized,
- focused on specific goals,
- includes a plan of action,
- task versus person oriented,
- designed for remediating deficits or reducing given behaviors versus reinforcing or enhancing existing strengths, and
- delivered by a trustworthy and respected authority.

Similar findings have been reported in psychotherapy research. As is introduced in Chapter 7, studies of *routine outcome monitoring*—soliciting feedback from clients on an ongoing and formal basis—have shown it decreases dropout and improves outcomes (Lambert, 2013; Østergård, Randa, & Hougaard, 2018; Schuckard, Miller, & Hubble, 2017; Tilden & Wampold, 2017). Consistent with results from the broader feedback literature, randomized controlled trials show routine outcome monitoring is most helpful for clients at risk for a negative or null outcome. It is less effective for therapies on track. Additionally, the impact increases when it is (a) delivered at the time the service is provided, (b) done consistently and frequently, (c) includes specific recommendations for improving care, and (d) deemed trustworthy by clinicians.

One note before moving on to the fourth and final component of DP. In the previous discussion of individualized objectives and coaching, a sharp distinction was drawn between learning and performance. The same applies to feedback. It is more effective when aimed at helping the individual correct and refine core skills rather than shape a final result. Consider comedian Chris Rock's learning regimen (Sims, 2010). Before appearing in large concert venues, he spends months and months developing, testing, and refining his routines in small venues around the country. While in this mode, he is everything but the "Chris Rock" most people know from HBO specials. Gone is the flashy suit, crazy vocal intonations, and funny facial expressions. Instead, he's informal, conversational, and preoccupied with scribbling notes on a legal pad. During a 45-minute appearance on stage, most of his jokes fall flat. It's no wonder his audiences are routinely disappointed. As far as he is concerned, that's fine. He's not focused on entertaining. He's there to *learn* what will entertain.

Successive Refinement

Martial arts enthusiasts are fond of quoting Lee Jun-Fan, better known as Bruce Lee. One, in particular—the source and occasion unknown—goes, "I fear not the man who has practiced 10,000 kicks, but I fear the man who has practiced one kick 10,000 times." The premise is accurate but only in part. Whatever is repeated will merely become automatic and enduring, not necessarily better; that is, unless the performer is (a) reaching for specific objectives just beyond their current abilities, (b) consulting a coach who identifies and isolates specific errors and develops a customized plan and training activities, and (c) receiving ongoing feedback about what they are doing and how they are doing it (Ericsson, 2006).

At this juncture, recall the results of Miller, Chow, et al. (2018), which found simply putting in time was half as effective as practicing deliberately. Successive refinement is not about clocking hours. Fundamentally, it's about change, directing time and effort toward modifying behaviors that have a clear relationship with performance.

The temptation to settle—to avoid working at the edge of one's ability—is both strong and understandable. The threat of failure is always present. It's far easier to stay in the comfort zone. There, anxiety decreases and confidence increases. To illustrate, Deakin and Cobley (2003) found ice skaters, despite their strong desire to improve, often devoted more time to practicing elements of their routine they had already mastered. The cost is, as Henry Ford is said to have stated, "If you always do what you've always done, you'll always get what you've always got."

COMMON MISUNDERSTANDINGS ABOUT DELIBERATE PRACTICE: A WORD OF CAUTION

It is what you don't expect . . . that most needs looking for.
—Neal Stephenson (2008, p. 30)

Three misunderstandings commonly arise as psychotherapists initially learn about and try to apply DP to their work and professional development. Take a moment to review each before proceeding.

Confusing Deliberate With Clinical Practice

DP is *not* clinical practice. Look up *practice* in an American English dictionary ("Practice," 1976), and one learns the word is both a verb and a noun, referring to either "repeated performance for the purpose of acquiring skill," or the pursuit of a "profession, art, or occupation." Obviously, the meanings are different. As such, it is easy to confuse the two. As the research reviewed in Chapter 2 plainly shows, while clinicians become more confident as years of working with clients accumulate, their effectiveness does not improve.

In British English, two spellings are used to distinguish between verb and noun, *practise* and *practice*, respectively. To keep "learning how to do therapy" separate from "the doing," it would be far better for practitioners to refer to their daily work with clients as a performance rather than a practice. Instead of stating, "I have been practicing," it is more accurate to say, "I have been performing therapy for 10 years." The term *deliberate practice* would only be used to refer to the time spent outside of sessions in activities specifically designed to become better therapists.

Believing Deliberate Practice Is a Special Set of Techniques

DP is not a set of techniques that, when learned and applied in the same way by everyone, leads to better results. The field of psychotherapy has a long history of selling formulaic approaches. Gift wrapped in books, manuals, workshops, and webinars, the promise is do this—whatever the "this" is—and you will be more effective. Decades of research have shown these claims to be empty.

By contrast, DP is not a formula to be followed but a form. The four building blocks provide a structure and discipline for organizing, advancing, and sustaining one's professional development. The particulars vary from person to person depending on what needs to be learned, the coach's input and feedback, the time devoted to successive refinement, and the progress achieved.

Applying Deliberate Practice to Mastering Treatment Models

Simply put, DP is not likely to improve effectiveness when it is applied to learning therapy models. One may become an expert, but why spend practice time mastering the elements of a particular approach when the evidence clearly shows adherence and competence contribute a negligible amount to outcome (Barber et al., 2006; Duncan, Miller, Wampold, & Hubble, 2010; Wampold & Imel, 2015; Webb, DeRubeis, & Barber, 2010)?

Consider a recent study out of the United Kingdom (Branson, Shafran, & Myles, 2015). There, massive amounts of money have been spent training clinicians to use cognitive behavioral therapy. The expenditure is part of a well-intentioned government program aimed at improving access to effective mental health services (S. Griffiths & Steen, 2013). Anyway, in the study, clinicians participated in a high-intensity course that included more than 300 hours of training, supervision, and practice. Competency in delivering cognitive behavior therapy was assessed at regular intervals and shown to improve significantly throughout the training. The tremendous investment of time, money, and resources notwithstanding, clinical outcomes did not improve.

Despite decades of similar findings, the allure of models (and promise of a shortcut to expertise) is so strong, we suspect we'll be seeing in the near future books, workshops, and articles claiming to apply the principles of DP to mastery of therapeutic techniques. The evidence, however, points in a different direction. Instead of focusing on how to do therapy, DP directs attention to the development of the therapist. To be sure, some clinicians may benefit from improving their ability to structure and organize the therapeutic hour using one of the hundreds of available approaches (Kaslow & Patterson, 2002; Miller, Duncan, & Hubble, 1995; Truscott, 2010). Nonetheless, as reviewed later in this volume, factors other than model and technique provide more potent alternatives.

TO SUM UP

Believing practice leads to improvement is neither new nor noteworthy. It is also untrue. Mere repetition does not lead to excellence. It simply makes what is repeated permanent. The key to improving therapeutic effectiveness is *deliberate* practice. Its building blocks include (a) individualized learning objectives, (b) use of a coach, (c) feedback, and (d) successive refinement through repetition.

WHAT TO DO RIGHT NOW

A journey of a thousand miles begins with a single step.
—LAO TZU (BERTRAND, 2017, PREFACE)

In the preceding chapters, the empirical foundation of DP practice was presented and described. Attention is now turned to its application in your own work, starting with establishing a baseline against which progress can be measured.

With that end in mind, before turning the page, take out the schematic or blueprint you created at the end of Chapter 3 for how you do therapy. With that in hand, and Figure 4.1 in mind, answer the following questions:

1. *Individualized learning objectives:* What aspects of your clinical work do you need to address to achieve better results?

2. *Coach:* To whom will you turn for guidance about improving your performance? How will you make your work available for your coach to observe, assess, and then provide corrective instruction?

3. *Feedback:* How will you stay focused on learning rather than the end performance when receiving critical feedback?

4. *Successive refinement:* What must you find in yourself and create in your environment to stay engaged in DP while working to refine and improve your work?

GETTING STARTED:
WHAT TO DO FIRST TO
ACHIEVE BETTER RESULTS

5

Baseline Matters

Without a clear, unbiased view of . . . performance, choosing the best practice activity will be impossible.

—GEOFF COLVIN (2009, p. 67)

Shaquille O'Neal and Wilt Chamberlain are two of the most celebrated basketball players in the history of the game. Known as "Wilt the Stilt" for his 7-foot-plus height, Chamberlain was the first to exceed 30,000 career points and the only player to score 100 points in a single game. Eighteen years after the Stilt's retirement, O'Neal came on the scene. Nicknamed "Shaq," he was a virtual juggernaut. One of the largest and heaviest ever to play in the NBA, he dominated the court, easily driving past opposing players to the hoop. Another testament to his physical prowess, he could extend 12-and-a-half feet from a standing position—the highest maximum vertical reach ever measured (B. A. Graham, 2013).

O'Neal and Chamberlain share one additional record. The two are the only players to miss more than 5,000 free throws! Given the ball during play, scoring was near inevitable. Take an uncontested shot standing a mere 15 feet from the basket, and their probability of success plummeted. In the case of O'Neal, other teams developed a specific defensive tactic to take advantage of just this fact. Called the "Hack-a-Shaq," players would purposefully foul him, in the process breaking his charge and forcing him to the free throw line, where baskets are worth only 1 point.

http://dx.doi.org/10.1037/0000191-005
Better Results: Using Deliberate Practice to Improve Therapeutic Effectiveness, by S. D. Miller, M. A. Hubble, and D. Chow

Similar to psychotherapy outcomes, the success rate of free throws has remained unchanged for 50 years (Branch, 2009). On average, NBA players sink 75%; their college counterparts, slightly less (approximately 70%). Shaq and Wilt rank among the game's *worst,* hitting only 50% of shots—a third less than average.

WHY BASELINE MATTERS

Statistics such as these are not insignificant details, subjects for pundits and sports fans to discuss and debate endlessly. Quite the contrary, access to valid and reliable baseline performance data facilitates two important objectives. First, such information serves as a standard against which the efficacy of any performance improvement effort may be evaluated. Second, and particularly obvious in the cases of O'Neal and Chamberlain, it permits the identification of deficits or weaknesses specific to the individual that then can be targeted for remediation.

It stands to reason. If one calls for directions to a particular destination, the first question likely to be heard is, "Where are you now?" As reviewed in Chapters 1 and 2, most practitioners have no hard data about their therapeutic effectiveness (Boswell, Kraus, Miller, & Lambert, 2015). Not knowing "where they are," they have no reference point for charting a course of professional development, much less determining the impact of any steps taken to improve.

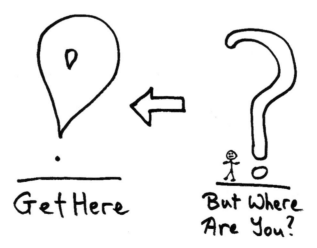

As also reported, therapists' personal appraisals are not reliable and thus cannot be counted on to provide direction. Clinicians believe themselves to be more effective than they are, chronically underestimate the number of clients who deteriorate while in their care, and think they are improving when they are not (Chow et al., 2015; Miller, Hubble, & Duncan, 2007; Walfish, McAlister,

O'Donnell, & Lambert, 2012). Critically, this "illusory superiority bias" is not self-correcting, despite time and experience in the field (Buunk & Van Yperen, 1991; Hannan et al., 2005; Kahneman, 2011; Kruger, 1999).

Back on the court, similar problems and biases plague basketball. The free throw has long been dismissed as an unimportant element of the game. Believed to require nothing in the way of real skill, it is regarded by many coaches and players with contempt. Even the name, as sportswriter Bill Modoono (1987) pointed out, conveys a lack of respect: "Free. . . . As in 'gratuitous.' . . . Throw. Not 'shoot' or 'launch' or even 'propel.' Just 'throw.'" In the same vein, even when provided with a scientifically superior free throw technique known as the "Granny Shot," both Chamberlin and O'Neal balked (Devlin, 2017). With so much prejudice arrayed against the free throw, few consider it worthy of the time or attention required for improvement.

DATA MATTERS

If we have data, let's look at data. If all we have are opinions, let's go with mine.
—Jim Barksdale (Theodore, 2017)

Looking at the facts about free throws in basketball, an altogether different understanding emerges. Data show improving success at the free throw line by a tiny percentage (4%) would on average lead a team to one more winning game per week. As it is, each season, many games are won or lost by a small margin, even a single point. For example, in 2013, the San Antonio Spurs lost the NBA championship when team members Manu Ginobili and Kawhi Leonard bungled two free throws in Game 6. Adapting Carl Rogers's famous maxim, ignoring the facts is never friendly. Indeed, as the Spurs know all too well, neglecting baseline performance data has major, real-world consequences.

Compared to the field of psychotherapy, professional basketball is in a very enviable position. While they may be ignored, statistics are constantly being accumulated, cataloged, dissected, and interpreted about both teams and individual players. Andre Drummond of the Detroit Pistons provides an excellent example of what can be accomplished when data are not only available but also put to use to improve effectiveness.

Drummond has the distinction of being the *worst* free throw shooter in the entire history of the NBA. Chamberlain and O'Neal were, by comparison, titans of the shot. Year after year, he sustained his dismal record—in his fourth season, succeeding only 36% of the time. Then, after opposing teams had invested 5 years singling him out for the "Hack-a-Shaq," Drummond more than doubled his success rate at the line, sinking 78% in one season (Ellentuck, 2017). Observers noted his entire form had changed: He stood differently, was more fluid, and exhibited greater finesse and comfort.

How Drummond achieved this remarkable improvement is no mystery. It is a textbook example of deliberate practice. According to his trainer, Idan

Ravin, the player spent "many, many, many weeks, and thousands of hours" developing a winning throw (Ellentuck, 2017). Critically, the entire process started with taking his numbers seriously—in short, attending to his baseline. Rather than being an asset, it was obvious to everyone he'd become a liability. Fouled so often and so quickly (in one game five times in 9 seconds), he was rendered unplayable. Certainly, the owners were motivated to give him extra training in foul shots. They'd invested $130 million in his contract! In the end, all decided a change was long overdue.

TOOLS FOR ESTABLISHING YOUR BASELINE

> I have been struck again and again by how important measurement is to improving the human condition.
>
> —Bill Gates (Soper, 2013)

For their part, practitioners of psychotherapy have, until very recently, not had the means to collect data pertinent to their practices and outcomes. Fortunately, several well-established measures for assessing therapeutic performance are now available (cf. Corcoran & Fischer, 2013; Froyd, Lambert, & Froyd, 1996; Ogles, Lambert, & Masters, 1996; Prescott, Maeschalck, & Miller, 2017). Computerized systems, moreover, have come online that automate the collection of data for agencies and individual clinicians, and facilitate comparisons with national and international benchmarks (cf. Lambert, 2012; Miller, Duncan, Sorrell, & Brown, 2005).

In the next chapter, instructions are provided for using one well-established system. Called the *Partners for Change Outcome Management System* (PCOMS; Bertolino & Miller, 2012; Miller et al., 2005), it was reviewed and listed on the Substance Abuse and Mental Health Services Administration's National Registry of Evidence-Based Programs and Practices (Prescott et al., 2017). Research to date documents PCOMS provides valid and reliable quality and outcome benchmarks (Schuckard, Miller, & Hubble, 2017). Developed and studied thoroughly by the authors, it is in use around the world, across diverse settings and treatment populations. Additionally, the method and included measures have proven to be simple to learn and incorporate into daily clinical practice (Miller et al., 2005).

TO SUM UP

Getting somewhere requires knowing your starting point. Using standardized measures to establish a baseline of your clinical effectiveness provides a reference for assessing progress and, as will be seen, guidance about *where* room for improvement exists, specifically, clues about the learning objectives you might most profitably pursue.

WHAT TO DO RIGHT NOW

There are no secrets to success. It is the result of preparation, hard work, and learning from failure.

—RETIRED GENERAL COLIN POWELL
(WASHINGTON SPEAKERS BUREAU, n.d.)

As practitioners begin using valid and reliable tools to measure their performance, many find their own informal assessment diverges significantly from the data they gather. For this reason, prior to reading further, turn back to the questions at the end of Chapter 1. If you haven't already answered them, take the time to do so now. To these, add your answers to the following:

- How many sessions do your clients attend on average?
- What percentage of your clients drop out after a single visit?
- What percentage of your clients deteriorate while in your care?

6

How to Find Your Baseline

Without data you're just another person with an opinion.
—W. EDWARDS DEMING (JONES & SILBERZAHN, 2016)

What constitutes "a result" in psychotherapy, and who gets to decide? What do we, as therapists, believe to be our raison d'être, our purpose or mission? What about the people in therapy, the recipients of care? Do they get a say? And, if so, what do they want and deem important? How about researchers? When they say psychotherapy "works," what exactly does that mean? Just what is "a good outcome?" And, if we can all agree on the answers to these questions, what in our performance best predicts engagement, effectiveness, and satisfaction for those involved?

"Measuring change in or outcome of psychotherapy," Ogles, Lambert, and Masters (1996) noted, "has proven to be a . . . complicated, multidimensional issue . . ." (p. 4). For the first 100 years of the profession, good results were literally whatever therapists said they were. Evaluations of benefit, if they occurred at all, were based on reviews of written case notes and clinical files. Much greater attention was directed to how treatment was done; fidelity in the application of a given theory and its methods was the primary concern.

http://dx.doi.org/10.1037/0000191-006
Better Results: Using Deliberate Practice to Improve Therapeutic Effectiveness, by S. D. Miller, M. A. Hubble, and D. Chow

THE EVOLUTION OF OUTCOME MEASUREMENT

Beginning in the 1950s, the customary ways of assessing effectiveness came under close scrutiny. Researchers within the emerging school of behavior therapy were harshly critical of claims made and methods used to determine outcome (Miller, Hubble, Chow, & Seidel, 2013). When Hans Eysenck (1952) analyzed 24 empirical studies of psychotherapy, he concluded the current methods were not only ineffective but potentially harmful. Needless to say, his report aroused both public and professional concern (Luborsky, 1954; Rosenzweig, 1954).

The field responded. Following Eysenck's (1952) critique, interest in improving the evaluation of therapy heightened among academicians and researchers. Variety and rigor increased. Still, it was largely business as usual. In particular, although more standardized measures were employed, the clinicians' perspective, informed by their preferred models and techniques, was still given pride of place (Ogles, 2013).

As the desire for greater thoroughness and precision grew, the early emphasis placed on theoretical orientation gave way to a search for a common diagnostic framework (e.g., the first edition of the *Diagnostic and Statistical Manual of Mental Disorders* [*DSM–1*]; American Psychiatric Association, 1952). The assumption was that a careful, accurate, and reliable delineation of the "targets" of treatment would, as it had done so well in the broader field of medicine, make determining effectiveness straightforward. In the case of strep throat, for example, the clinician's opinion matters little. The proof of cure is the elimination of the infection.

Similarly in psychotherapy, studies began using measures designed to assess change in symptoms specific to a given diagnosis (e.g., Beck Depression Inventory; Beck, Ward, Mendelson, Mock, & Erbaugh, 1961). In short, the reduction or elimination of symptoms served as the benchmark for assessing the success of care. The addition of measures completed by other stakeholders (e.g., supervisors, independent raters, patients, significant others) provided collateral evidence of effectiveness. The focus on assessing symptom relief has endured to the present, resulting in the development of literally hundreds of scales (Ogles, 2013; Ogles et al., 1996).

A less popular alternative, and consequently smaller number of measures, directs attention to clients' well-being and overall quality of life. The Global Assessment of Functioning Scale, introduced in the *Diagnostic and Statistical Manual III-R* (third ed., rev. [*DSM–III–R*]; American Psychiatric Association, 1987), is one example most clinicians know. Others include the Quality of Life Index (Spitzer, 1981) and the WHO Psychiatric Disability Assessment Schedule (World Health Organization, 1988; see Figure 6.1). The premise underlying these scales is that people are more than their symptoms. For change to be considered meaningful, a real improvement in individual, social, and occupational functioning must take place (Ogles, 2013; Pavot & Diener, 2004; World Health Organization, 1946).

FIGURE 6.1. Measurement of Symptoms Versus Measurement of Global Well-Being

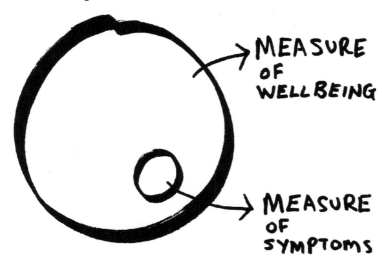

For all the attention paid to effectiveness since Eysenck, one fact is evident: Until very recently, modern measurement methods have principally reflected the needs, interests, and goals of researchers. Surveys indicate clinicians *are* truly interested in obtaining reliable outcome data (Bickman et al., 2000; Hatfield & Ogles, 2004). The same surveys show therapists regard existing scales as impractical and, more importantly, of little clinical value.

Thankfully, the divide between practitioners and researchers is closing. Mindful of practical considerations, measurement systems have come online that are far more feasible for use in real-world practice. They take but a few minutes to complete, are easy to understand and administer, and apply across a wide range of presenting problems and clinical settings. These instruments also provide reliable and valid estimates of progress, give warnings when treatment is at risk for a negative outcome, and furnish detailed metrics for profiling a clinician's strengths and weaknesses. Even more, they make the assessment of the client's experience central to the measurement—after all, without satisfied customers, a practitioner is unlikely to be successful.

PARTNERS FOR CHANGE OUTCOME MANAGEMENT SYSTEM

> Alone we can do so little, together we can do so much.
> —Helen Keller (Helen Keller International, n.d.)

As introduced at the end of the preceding chapter, the Partners for Change Outcome Management System (PCOMS; Miller, Duncan, Sorrell, & Brown, 2005) is one example of the new generation of practical, user-friendly, and client-oriented methods for measuring effectiveness. It consists of two simple scales: the Outcome Rating Scale (ORS; Miller & Duncan, 2000) and the Session Rating Scale (SRS; Miller, Duncan, & Johnson, 2000). In order, the SRS and ORS assess clients' experience of the quality of the relationship (i.e., the working alliance) with their therapist and the current state of their well-being in day-to-day life. Both scales are short, four-item, self-report instruments that have been tested in numerous studies and shown to have solid reliability and validity (Schuckard, Miller, & Hubble, 2017). In wide use around the world, the measures have been translated into 30 languages and are available in versions for adults, adolescents, and children. Individual practitioners can begin using the tools by registering at https://scott-d-miller-ph-d.myshopify.com/collections/performance-metrics/products/performance-metrics-licenses-for-the-ors-and-srs for a free license.

Administering and scoring the measures is simple and straightforward. The ORS is completed at the beginning of each session. As can be seen in Figure 6.2, the scale asks those in care to think back over the prior week (or since the last visit) and place a hash mark (or *x*) on four different lines, each representing a different area of well-being (e.g., individually, interpersonally, socially, and overall). Hand-scoring is a simple matter of determining the distance in centimeters (to the nearest millimeter) between the left pole and the client's mark on each individual item. The four numbers are then added together to obtain the total score.

Assessments of well-being have several advantages over measures linked to a particular diagnosis or limited to assessing symptoms. First, scales like the ORS can be administered to clients regardless of their presenting problem, thereby saving time and eliminating the need to master a battery of tests (Duncan, Miller, & Sparks, 2004). Second, it turns out well-being, in contrast to mere symptom reduction, is highly predictive of several positive life outcomes. As well-being increases, for instance, people exercise more, drink less, and abstain from tobacco. Not surprisingly, they enjoy better physical health and live longer lives. Additionally, greater well-being is associated with personal goal achievement, better social relationships, and work performance (Diener, Oishi, & Tay, 2018; Holt-Lunstad, Smith, Baker, Harris, & Stephenson, 2015; Holt-Lunstad, Smith, & Layton, 2010).

At the end of each session, the SRS is administered (see Figure 6.3). Items on the scale assess the quality of the relationship, reflecting the classic definition first proposed by Bordin (1979). In particular, it gauges clients' experience of four interacting elements: the quality of the relational bond and the degree of agreement between the client and therapist on the goals, methods, and overall approach of therapy. Scoring of the SRS is identical to that of the ORS.

Why Measure the Alliance?

Before proceeding, it is reasonable to ask, among the universe of variables pertaining to a clinician's baseline performance, "Why measure the quality of the therapeutic relationship?" First and foremost, decades of research have

FIGURE 6.2. The Outcome Rating Scale

Outcome Rating Scale (ORS)

Name _____ Age (Yrs):____ Gender_____
Session# ____ Date:_____
Who is filling out this form? Please check one: Self_____   Other_____
If other, what is your relationship to this person?_____

Looking back over the last week, including today, help us understand how you have been feeling by rating left represent low levels and marks to the following areas of your life, where marks to the left represent low levels and no marks to the right indicate high levels. *If you are filling out this form for another person, please fill out according to how you think he or she is doing.*

Individually
(Personal well-being)

|---|

Interpersonally
(Family, close relationships)

|---|

Socially
(Work, school, friendships)

|---|

Overall
(General sense of well-being)

|---|

International Center for Clinical Excellence

www.scottdmiller.com

From *The Outcome Rating Scale*, by S. D. Miller and B. L. Duncan, 2000, Chicago, IL: Author. Copyright 2000 by Scott D. Miller and Barry L. Duncan. Reprinted with permission.

shown it to be one of the most robust predictors of treatment outcome (Norcross, 2010; Wampold & Imel, 2015). Figure 6.4 graphically depicts just how much more relational elements affect the effectiveness of psychotherapy over variables long thought to be more important. Mindful of such data, time spent in efforts to achieve better results would be best allocated to improving one's ability to convey understanding and empathy than to mastering a new treatment model (Elliott, Bohart, Watson, & Greenberg, 2011).

FIGURE 6.3. The Session Rating Scale

Session Rating Scale (SRS V.3.0)

Name _____ Age (Yrs):____

ID# _____ Gender:_____

Session # ____ Date: _____

Please rate today's session by placing a mark on the line nearest to the description that best fits your experience.

Relationship

I did not feel heard, understood, and respected. |--| I felt heard, understood, and respected.

Goals and Topics

We did *not* work on or talk about what I wanted to work on and talk about. |--| We worked on and talked about what I wanted to work on and talk about.

Approach or Method

The therapist's approach is not a good fit for me. |--| The therapist's approach is a good fit for me.

Overall

There was something missing in the session today. |--| Overall, today's session was right for me.

International Center for Clinical Excellence

www.scottdmiller.com

From *The Session Rating Scale 3.0*, by S. D. Miller, B. L. Duncan, and L. D. Johnson, 2002, Chicago, IL: Author. Copyright 2002 by Scott D. Miller, Barry L. Duncan, and Lynn D. Johnson. Reprinted with permission.

FIGURE 6.4. The Effect Size of Factors Affecting the Outcome of Psychotherapy

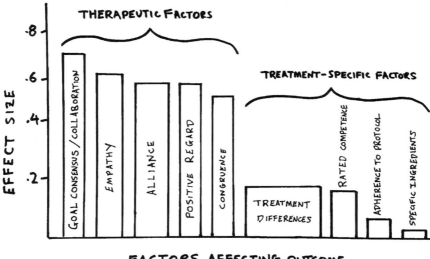

Width of bars reflects the number of studies reflecting effect sizes for each therapeutic factor. From *The Great Psychotherapy Debate: The Evidence for What Makes Psychotherapy Work* (2nd ed., p. 258), by B. E. Wampold and Z. E. Imel, 2015, New York, NY: Routledge. Copyright 2015 by Bruce E. Wampold and Zac E. Imel. Adapted with permission.

Second, the evidence confirms what everyone already knows but rarely discusses openly: (a) Some therapists are better than others at establishing and sustaining helpful relationships and (b) no practitioner, no matter how effective, connects with everyone they see in their practice (T. Anderson, Crowley, Himawan, Holmberg, & Uhlin, 2016; T. Anderson, Ogles, Patterson, Lambert, & Vermeersch, 2009; Baldwin, Wampold, & Imel, 2007). As will be discussed in Chapter 8, being able to compare one's relational ability to other clinicians and pinpoint when and with whom one connects or not, enables the identification of individual strengths and weaknesses. The information, in turn, can be used to develop a personalized professional development plan.

All's Well That *Begins* Well

Obtaining valid and reliable data regarding baseline performance starts with creating an environment conducive to sharing and participation. Beyond displaying an attitude of openness and receptivity, taking time to introduce the measures in a thoughtful and thorough manner fosters the development of a culture of feedback (Schuckard et al., 2017). This is a critical step. Clients need to feel free to rate their experience of the process and outcome of services without fear of criticism or other adverse repercussions.

Experience and research strongly support providing a rationale for using the tools. When introducing the measures at the outset of a new episode of care, the therapist can say,

> I work a little differently at [this agency or practice]. My first priority is making sure that you get the results you want. For this reason, it is important that you are involved in monitoring our progress. To do this, I use a brief measure called the Outcome Rating Scale. It takes about a minute to complete. I'll ask you to fill it out at the beginning of each session and then we'll talk about the results. A fair amount of research shows that if we are going to be successful in our work together, we should see signs of improvement sooner rather than later. If what we're doing works, then we'll continue. If not, then we'll work together to figure out what can do differently. If things still don't improve, then we'll find someone or someplace else for you to get the help you want. Does this make sense to you? (Bargmann & Robinson, 2012, p. 9)[1]

At the end of each session, the therapist administers the SRS. As with the ORS, the purpose of the tool is explained:

> I'd like to ask you to fill out one additional form. This is called the Session Rating Scale. A great deal of research shows that your experience of our work together— did you feel understood, did we focus on what was important to you, did the approach I'm taking make sense and feel right—is a good predictor of whether we'll be successful. I want to emphasize that I'm not aiming for a perfect score— a 10 out of 10. Life isn't perfect and neither am I. What I'm aiming for is your feedback about even the smallest things—even if it seems unimportant—so we can adjust our work and make sure we don't steer off course. Whatever it might be, I promise I won't take it personally. I'm always learning, and am curious about any feedback from you that will in time help me improve so I can better help you. Does this make sense? (Bargmann & Robinson, 2012, p. 14)

Integration of the Measures Into Therapy

When first using the scales, it is not uncommon for clinicians to be anxious and even report difficulties gaining client compliance. We hear: Could this alienate people—after all, they already have to complete tons of paperwork? Might it interfere with clinical work? What if my client refuses? All such concerns are understandable. And yet, as with any new undertaking, integrating the use of standardized questionnaires into routine practice, no matter how simple or brief, takes time, patience, and persistence. In reality, existing evidence indicates most worries and objections originate with therapists, *not* clients. When polled, 92% of those receiving psychological care approved of measures that tracked their progress and solicited their perspective (Lutz, 2014; Miller, 2014). Bearing this in mind, with few exceptions, any challenges are best viewed as a learning opportunity—a call to review and refine one's presentation of the tools.

---

[1]This and the following quote are from "Manual 2—Feedback-Informed Clinical Work: The Basics," by S. Bargmann and B. Robinson, in *The ICCE Manuals on Feedback-Informed Treatment (FIT)* (pp. 9 and 14), by B. Bertolino and S. D. Miller (Eds.), 2012, Chicago, IL: International Centre for Clinical Excellence. Copyright 2012 by the International Centre for Clinical Excellence. Reprinted with permission.

Our experience shows two common causes are behind the difficulties therapists voice when first using the scales: (a) acting as though one is "proctoring" an exam and (b) communicating, albeit indirectly, that the measures are a chore, irrelevant to the work client and therapist will do together. As Schafer (1954) long ago observed, it is a mistake to treat the administration of measures as "an impersonal getting-together of two people in order that one, with the help of a little 'rapport,' may gain some 'objective' test responses from the other" (p. 6). We've heard therapists argue, out of concern a client will not provide an accurate or honest answer, or be unduly influenced in responding, that they must assume an aloof or distant stance. Some even consider turning over the administration of the tools to another (e.g., support staff). This is a mistake. Viewing the measures as a part of, rather than apart from, the work is the solution.

TO SUM UP

The ability to assess the quality and outcome of psychological care has come of age. No longer relegated to researchers or diagnosticians, the development of valid, reliable, and simple-to-use tools has made it possible for clinicians to obtain feedback in real time. Access to such information improves outcomes and, as will be shown, identifies targets for deliberate practice. What is more, the evidence shows the majority of consumers do not object. Paying attention to how the forms are introduced and utilized further ensures their acceptance as an integral part of the work.

In the next chapter, attention is directed toward making sense of the data produced by the measures. Several performance metrics are introduced and explained. You will learn how to determine just how effective you are as a therapist. You will be able to discover with whom you work well, including their age, gender, cultural background, and presenting problem, as well as how long your clients stay in treatment, their rate of change, and who drops out and when. At length, you will also be able to see how your clinical performance compares with that of others.

WHAT TO DO RIGHT NOW

If you want to run, run a mile. If you want to experience a different life, run a marathon.

—EMIL ZÁTOPEK (ELLICK, 2001)

(continues)

WHAT TO DO RIGHT NOW (*Continued*)

Deliberate practice is a marathon, not a sprint. It takes time and effort, as well as a willingness, to forgo immediate rewards. As all long-distance runners know, the key to success is endurance—burning long rather than brightly. For these reasons, although it may be tempting to jump right into the next chapter, we recommend pacing yourself. With the next 10 new clients you see:

1. Use the ORS and SRS at each and every session. For now, stick to the scripts provided, even reading them word-for-word from the text.

2. Keep in mind while administering the scales, physicians do not treat their stethoscope as separate from, but integral to, the care they provide. Look for opportunities to weave your clients' responses to the measures into your therapeutic work.

3. Make note of what, if anything, you discover about yourself and your clients as a result of using the scales.

7

Making Sense of Your Baseline

When you have mastered numbers, you will in fact no longer be reading numbers, any more than you read words when reading books. You will be reading meanings.
—HAROLD GENEEN (1984, p. 151)

Michael Lambert is one of the field's most influential outcome research-ers. He has devoted his career to exploring what works in psychother-apy (Lambert, 2013). More, he was among the first to raise concerns about negative treatment effects, calling attention 4 decades ago to the then "ample evidence that psychotherapy can and does cause harm to a portion of those it is intended to help" (Lambert, 1979, p. 6). Alarmed by these findings—and the field's relative indifference—he went to work, developing a system for alerting therapists to cases at risk of deterioration or dropout (Lambert, 2010a, 2010b; Lambert, Harmon, Slade, Whipple, & Hawkins, 2005). In the ensuing time, numerous, large-scale randomized clinical trials published by interna-tional teams not only confirmed Lambert's concerns but also validated his proposed solution. It is now well-established that providing real-time feed-back about progress and the strength of the working alliance reduces deterio-ration and premature termination while improving the overall effectiveness of psychotherapy (Schuckard, Miller, & Hubble, 2017).

Despite these positive results, within a short period, Lambert began noticing something unsettling: Therapists were not learning from the feedback provided

http://dx.doi.org/10.1037/0000191-007
Better Results: Using Deliberate Practice to Improve Therapeutic Effectiveness, by S. D. Miller, M. A. Hubble, and D. Chow

(Miller, Hubble, & Duncan, 2007). How did he come to this finding? Research, of course!

In a series of ingenious studies, therapists received feedback on *half* of their cases. With the other half, the measures were administered, but no feedback was provided. Consistent with findings from prior studies, outcomes improved when data from the measures were made available to clinicians in real time. However, when progress information was withheld, no improvement occurred. Therapists were not able to generalize lessons learned from the cases in which feedback was provided to those where none was made available. Observed Lambert, "Even though therapists ha[d] gotten feedback on half their cases for over three years, . . . [they did] not learn how to detect failing cases" (Miller, Duncan, & Hubble, 2004, p. 16). In short, ongoing feedback only served to help clinicians adjust in the moment. For whatever reason, they did not learn anything that carried over to and helped their other cases.

It was a baffling result. The participants in Lambert's studies were all intelligent, thoughtful practitioners who fully understood the purpose and importance of the research. The whole point was to identify people at risk for deterioration or dropout and then take steps to prevent these undesirable outcomes. A reasonable person would expect that, with time and experience, therapists would become sensitive to the "tells"—verbal or otherwise— indicative of potential negative results. After all, the measures and feedback were fairly straightforward, even basic in nature: Is therapy working or not? Are the therapist and client in sync with one another or not?

At this point, some might ask, "So what?" We don't expect physicians to be able to determine a person's blood pressure without a sphygmomanometer, nor would one expect health care professionals to detect bacterial infections without obvious visible clues or medical testing. Why on earth would we expect psychotherapists to be any different? And yet, some are, and reliably so.

TOP PERFORMERS POINT THE WAY

> Actions speak louder than words, but not nearly as often.
> —Attributed to Mark Twain

In his thought-provoking book *Sources of Power: How People Make Decisions*, cognitive psychologist Gary Klein (1998) tells the story of a select group of nurses who, by simply looking at a premature infant—even "micro-premies" less than 800 grams or 26 weeks gestation at birth—can tell the child is developing a life-threatening infection. "When babies this small develop an infection," Klein pointed out, "it can spread through their entire body and kill them before the antibiotics can stop it" (p. 42). Therefore, the ability to discern the presence of a disease process before confirmation by medical testing, and even when such tests return false negatives, is critical for saving infants who otherwise would die.

The findings from the "infected babies project" were initially viewed as inexplicable, if not magical. To the nurses, it was equally puzzling. When asked, they chalked it up either to intuition or possessing a "special sense." It was neither. Eventually, researchers decoded the method behind the magic. The key was the time nurses spent reflecting, almost to the point of obsession, on their results. And not just any results, but on the babies who died or came close to dying in their care. Although outside of their direct awareness, the process of mulling over, thinking and rethinking, in time gave rise to an internal catalog of clues—a mental map, so to speak—pointing to the presence of the underlying, life-threatening infection. By interviewing the nurses, researchers eventually developed and published a master list of cues and patterns of cues, half of which were previously unknown to medical science and, in some instances, were the opposite of what one would see in adults.

Similar findings have long been reported in psychotherapy. To wit, some practitioners possess an uncanny ability to help others. Not only does this group achieve better results, but also they are better at connecting with people regardless of clinical presentation. Psychologist David F. Ricks (1974) was the first to publish an actual study on this class of exceptional therapists— practitioners who stand head and shoulders above the rest. His investigation examined the long-term outcomes of a group of "highly disturbed" adolescents. When later interviewed as adults, Ricks found some had been far more successful than others in their posttreatment life adjustment. What accounted for the difference? Contrary to what one might expect, it was not the clients' history, level of impairment, or therapeutic model employed. Rather, it was *who* had provided their treatment.

Had the kids been asked at the time, the field would not have had to wait so long to discover the factor responsible for their success. Indeed, all were aware of the important role their therapist played in their lives. Looking back as adults, they affectionately recalled referring to the clinician who had treated them as "the supershrink"—even going so far as to encourage other kids to seek out this particular person for help.

Sadly, another 3 decades would pass before the subject was revisited by psychotherapy researchers. Every so often, an article would appear examining the impact of the individual therapist on outcome or identifying personal traits and characteristics assumed to be associated with being an effective practitioner. However, compared to the number of studies focused on models and methods, providers of therapy barely even registered as subjects worthy of study. In 1997, veteran psychotherapy researcher Sol Garfield called the therapist "*The* Neglected Variable" (italics added).

As the new millennium began, the "era of indifference" finally came to an end. In 2003, Lambert, together with colleagues (Okiishi, Lambert, Nielsen, & Ogles, 2003), published the first large-scale empirical analysis of therapist effects. Data gathered over a 2 1/2-year period from nearly 2,000 clients and 91 therapists documented significant variation in effectiveness among the clinicians in the study. Indeed, clients of the most effective therapists experienced 10 times greater rates of change than the mean of the complete sample.

Despite these dramatic results, the researchers were at a loss to explain what the most effective actually "did to be 'supershrinks,'" ending the article calling it a "mystery" (p. 372).

The answer came 3 years later. In a piece titled "Supershrinks: What's the Secret of Their Success?," Miller et al. (2007) reported that the difference between the best and the rest was "the amount of time specifically devoted to reaching for objectives *just beyond one's level of proficiency*" (p. 30, italics in original). Although this assertion was new to psychotherapy, it was a fact well known to researchers investigating the development of expertise across various and diverse domains of human performance (Ericsson, Charness, Feltovich, & Hoffman, 2006; Ericsson, Hoffman, Kozbelt, & Williams, 2018). To achieve better results, individuals need to identify where and when their usual, effective pattern of practice falls short and then develop, rehearse, and refine a plan for improvement (Miller, Hubble, Chow, & Seidel, 2015). In 2015, Chow et al. found in the first 8 years of professional practice that the most effective practitioners devote 2 1/2 times more hours to deliberately working at improving their skills than their average counterparts (see Figure 7.1).

FIGURE 7.1. Comparison of Therapists From the Top Quartile With the Others in the Lower Quartiles Based on Their Adjusted Client Outcomes, as a Function of Estimated Time Spent on Deliberate Practice Alone Per Typical Work Week

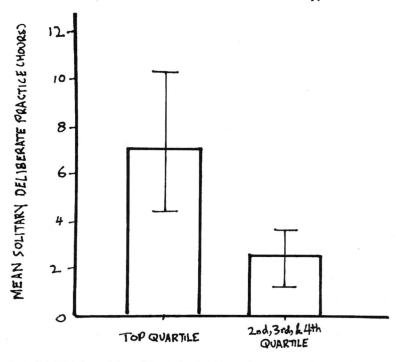

Error bars: ± 1 SE. Adapted from "The Role of Deliberate Practice in the Development of Highly Effective Psychotherapists," by D. L. Chow, S. D. Miller, J. A. Seidel, R. T. Kane, J. A. Thornton, and W. P. Andrews, 2015, *Psychotherapy, 52,* p. 342. Copyright 2015 by the American Psychological Association.

What follows next rests on the assumption that you, the reader, have begun using measures at every session with all of your clients, as we suggested at the end of Chapter 6. If you have, then naturally, data are accumulating. Combining or aggregating the information across clients over time makes it possible to calculate a number of metrics reflecting one's baseline level of performance. First, we define each index and its relevance to clinical practice. Next, we explain what it reveals about how your work measures up against established norms. The overall goal, of course, is to identify what can be improved in your workflow to achieve better results.

Before moving on, we wish to pay homage to the psychologist whose research was the first to draw attention to expert therapists. David F. Ricks died in 2004, just a few years before his investigation would become widely recognized as the first empirical study of expertise in psychotherapy. Other than a brief obituary, virtually no other information about him—not even a photo—was available online.

A bit of detective work combined with good luck eventually led us to one of his adult children. In multiple phone calls, she talked at length about her father. Turns out, although he would never have said so himself, he was a remarkable person. Born in 1927 in Wilson, Wyoming (population: 32), his log cabin had no indoor plumbing or electricity. He literally rode a horse to and from the one-room school house he attended—that is, until the family was forced by the Great Depression to move south in search of economic opportunities. There, the hardships continued: His father died when he was 15, his mother was often ill, and the family remained poor.

Although an elementary school teacher once told his parents, "David can't learn," he was awarded a full scholarship to attend college, eventually earning a PhD in psychology from the University of Chicago. Over the course of his career, he taught, did research, and was a professor at Harvard, Cornell, and eventually, the University of Cincinnati. Academic achievements aside, in a personal history penned for his grandchildren, he wrote that life had taught him to value, above all else, honesty and courage.

KEY BASELINE METRICS: HOW DO *YOU* DO?

Know thyself.

—Ancient Greek Maxim

Even though the indices described in this section are not exhaustive, all have been used in outcome research for decades and, more important, have known ranges and values. Once more, the information obtained will allow you to see how your work compares with your peers. Any guesswork about how effective you are is removed.

Of the eight metrics to be reviewed, no one should be considered more important than any other. Rather, each provides valuable data regarding a

specific aspect of clinical performance. It is when they are used in combination that a more complete and nuanced picture of your individual strengths and weaknesses emerges—the latter which, of course, may be useful in establishing individualized learning objectives.

As will be seen, some of the metrics are easily computed using a handheld calculator and basic math. Others require the use of sophisticated analyses that, for most, will necessitate utilizing a statistical consultant or accessing online outcome management software.

1. Effect Size

In the context of psychotherapy, *effect size* (ES) is a quantitative measure of the impact of treatment, and specifically, the magnitude of each client's response to your services. To compute, scores from whatever outcome tool is used are first standardized, transforming them into a common scale with an average of 0 and standard deviation (σ) of 1. Doing so makes it possible to compare your outcomes with established levels of effectiveness for the profession.

For those statistically inclined, the computation begins with subtracting the mean of your clients' posttreatment scores on whatever outcome tool is being used (e.g., Outcome Rating Scale [ORS]; Miller & Duncan, 2000) from the mean of their pretreatment scores, and then dividing the resulting number by the standard deviation of the entire sample (a brief description of, and formula for calculating the standard deviation can be found in Appendix B).

The complete equation for ES is as follows:

$$\frac{[\text{Posttreatment mean}] - [\text{Pretreatment mean}]}{\text{Standard deviation of the clinical sample}}$$

Over the past 4 decades, the ES for people who receive no treatment (i.e., waitlist controls) typically falls between .0 and .2 σ. Since the mid-1970s, the average ES of psychotherapy has hovered around .8 σ (see Figure 7.2; Smith

FIGURE 7.2. Normal Distribution and Effect Size of Recipients of Psychotherapy

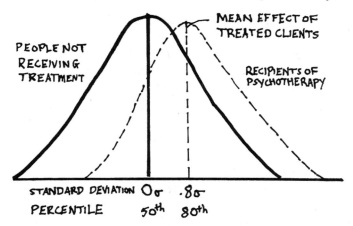

Data from Smith and Glass (1977) and Wampold and Imel (2015).

& Glass, 1977; Wampold & Imel, 2015). Therefore, when considering your own ES, any number greater than .2 σ indicates people in your care are improving more than those not in treatment. Numbers at or near .8 σ show your results are on par with outcomes typical for the field.

While it is possible for solo practitioners to compute their ES in the manner described here, it is not the best method for other settings or applications. To illustrate, in a large, busy practice or agency setting, computing ESs for each therapist can be quite time consuming. More important, a variety of factors other than the actual effectiveness of the treatment provided can affect the validity of the index. As everyone knows, outcomes vary depending on the severity of the problems a clinician treats. Unless statistically adjusted, those working with comparatively healthy people will end up looking more effective than those treating more difficult and complex problems, and vice versa.

Fortunately, several systems are available for generating accurate estimates of ES (e.g., Partners for Change Outcome Management System [PCOMS; Miller, Duncan, Sorrell, & Brown, 2005; Prescott, Maeschalck, & Miller, 2017]; Outcome Questionnaire–Analyst [OQ-Analyst; Lambert et al., 2004]; Contextualized Feedback Systems [Bickman, Kelley, & Athay, 2012]; Systemic Therapy Inventory of Change [Pinsof, 2017]). All automate data collection and analysis, and rely on large, international samples and sophisticated statistical procedures to correct for variables that can skew the results in one direction or another. The metrics associated with the PCOMS measures discussed in the previous two chapters can be accessed via three proprietary websites that are compliant with the Health Insurance Portability and Accountability Act of 1996: MyOutcomes (see https://www.myoutcomes.com), FIT-Outcomes (see https://www.fit-outcomes.com), and OpenFIT (see https://www.openfitapp.com).

2. Relative Effect Size

If ES reveals the effectiveness of your work compared with the field's overall historic performance, *relative effect size* (RES) shows how your outcomes compare with those obtained by other clinicians. This is the metric most practitioners want to know: How good am I compared with my peers? While the math needed to determine RES is not difficult, two obstacles prevent most from doing the necessary computations: (a) gaining access to a comparison group (i.e., data generated by other clinicians) and (b) proficiency with the statistical procedures needed to ensure you are comparing your results with those of therapists treating clients with similar problems or levels of functioning (known as *case-mix adjustment*).

As a practical matter, most practitioners and agencies will choose to use an online outcome management system, which permits valid comparisons with the outcomes of other providers. For instance, the RES calculated by the websites using PCOMS are based on a sample of literally thousands of clinicians, and more than a million clients, treated in diverse settings, around the world (Miller, 2011a). Scores are reported on a standardized scale, with an average of 0 ($\bar{x} = 0$), and standard deviation (σ) of 1. In this instance, a zero means your results are on par with clinicians in the normative sample. Deviations above or below indicate better or worse performance, respectively.

When assessing your RES, keep in mind that although variability exists between clinicians, the range is small. Like it or not, most are us hover near the average in terms of results. To illustrate, in the normative sample used in PCOMS, the majority fall within −.3 σ and +.3 σ. Few land outside of this range. See Figure 7.3 to get a sense of just how similar we therapists are to one another.

FIGURE 7.3. Distribution of Relative Effect Sizes of Practicing Clinicians in the Partners for Change Outcome Management System Database

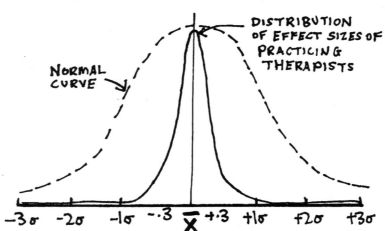

Data from Miller, Duncan, Sorrell, and Brown (2005).

In our experience, practitioners are apt to feel discouraged on learning they are no more effective than anyone else. Recall the findings reported earlier (see Chapter 2), documenting the tendency we therapists have for overestimating our effectiveness (by as much as 65%). Be that as it may, an RES of 0 does not mean you are "a zero." In our craft, average results are good. Indeed, what we do is equivalent to or better than the results of many accepted health care procedures. As mentioned earlier, psychotherapy is just as effective as coronary artery bypass surgery and has an ES 4 times greater than fluoride in the prevention of dental caries.

Still, room for improvement always exists. Across the range of human performance, simple observation, research, and experience confirm how small differences can make a big difference. In sports, a fraction of a second or one tenth of a millimeter is often what separates the best from the rest. Two tenths of a second—about the time it takes a hummingbird to flap its wings—is all that kept Dutch speed skater, Annette Gerritsen, from taking the gold in the 2010 Winter Olympics in Vancouver ("Fractions of a Second," 2010).

In our profession, small differences have also been shown to have a profound impact. Researchers Imel, Sheng, Baldwin, and Atkins (2015) found that a razor-thin difference in effectiveness between clinicians resulted in 4 times more people reaching recovery over a decade. The implication is obvious: A barely measurable improvement in your performance will help many more clients.

3. Percentage Achieving Reliable Change/Clinically Significant Change

When your clients improve, it is essential to know whether it's because of the care you are providing or the consequence of some other unrelated factors. The passage of time, occurrence of chance, change-producing events, and imprecision in the measurement process can all affect outcome scores. In such circumstances, while the client may be better, it would be a mistake to give the credit to the therapy. Doing so invites superstitious thinking—assuming a causal relationship between our actions and the outcome when none exists.

In 1984, researchers Jacobson, Follette, and Revenstorf recognized this problem and proposed formulas for determining when changes in therapy can confidently be attributed to the treatment. The Reliable Change Index (RCI), as Jacobson and Truax (1991) later called it, can be found in the administration and scoring manual of most commonly used outcome tools. Returning to PCOMS, Bertolino and Miller (2012) reported an RCI of 5 for the ORS (Miller & Duncan, 2000). In application, any difference in the total score exceeding 5 points, either from the first to the last session, or between visits, meets the benchmark for reliable change. When positive, it can be inferred clients are improving as a result of treatment. Negative scores, on the other hand, indicate what you are doing is actually making the client worse.

According to Jacobson and Truax (1991), *clinically significant change* is "the extent to which therapy moves someone outside the range of the dysfunctional population or within the range of the functional population" (p. 12). Briefly, change is deemed clinically significant when (a) it exceeds the RCI and (b) falls above the clinical cutoff established for whatever outcome measure is being used. On the ORS, research has determined the cutoff—the dividing line between a clinical and nonclinical level of distress or functioning—is 25 (Bertolino & Miller, 2012; Miller, Duncan, Brown, Sparks, & Claud, 2003).

A simple tool for quickly determining which of your clients has achieved either reliable or clinically significant change can be found in Appendix A. To avoid having to flip back and forth, you might want to make a copy of that page before reading further. Known as a *reliable change chart*, it works by crossing your client's pretreatment score (along on the horizontal axis) with their current or posttreatment score (the vertical axis). The titles in the area where the lines intersect instantly show whether a reliable improvement or worsening has occurred. Should the lines meet in the area labeled "no reliable change" (representing the RCI), then it can be inferred change is insufficient to be attributed to therapy ($\leq \pm 5$ points). A difference in scores falling in the area labeled "reliable change" can indicate an improvement is both reliable (> + 5 points) and even clinically significant (> + 5 points and above the clinical cutoff of 25).

As an illustration, consult the results plotted in Figure 7.4, showing the outcomes of a sample clinician. With the diamonds representing individual

FIGURE 7.4. Plot of a Sample Clinician's Outcomes on the Reliable Change Chart Using the Outcome Rating Scale

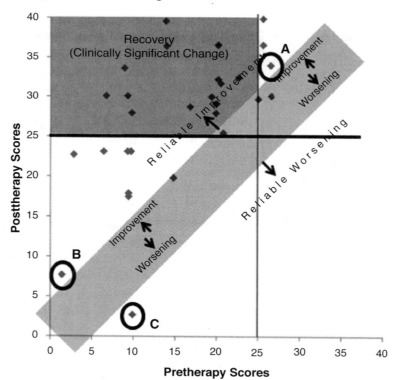

See Miller & Duncan (2000).

clients, the percentages for each category of change can be determined by dividing the number of cases found in any particular area or zone by the total number of clients. Accordingly, 48% of the people treated by this therapist are or have achieved a clinically significant change (14 out of 29)—a figure in line with results reported in randomized clinical trials (approximately 51%; Springer, Levy, & Tolin, 2018). An additional 34% (10 out of 29) have reliably benefited from the care but do not meet criteria to be described as recovered. If this result strikes you as high, you are correct. It's about 70% higher than rates seen in large, international normative samples (approximately 64%–74%; cf. Chow et al., 2015; Lambert, 2010b; Stiles, Barkham, Mellor-Clark, & Connell, 2008; Stiles, Barkham, & Wheeler, 2015). We'll explain why shortly.

Returning to the graph, approximately 14% (four out of 29) of this therapist's clients are neither better nor worse. And, one out of the 29 has deteriorated (see diamond labeled "C"), a rate of 3.5%—below the range of 5% to 10% reported in the outcome literature (Lambert, 2010b).

As noted above, the percentage of clients achieving a reliable change with this therapist is significantly higher than average. What might explain this? Perhaps the practitioner is exceptional. In this case, however, a statistical artifact is more likely the cause of the results. Think of it this way: The RCI is but an average. It is not specific to the individual client. Rather, it is an estimate based on all clients in the instrument's normative sample. Depending on the level of distress or functioning at intake, the exact amount of change necessary for any individual to be considered reliably changed will vary. For some, the RCI will be an overestimate (i.e., those who are more functional and less distressed at intake; see diamond "A" in Figure 7.4), whereas for others, it will be an underestimate (i.e., clients who are less functional and more distressed at the outset of services; see diamond "B" in Figure 7.4).

To better understand the shortcoming associated with using the RCI across clients, consider an analogy to a shoe store. Retailers often rely on averages when making decisions about what sizes to stock. For the majority of customers—say, men with a shoe size of 9 to 10.5—this process works well. If you are an average male, you are likely to find a shoe that fits. For a significant percentage (i.e., ± 1 σ, or approximately 34%), however, the shoes available will either be too big or too small.

What is the solution? As is the case with most of the performance indices described in this chapter, efficiency and accuracy is better achieved by using one of the existing computerized outcome management systems. Sites using the PCOMS measures (ORS and the Session Rating Scale; Miller, Duncan, & Johnson, 2000), for example, automatically calculate an RCI specific to each client. Back to the shoe store, using an automated system is akin to footwear being tailored to the individual rather than the individual being fitted into whatever product is on the shelves.

4. Deterioration Rate

Researcher Michael Lambert, whose work and thinking we cited at the beginning of this chapter, was absolutely right. People can, and do, deteriorate in and as a result of psychotherapy. As much as the evidence shows that what we do works, between 5% and 10% of clients end worse off than they were at the beginning of treatment (Lambert, 2010b)—a fact long overlooked, if not lost, amid enthusiastic claims that "everyone can benefit" from psychotherapy (Flor, 2016; Lazar, 2017; Moore, 2010).

To calculate your overall deterioration rate, you simply divide the number of clients whose scores at termination fall below the RCI by the total number of people who have completed therapy. In the results displayed in Figure 7.4, the diamond labeled "C" counts as the lone reliably deteriorated case. That particular person started with an ORS score of 10 and ended with a 3, a change greater than −5 points, the RCI for that measure.

5. Length and Amount of Therapy

Despite continuing debates over the appropriate dose of psychotherapy (e.g., brief versus long-term, weekly or monthly, or protocols specifying the number of visits clients should attend), both the average number of sessions and length of time people engage in treatment is relatively short. In 1978, Garfield summarized results from a "representative number of investigations carried out in several types of clinics" and found a "clustering around 6 interviews" (p. 195). Thirty-seven years later, using a sample of more than 20,000 clients, Erekson, Lambert, and Eggett (2015) reported a mean of 5.8 sessions, delivered over an average of 9.1 weeks of contact. Roughly similar results have been reported in other studies with large and diverse samples (cf. Baldwin, Berkeljon, Atkins, Olsen, & Nielsen, 2009; Stiles et al., 2015).

Over the past 4 decades, data regarding the modal number of visits—that is, the value that appears most often in a distribution—have also been remarkably consistent. About 30% of clients attend only a single session (Chow, 2018a; Connolly Gibbons et al., 2011; Garfield, 1978; Hansen, Lambert, & Forman, 2002). While some have argued that "most . . . who quit . . . do so because they have accomplished what they intended" (Talmon, 1990, p. xi), available evidence actually indicates otherwise. While the follow-up research is admittedly limited, what it does show is that a sizable number of people who discontinue (approximately 50% or more) leave feeling dissatisfied, unchanged, or worse off (Miller et al., 2005; Swift & Greenberg, 2015).

Of the performance metrics reviewed thus far, calculating your average treatment duration and number of sessions is perhaps the simplest. For this, you will use the data from clients who have ended treatment. Include all clients, regardless of whether they attended only a single visit, terminated formally, or dropped out, as well as those with whom you've had no contact for at least 2 months. Now, count the number of weeks and sessions each client attended. Divide each figure by the total number of clients.

It's important to keep in mind averages are skewed by extreme values. As reported previously, many therapists' data are affected by a large number of clients who do not return after a single visit. Others have a handful of clients whom they've met with on and off for years. In such instances, determining the median rather than mean number of sessions and weeks you meet with clients will provide a more accurate picture of your usual baseline performance. To find the median, first create two lists. One is the number of weeks you met each of your clients that have now ended therapy. The other is how many times you met. Next, put the numbers in each list in numerical order from lowest to highest. Once done, count how many numbers are on each list. If the resulting value is odd, the median will be the middle number. If even, the median is the number halfway between the two numbers in the center. Add those numbers together and divide by two (for a faster way to calculate your mean, median, and modal number of sessions, use this spreadsheet: http://bit.ly/sessionnumber).

As is the case with all of the metrics presented to this point, rather than doing the necessary calculations on one's own, many clinicians and agencies choose to use one of the existing computerized outcome management systems. Doing so is not only more convenient and efficient, it also provides access to more sophisticated normative comparisons. Research shows, for example, that treatment length is affected by a variety factors, including age, gender, socioeconomic status, race, and practice setting (i.e., private or public; Swift & Greenberg, 2015). Without access to large samples and fairly advanced statistical skill, most will not be able to determine if and how these factors may be influencing the average length of time and number of sessions your clients remain in treatment.

6. Dropout

According to Swift, Greenberg, Tompkins, and Parkin (2017), dropout occurs "whenever a client begins an intervention, but then unilaterally terminates . . . prior to recovering from the problems that led him or her to seek treatment in the first place" (p. 48). Their research documents 20% to 22% of people who initiate services will stop attending prior to benefiting from care. Given the weight of such findings, these figures serve as an important benchmark for assessing a clinician's baseline performance.

To compute your dropout rate, first identify those clients who quit without telling you; second, within that group, count the number of those whose outcomes scores on whatever measure you are using do not exceed the RCI; third, divide the resulting figure by the total number of clients who have finished treatment.

7. Planned Versus Unplanned Terminations

Better outcomes are associated with therapies in which the client and therapist jointly decide to end treatment. As it turns out, studies of highly effective practitioners show they have more planned endings than clinicians with average results. In a sample consisting of 4,580 clients, seen by 69 therapists, Chow (2014a) found the most effective therapists (i.e., first quartile) had more than 3 times as many planned endings than the least effective therapists (i.e., fourth quartile; see Table 7.1).

Given such findings, it is not surprising Saxon, Ricketts, and Heywood (2010) concluded, "Unplanned endings, where clients unilaterally end therapy, are of concern" (p. 13). In their analysis of counseling services in a primary care setting, more than a third of 1,254 clients (432 [34%]) had an unplanned termination of therapy. Their data showed unplanned endings tended to happen early in the treatment process, with the mean number of sessions attended by those with a planned versus unplanned ending being 6.3 ($SD = 1.9$) and 2.9 ($SD = 1.9$) sessions, respectively.

To compute your planned terminations, count the number of cases when both parties agreed to end treatment. Likewise, for unplanned terminations, count the number of cases that unexpectedly did not return for therapy. Divide each of the two figures by the number of cases you've seen to obtain the planned and unplanned termination cases.

8. Average First Session Alliance Score

Research conducted over the past 40 years documents a robust, positive association between the therapeutic alliance and outcome (Bachelor & Horvath, 1999; Norcross, 2011; Wampold & Imel, 2015). The most recent meta-analysis of 295 independent studies (conducted between 1978 and 2017) including more than 30,000 clients strongly affirms the power of the working relationship in face-to-face therapy (Flückiger, Del Re, Wampold, & Horvath, 2018). Client characteristics, the country in which the research was conducted, type of measure or treatment approach used, and the person who completed the measure (i.e., client, therapists, other observers or participants) did not moderate or significantly influence the findings.

Studies have further shown the trajectory of the alliance scores is predictive of ES (Miller et al., 2007; Owen, Miller, Seidel, & Chow, 2016). As can be seen in the first bar of Figure 7.5, scores indicative of a good alliance from the

TABLE 7.1. Therapists Grouped Into Quartiles Based on Their Performance and Their Planned/Unplanned Endings of Psychotherapy

Therapist's ranking	Percent planned endings	Percent unplanned endings
Quartile 1	73.39	12.16
Quartile 2	60.51	15.72
Quartile 3	51.68	23.34
Quartile 4	27.68	22.45

Note. The first quartile is made up of the most effective therapists, and the fourth quartile is the least effective group. From *The Study of Supershrinks: Development and Deliberate Practices of Highly Effective Psychotherapists* (Doctoral dissertation, p. 91), by D. Chow, 2014, Curtin University, Australia. Copyright 2014 by Daryl Chow. Reprinted with permission.

FIGURE 7.5. Association Between First and Last Session Alliance Scores and Severity Adjusted Effect Size in a Sample of 9,000 Youths Between the Ages of 12 And 18

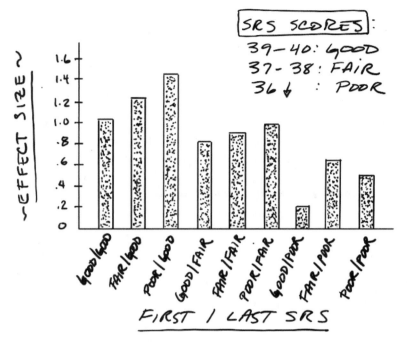

SRS = Session Rating Scale. Data from Miller, Hubble, and Duncan (2007); and Owen et al. (2016).

first to the last administration of the measure are associated with an ES roughly equivalent to the average overall effectiveness of psychotherapy (as reported earlier: .8 σ). Continuing, any drop in scores is a cause for concern as lower ESs can be expected (see Bars 4 and 7). The best results (see Bars 2, 3, and 6), are linked to alliance scores that improve with time, with the largest treatment effects (1.42 σ) resulting from alliances that start poor and end good.

While such results may, at first glance, seem counterintuitive, a similar pattern has been observed in other professions. In the business literature, for example, researchers Fleming and Asplund (2007) reported that dissatisfied customers are more likely to become loyal to a particular product or service when they feel any concerns they have are heard and handled respectfully. In fact, they demonstrate more commitment than customers who never complain to begin with—even when the issue is not resolved in their favor.

The takeaway is clear: Complaints are opportunities to foster the development of a stronger, more enduring, and effective relationship. Therefore, for the purpose of benchmarking, lower initial scores on an alliance measure can be considered a good indicator of future progress. To illustrate, with PCOMS, scores on the SRS are considered poor when they fall at or below 36 (or the

75th percentile; Bertolino & Miller, 2012). To calculate the average initial SRS score for your practice, simply divide the sum of all first-session SRS scores by the total number of clients for whom you have results.

TO SUM UP

By now, you have hopefully been using measures at every session with all of your clients. As a result, data are accumulating. Aggregating the information provided by the measures makes it possible to calculate a number of metrics reflecting your baseline level of clinical performance. In this chapter, much information was provided about how to calculate the various indices. For easy reference, a summary can be found in Table 7.2.

TABLE 7.2. Summary of Performance Benchmarks

Metric	Benchmark	Notes
Average intake Outcome Rating Scale (Miller & Duncan, 2000)	19	The first score of the ORS; *SD* range is approximately 6.5–7.5 for first ORS
Effect size	0.8–1.2	The amount of change due to treatment compared to no treatment; the figure is expressed in standard deviations; raw ES = (post-ORS − PreORS)/*SD* of pre-ORS
Relative effect size	0	This compares the ES of a given clinician or agency to the grand mean ES of the normative sample; a positive RES means an effect above average; a negative RES means an effect below average; a 0 means the effect is average compared to the norm
		(This figure is provided in outcome systems like MyOutcomes [see https://www.myoutcomes.com], FIT-Outcomes [see https://www.fit-outcomes.com], and OpenFIT [see https://www.openfitapp.com])
		In the normative sample used in these systems, the majority fall within −.3 σ and +3 σ
Reliable change index	64%–74%	A 5-point or more increase in the ORS (Jacobson & Truax, 1991; Miller, Duncan, Brown, Sparks, & Claud, 2003); this is often referred to as *reliable improvement* in systems like MyOutcomes (see https://www.myoutcomes.com), FIT-Outcomes (see https://www.fit-outcomes.com), or Open-FIT (see https://www.openfitapp.com)

TABLE 7.2. Summary of Performance Benchmarks (*Continued*)

Metric	Benchmark	Notes
Clinically significant change	Approximately 25%–40%	Two criteria must be met: (a) client experienced reliable change and (b) client started treatment within the clinical range, i.e., ORS below 25, and concluded in the nonclinical range (Jacobson & Truax, 1991); this is often referred to as *reliable recovery*
Deterioration rate	5%–10%	The percentage of people who are reliably worse while in treatment
Average number of sessions	4–6 sessions	Based on a large international normative sample, the average number of visits people attend is 5.8 visits ($SD = 4.2$)
Modal number of sessions	1	A large percentage of clients attend only 1 session (> 30%)
Dropout rate	20%–22%	The percentage of people who discontinue unilaterally without experiencing a reliable improvement; about 1 in 5 clients drop out, but note a huge variance exists between studies, ranging from 5% to 70%; dropout rates are typically higher in child and adolescent population (40%–60%)
Planned versus unplanned termination	PT: Approximately 50%–64% UT: Approximately 20%–34%	Highly effective therapists have more planned endings than average performers (Chow, 2014a); Saxon, Ricketts, and Heywood (2010) reported mean and standard deviations for numbers of sessions attended by those who had a planned versus unplanned ending: 6.3 ($SD = 1.9$) and 2.9 ($SD = 1.9$) sessions respectively; aim to have approximately 12%–15% of unplanned termination
Cutoff for Session Rating Scale (Miller, Duncan, & Johnson, 2000)	36	75% of clients score higher than 36 (Bertolino & Miller, 2012); however, lower initial SRS scores can be considered a good indicator of future progress

Note. ES = effect size; ORS = Outcome Rating Scale; PT = planned termination; RES = relative effect size; SRS = Session Rating Scale; UT = unplanned termination.

WHAT TO DO RIGHT NOW

Act now without delay.

—SIMONE DE BEAUVOIR (COOK, 2007, p. 548)

Right now, take the time to calculate the performance metrics outlined in this chapter. Recall:

- The numbers can be computed by hand or by entering your data into a proprietary outcome monitoring system and letting it do the work.

- To draw sensible conclusions about your effectiveness, it's important to have a sufficient number of cases. In the manual for the ORS, Bertolino and Miller (2012) reported the likelihood your metrics are reliable is 70% once you complete 40 cases. With 60, the figure rises 90%.

- Measuring outcomes can trigger anxiety. Our advice is to let the data accumulate. Keep a running count of the number of cases but, for now, don't give into temptation to scrutinize your overall results.

IV

MOVING FORWARD: IDENTIFYING WHAT TO DELIBERATELY PRACTICE

8

Mining Your Data for Better Results

The goal is to turn data into information, and information into insight.
—CARLY FIORINA (LLOYD, 2016)

Does the name Barry Marshall ring a bell? Probably not if you are a mental health professional. For decades, the Australian physician was persona non grata in the field of medicine—or perhaps stated more accurately, *persona sciocca*, a fool. Beginning in the early 1980s, Marshall, together with colleague Robin Warren, advanced the hypothesis that the bacteria *Helicobacter pylori* was at the root of most stomach ulcers. That idea proved exceptionally controversial flying, as it did, in the face of years of accepted practice and wisdom. Ulcers caused by something as simple and obvious as a bacterial infection? *Bunk*, the medical community responded, in the process, lampooning the two researchers. After all, everyone *knew* stress was the real culprit. They also *knew* the cure: certainly *not* antibiotics, but, rather, antacids, sedatives, psychotherapy, and, in the more chronic and serious cases, gastrectomy—a surgical procedure involving the removal of the lower third of the stomach.

A popular textbook used in introductory psychology courses throughout the 1970s and 1980s boldly declared, "Emotional stress is now known to relate to . . . such illnesses as . . . ulcers" (Braun & Linder, 1979, p. 343). The chapter on the subject in that volume was full of stories of people whose busy, emotionally demanding lives "caused" their stomach problems. Students reading the text at the time would dutifully overline the relevant sections. For

http://dx.doi.org/10.1037/0000191-008
Better Results: Using Deliberate Practice to Improve Therapeutic Effectiveness, by S. D. Miller, M. A. Hubble, and D. Chow

several decades, graduates confidently interpreted stomach problems as stress related and, not surprisingly, intervened with "stress management" strategies. It was a slam dunk. Everybody *knew* what to do.

The only problem is that what everyone knew to be true was wrong, patently wrong. Stress was not responsible for stomach ulcers. And no, antacids, sedatives, surgery, and psychotherapy were not the best treatments. The problem, as research by Marshall and Warren eventually and conclusively proved (see Klein, 2013), could be cured efficiently and effectively with a standard course of antibiotics, many of which had been available since the 1960s (see Klein, 2013)! The cure had been within reach all along—which begs the question: How could health care professionals and researchers have overlooked it?

Truth is, Marshall and Warren narrowly missed making this ground-breaking discovery themselves. After noticing a high instance of a corkscrew shaped bacteria (see Figure 8.1) in the stomachs of patients referred for cancer screening—all biopsies of which proved negative—the two decided to do a proper study (Klein, 2013). Did a connection, they wondered, exist between the presence of the bacteria and the genesis of gastric distress?

Marshall and Warren had reason to be hopeful. Their review of the medical literature uncovered reports about the spiral gastric bacterium dating back to 1892! And yet, the first 30 ulcer patients they examined showed no signs of the infection whatsoever (Klein, 2013). To any observer, the result would be discouraging. What could have gone wrong? After all, the samples had

FIGURE 8.1. Microscopic Picture of the *Helicobacter Pylori* Bacteria

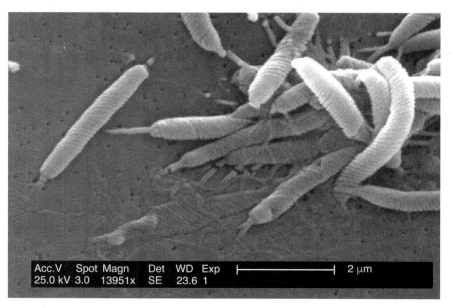

From Centers for Disease Control/Dr. Patricia Fields, Dr. Collette Fitzgerald, 2004. Photo credit: Janice Carr. See https://phil.cdc.gov/Details.aspx?pid=5715. In the public domain.

been taken appropriately, sent to the lab, and cultured according to protocols for other bacterial organisms (e.g., streptococcus).

The story might have ended there had the lab doing the analyses not been unexpectedly inundated with other work owing to an outbreak of a superbug. As a result, the Petri dishes containing Marshall and Warren's next samples ended up sitting around 3 days longer than the prescribed period. Those cultures, as well as 13 subsequently collected, all tested positive for *H. pylori* (Klein, 2013).

Over time, additional data confirmed these initial results. Decades later, in 2005, the researchers' pioneering work earned both the Nobel Prize in Physiology or Medicine (Nobel Media, 2005). Despite the eventual recognition, during much of the intervening period, their results continued to be ignored, ridiculed, or dismissed by the larger medical community.

FOLLOW THE DATA

> It doesn't matter how beautiful your theory is, it doesn't matter how smart you are. If it doesn't agree with experiment, it's wrong.
> —Richard P. Feynman (Sképseis, 2013)

It might be tempting to see the story of Marshall and Warren as just another instance of the "it pays to be persistent" or "just hang in there and eventually you'll succeed" meme. On the contrary, the larger lesson, as it pertains to achieving better results, is to embrace the data and follow wherever they lead. When it comes to advancing knowledge, what we hold to be true can get in the way of learning something new. No one believed bacteria could survive in the highly corrosive gastric juices of the stomach—a view that continued to hold sway for several decades even in the face of definitive, contradictory evidence.

Our own profession is not immune to the same phenomenon. Throughout its history, the effectiveness of psychotherapy has been checked by beliefs and practices that, while making perfect sense at the time, were later shown to be wrong, misleading, or, at a minimum, unhelpful. A particularly glaring example can be found in the explanations routinely provided for poor outcomes. Over the years, dropout, lack of progress, and deterioration in treatment have frequently been attributed to the client—their traits, behaviors, and life circumstances. The list is long and familiar. To name a few: resistance, lack of motivation, unwillingness to change, secondary gain, attachment or other interpersonal impairments, functional disturbance or symptomatology, limited psychological mindedness, low socioeconomic status, culture or ethnic background, and so on.

A review of the research shows the evidence behind these beliefs is scant, inconsistent or, in some instances, contradicts the prevailing point of view. For example, the latest and most comprehensive meta-analysis examining the link between dropout and a host of client variables (e.g., socioeconomic status, education, ethnicity/minority status) reveals *no* relationship (Swift &

Greenberg, 2012). Granted, studies exist documenting an association between poorer treatment outcomes and clients presenting with more severe problems, a higher degree of comorbidity, lower motivation for treatment, and attachment-related difficulties (Bohart & Wade, 2013). And yet, as any new student of statistics knows: Correlation is not causation. Bearing this maxim in mind, such findings can be construed as having as much to say about the impact of therapist, and the therapy offered, as they do about clients.

To illustrate, why assume a client's apparent lack of motivation is at the root of a poor therapeutic response rather than a therapist's inability to engage the people they treat in a productive working alliance? Just as it was in the case of ulcers, both the nature and target of any efforts to improve outcomes will vary greatly depending on the perspective one takes. If poor outcomes or high dropout rates are attributed to an unmotivated client, the target of therapeutic efforts—not surprisingly—will be directed toward the recipient of care. "How can I motivate my client?" becomes the guiding question. Confrontation, pep talks, letting them hit bottom, or, more recently, exploring their ambivalence regarding change all qualify as potentially "correct" interventions. On the other hand, if seen as resulting from the actions taken (or not) by the individual practitioner, the question becomes, "What about me is getting in the way of my client's participation?"

ETTA'S METRICS: AN EXAMPLE OF MINING YOUR DATA

Etta[1] is a well-respected psychologist, known specifically for her work with eating disorders. Data from her practice, gathered on a session-by-session basis over the past year, showed she was effective, with 65% of her clients

---

[1]Etta is a fictitious case example created from the authors' real-world experience providing consultations. The test developer is one of the authors (SDM).

achieving reliable change within an average of seven visits. These favorable results stood in marked contrast to her dropout and deterioration rates, both falling outside established benchmarks. Specifically, 28% of those Etta begins treating (compared with an international average of 20%) terminate without notice before realizing any measurable improvement. Among those who do continue, 15% worsen over the course of care (compared with the benchmark of 5%–10%).

A dedicated clinician, Etta turned to the literature, eager to find answers for reducing the percentage of people who drop out or deteriorate on her caseload. She also sought out supervision with a senior colleague. Both experiences confirmed what her data appeared to suggest, namely, people with eating disorders are difficult to treat, notoriously resistant to change, and often get worse before they get better. As such, it seemed her only recourse was to face facts: Progress takes years (7–10; Strober, Freeman, & Morrell, 1997) and is frequently uneven, and both dropout and relapse are simply par for the course (American Psychiatric Association, 2010; DeJong, Broadbent, & Schmidt, 2012; Kahn & Pike, 2001; Richards et al., 2000). In the words of her supervisor, "Stop blaming yourself. It's not your fault."

According to Etta, although she was initially reassured, "The problems continued to 'eat away' at me. It was like I was settling, giving up, and I wasn't ready to do that." Supposing clues might be found in the metrics provided by the measures, she reached out to the developer of the instruments. "I have to admit, I was a bit nervous," she later recalled. "He lived in a different country and our primary languages were different." Undaunted, she decided to proceed and was pleasantly surprised when he agreed to meet over an online, video conferencing site. He asked that she send a screenshot of her data summary before the meeting. In the interest of having a fresh or unbiased look, he also requested she keep any interpretations or concerns about her performance to herself.

Before reading any further, take a moment to examine the data summarized in Table 8.1 (note results are provided both for Etta's current or "active" clients as well as former or "inactive"). Next, compare the values reported to the benchmarks discussed in the previous chapter. Once done, consider the following questions:

- Do the data provide a reliable estimate of Etta's performance as a therapist? Yes or no? And why?

- Do the data provide clues about what might be contributing to Etta's higher than average dropout and deterioration rates?

"Whenever I look at a clinician's results, I always start with the number of completed cases," the test developer began. "If there are fewer than 60, there's really no reason to look any further; in fact, it can be seriously misleading as the data just don't give us a reliable enough picture of the clinician's performance." Following a brief pause, "With 150 cases, of course, your numbers are more than sufficient to trust the indices."

TABLE 8.1. Etta's Performance Metrics

Key baseline metric	Active clients	Former clients
Effect size	.5	.8
Relative effect size	.15	.0
Percentage of clients achieving reliable change	54%	65%
Percentage of clients achieving clinically significant change	41%	49%
Deterioration	12%	15%
Average number of sessions	5	7
Duration of treatment (weeks)	4.2	6.4
Dropout	N/A	28%
Planned versus unplanned termination	N/A	PT = 42%
		UT = 58%
Average intake SRS	40	40

Note. PT = planned termination; SRS = Session Rating Scale; UT = unplanned termination.

He went on, "Your outcomes are quite good. The effect size, average number of sessions, average treatment length, and percentage reaching reliable and clinically significant change, are in the range of what we hope to see." He continued, "Also, your intake score on the ORS [Outcome Rating Scale (Miller & Duncan, 2000)] is consistent with large, mental health outpatient samples. So, your clients are in the right place."

At this point, he stopped. Etta waited as the developer looked over the remaining indices. "On the other hand, your drop and deterioration rates are on the high side."

"That's what I'm concerned about," Etta replied, "It's the reason I emailed you."

"Great. So, in looking at your data, do you have any thoughts about why that might be?"

Etta hesitated. "No. No, I don't. I've looked and looked. I went to supervision. I've been reading up on people with eating problems, but . . ."

"Got it," he acknowledged. "Sometimes these numbers can all blend together and then it's difficult to see the forest for the trees. Tell you what, let's take a look at your average intake SRS [Session Rating Scale (Miller, Duncan, & Johnson, 2000)] score. What do you notice?"

"It's good," Etta observed, and then, with a question in her voice, "Maybe, maybe . . . too good?"

"Exactly. Now, we can't be 100% sure, as many factors can play a role, but several studies show SRS scores that *improve* over time are associated with better outcomes," adding, "nearly 50% better."

"Hmm," Etta responded.

"And when you start at 40, which is your average intake SRS score for both your current and completed clients, there's not much room for improvement."

Thinking back on the new client she'd met before the consultation, Etta wondered, "So, it's better when the scores start lower?"

"Ha!" the developer laughed. "Now, this may be a bit confusing, but we want the intake SRS to be lower *if*, in fact, a reason exists for it to be lower," adding, "getting people to share their honest reaction, we've found, depends a great deal on the therapist using the scale."

For Etta, any uncertainty quickly dissipated. The message was loud and clear: High scores may have less to do with her clients than with her. "I have to confess," she replied, "if it's me, I'm not sure what I need do differently."

"That's why we're talking," the test developer offered. "Don't feel bad. Getting negative feedback is a skill, one that's not taught in graduate school, but really worth the effort to acquire," After a pause, he resumed, "So, let me suggest something. We've got a potential clue about what might be going on. We just need more information." The developer then asked Etta to begin recording and transcribing how she introduced and discussed the SRS during sessions with new clients.

"How long will it take you," he asked, "to have three or four cases to review?"

Averaging one new client a week, Etta suggested scheduling an appointment in a month.

On the next call, the two reviewed the transcripts together. The developer complimented Etta for the thorough explanation she gave for using the tool. He also noted being positively impressed with how she provided "room and space" in the conversation for her clients to speak about their experience.

"I *am* noticing something, Etta, that, if changed, we've found increases the likelihood of clients giving more critical feedback."

Intrigued and excited, Etta said, "Tell me."

"Well," he began, "Look at what you say when you start introducing the scale. Each time, you comment on how much you've enjoyed meeting and getting to know the client." He went on, "Now, I know you mean it, but in many cultures, it's customary for people to reciprocate when someone says something nice to them."

The developer's comments made perfect sense. Etta realized her kind words, mostly voiced out of habit, might be having an influence.

"I suggest skipping the niceties," he offered, "and asking directly for feedback."

Etta took notes as the developer modeled a different way to introduce the measure. "We've come to that point in the visit," he started, "where I need your help. I want you to know, I'm very interested in how you felt our visit went today. Life's not perfect, and neither am I."

He then said, "So, when you are filling out the scale, I'm not looking for high marks. It's not about that. It's really about finding out, is there something that, from your point of view, I need to know about—maybe something I missed."

"You may also think it went quite well. Sometimes when people think that, they are tempted to gloss over or not mention something small that actually, at the moment, didn't feel right. You don't do need to do that," he advised. "Small or large, I'm interested. Whatever it is, we can talk about it and, together, decide how make this experience a better fit for you."

The second call ended with Etta's agreeing to write out and memorize a script for introducing the SRS in her own words, and then noting the responses she received. The two then agreed to meet again in a month.

"It's really amazing," she reported when they next spoke, "the difference such a small change could make." In the interim, Etta had met with five new clients, introducing the tool in a manner consistent with the developer's feedback. None rated the initial visit a 40. Two had even given scores falling below the clinical cutoff of 36.

"I would never have been happy about such results had we not spoken," she remarked, adding, "and I can see now where not only a habit of speech, but also *my* expectations, and I'm not sure how to say this, but my hope they'd had a good experience had gotten in the way, preventing them from sharing how they felt."

"Have you met with any of these new clients more than once?" the developer inquired.

"That's also interesting," Etta answered. "Yes, all of them, at least twice, so it looks like it's also affecting my retention rates in a good way."

"That's great to hear," the developer responded, "but before we draw any firm conclusions, let's wait to see if this continues."

Together, the two reviewed the transcripts of Etta's administrations of the SRS. The developer made an additional suggestion for tweaking how she used the form in the session. Turning to one of the five cases, he stated, "Look here, this time after you introduce the SRS, your client, in the middle of filling it out, says, 'Hmm.' From the transcript, it doesn't look like you responded. Am I reading that right?"

"Yes, that's right. . . ."

"Because in the next line," he continued, "your client says, 'Now, this is interesting,' but again no response from you."

"That's correct," Etta inserted, explaining, "I didn't say anything because she wasn't speaking directly to me. She was kind of reading the items and mumbling under her breath."

"Oookaaay," the developer said, slowly.

Etta immediately recognized the missed opportunity. "I could have picked up on that, to ask her what she was thinking?"

"Yeah," he answered. "It's a different way of thinking about administering scales. Unlike traditional psychological tests, where you try to minimize your influence, here you want to help your client give voice to any thoughts they have about the session, good or bad, but especially, the bad."

At the close of the consultation, the developer and Etta decided to meet once a month and monitor her work with the measure. The process was similar each time. First, they carefully reviewed her transcripts. Next, they looked for ways to enhance her performance, often experimenting with changes of a word here or there. At the end of 5 months, Etta's dropout and deterioration rates had significantly declined (15% and 13%, respectively). Her goal largely accomplished, and feeling she knew how to proceed on her own, they ended the consultations with the understanding she could reach out in the future, if desired.

Half a year passed before Etta contacted the test developer again. In her correspondence, she noted continued improvement in a number of her performance metrics. For all that, she was feeling discouraged. No longer was she seeing as much improvement. "At first, I thought, this is, well, you know, 'as good as it gets.' You can only squeeze so much juice out of an orange!" Based on his work with other clinicians, the developer had a different idea. We'll return to Etta in the next chapter to see how her work with the developer played out.

Before proceeding, take a moment to review Etta's experience in light of the building blocks of deliberate practice (DP) presented in Chapter 4 (see Figure 4.1). All four are present in the story. To begin, noticing a deficit in her performance, Etta sought out and eventually found a knowledgeable coach. Next, using her data as a guide, he gently shifted the focus of their work together away from the results of her performance (e.g., dropout rate) and toward the identification of a small learning objective (i.e., obtaining more negative feedback via the SRS). Detailed instruction and feedback followed. Subsequent consultations helped Etta refine her knowledge and skills.

WHAT ARE YOUR NUMBERS?

> You have to be absolutely frank with yourself.
> —Audrey Hepburn (Paris, 1996, p. 108)

In future chapters, we return to the four building blocks as you work to integrate DP into your professional development efforts. In the meantime, take time now to plot the metrics from your own work in Exhibit 8.1. Use the last column to indicate whether the data show you are performing above (+), below (−), or on par (=) with the established benchmarks. As you do, please note that finding more minuses than plusses does not mean you need to "hang up your hat" as a therapist, any more than a preponderance of higher values indicate you are a "supershrink." Rather, both positive and negative indices can point to potential opportunities for development.

Consider a hypothetical example. Let's suppose your metrics indicate 90% of your clients achieve reliable change. Given the expected range of 64% to 74%, the figure could mean you help significantly more people than most clinicians. Caution would be warranted, however, as this particular index is known to be affected by the interaction between the length of treatment and the level of distress clients report at intake. In particular, longer than average lengths of stay are associated with higher rates of reliable change, especially

EXHIBIT 8.1

Comparing Your Performance Data Against Established Benchmarks

Key baseline metric	Established benchmarks	Your performance metrics	Rate: Above (+) Below (−) On par (=)
Effect size	$\overline{X} = .8$		
Relative effect size	$\overline{X} = .0$		
Percentage of clients achieving reliable change	$\overline{X} = 64\%–74\%$		
Percentage of clients achieving clinically significant change	$\overline{X} = 25\%–40\%$		
Deterioration	$\overline{X} = 5\%–10\%$		
Average number of sessions	$\overline{X} = 6$ sessions		
	Median = 5		
	Mode = 1		
Duration of treatment	9 weeks		
Dropout	$\overline{X} = 20\%–22\%$		
Planned versus unplanned termination	PT = 50%–64%		
	UT = 20%–34%		
Average intake SRS	Range = 34–36		

Note. PT = planned termination; SRS = Session Rating Scale; UT = unplanned termination.

among clients who present with higher ORS scores (e.g., more functional) at intake. An analogy: Hot water not only comes to boil more quickly but easily transforms into steam the longer it's kept on the burner. In short, keeping functional clients longer may be more responsible for the high percentage of those reporting improvement than anything you are doing in the course of treatment. On the other hand, among clients who score very low on the ORS at intake, shorter lengths of stay can artificially inflate the percentage achieving reliable change. Think of it this way, at the bottom, up is the only way to go.

Given the foregoing, a good rule to follow is to approach your data with the purpose of generating questions about your performance rather than confirming or disconfirming your effectiveness. Be sure your numbers are complete. Go back and compute any missing values before proceeding. It can't be said enough: If you don't have sufficient data for calculating *all* the metrics (between 40 and 60 completed cases if using the ORS), wait and continue collecting.

Next, carefully review each index one by one. Note which, if any, stand out, that is, trigger an emotional response, curiosity, surprise, discouragement, or inspiration. Consider whether any strike you as too good to be true or too bad to be believable. Importantly, at this juncture, resist the temptation to explain the results. Recalling the words of the fictional detective Sherlock Holmes in *A Scandal in Bohemia*, "It is a capital mistake to theorize before one has data. Insensibly, one begins to twist facts to suit theories, instead of theories to suit facts" (Baring-Gould, 1967, pp. 349–350). Once more, use your feelings to generate questions for further reflection and exploration. Be sure to write them down.

As an aid, here are a few examples:

- *Is my effect size higher (or lower) than average? What am I doing that might be responsible? What process do I use in making clinical decisions?* (If you haven't already done so, now is a good time to create a detailed and explicit map of how you work, making transparent what, with time and experience, has become automatic and unconscious.)

- *Am I more (or less) effective than my peers?* (*Note.* All things being equal, as they are still in treatment, active clients should have a lower effect and relative effect size than the inactive.)

- *Are more (or fewer) of my clients dropping out or deteriorating than expected?* (Hint: Look for commonalities among groups or subgroups of the clients who make up these figures.)

- *How many times, on average, am I meeting with clients?* (Be aware: Research shows the probability of change decreases as time in care lengthens; Duncan, Miller, Wampold, & Hubble, 2010.)

- *Is there a difference in the length of time in treatment between my active and inactive clients? Who are the people I tend to keep longer than usual?* (Clue: Therapists tend to keep nonprogressing clients in treatment, hoping they will eventually experience change.)

- *What is the percentage of clients with whom I hold a formal termination session?* (Research shows that such cases have better outcomes; Chow, 2014a.)

- *Do my clients provide constructive criticism? What am I doing to support or prevent them from doing so?* (Recall: The evidence shows alliance scores that improve are associated with better outcomes; Owen, Miller, Seidel, & Chow, 2016.)

TO SUM UP

Your best shot at becoming a more effective therapist is to follow your data. Leave theories, assumptions, and presuppositions—whatever you may already have decided about your particular strengths and weaknesses— at the door. As Etta's example shows, your metrics provide an evidence-based window into what you can do to develop and improve your skills and abilities.

WHAT TO DO RIGHT NOW

There are no shortcuts to true excellence.

—ANGELA DUCKWORTH (HILMANTEL, 2016)

Congratulations! In mining your data, you've taken the first, critical step toward better results. What you've learned will be used to inform your individualized DP plan. Two pieces of advice can be given at this point:

1. Resist the temptation to rely on inspiration over perspiration. Do the work. Use the measures. Crunch the numbers. Reflect on your data, giving thought in particular to how your performance metrics differ from the estimates you gave at the end of the first chapter and where your first opportunities for growth and development exist.

2. Stay focused on small, individualized learning objectives rather than on boosting your overall performance metrics. While establishing a baseline is critical for assessing progress, increases in effectiveness occur very slowly over a long period. Constantly monitoring the bottom line or comparing your results with others' is likely to have a negative impact on motivation. Indeed, research shows doing so often cripples development (Soderstrom & Bjork, 2015).

9

How Average Leads to Better Results

We're taught to fear the thought of being average. But maybe it's time to have another look at what that means.

—VIVIAN CHENG (2016)

ew would argue with the success of the hamburger. Although its exact origin is uncertain, sometimes disputed, it has become a staple of the American diet. A staggering 71% of all beef consumed in the country is served between two buns, with citizens eating an average of three per week. Laid end-to-end, that's enough burgers to circle the earth more than 32 times (Baidya, 2014)!

Vendors are everywhere, off nearly every highway exit, in most food courts, strip malls, and airports. Wherever you go—be it down the street, across the country, and now even around the world—there they are. Standing out among the many choices is McDonald's. The "Golden Arches" are everywhere. Each year, the company generates approximately $20 billion in revenue (Statista, 2019). Regardless of how you might feel about the chain, someone— actually many—are consuming its products.

It wasn't always that way. The global empire had very humble beginnings, starting out in the 1940s as a small, nondescript "Bar-B-Q" restaurant in San Bernardino, California. A few years into their business, something grabbed the attention of the owners Mac and Dick McDonald. Most of their profits

http://dx.doi.org/10.1037/0000191-009
Better Results: Using Deliberate Practice to Improve Therapeutic Effectiveness, by S. D. Miller, M. A. Hubble, and D. Chow

came from selling hamburgers. Despite their success at the time, they took a bold step. Following their "data," they closed and completely redesigned the restaurant. Gone were the majority of menu items as well as the iconic carhops who waited on customers. In their place was a walk-up, self-service counter and system for producing hamburgers, fries, and milkshakes efficiently and consistently.

From our current vantage point, it can be hard to appreciate the revolutionary changes put into place by the McDonald brothers. While burger joints were, like now, ubiquitous across the American landscape, the quality of the product and service varied considerably one to the next, and even day to day at the same location. Whatever one's tastes may be when it comes to a hamburger, it's difficult to dispute the uniform quality and service of McDonald's—a standard now reflected and expected throughout the fast-food industry. And while it has become fashionable in some circles to be critical of the Golden Arches, the link between their products and health-related concerns is far less certain than assumed (Chandler, 2019). More to the point, as comedian Jim Gaffigan wryly observed, even though "no one admits going to McDonald's, they sell 6 billion hamburgers a day. There's only 300 million people in this country. So, I'm not a calculus teacher, but I think everyone's lying" (Tremonti, 2017).

CONSISTENCY AND EFFECTIVENESS IN THE DELIVERY OF PSYCHOTHERAPY

You may wonder what this story has to do with psychotherapy. Like burgers from the pre-McDonald's era, therapists vary in terms of effectiveness (Baldwin & Imel, 2013; Johns, Barkham, Kellett, & Saxon, 2019; Okiishi, Lambert, Nielsen, & Ogles, 2003). Indeed, in a study of 119 real-world practitioners and more than 10,000 clients, Saxon and Barkham (2012) found recovery rates of individual therapists ranged from 23.5% to 95.6%! Other research reveals, and clinical experience confirms, practitioners even vary in their effectiveness from hour to hour and client to client (Goldberg, Hoyt, Nissen-Lie, Nielsen, & Wampold, 2018; Lambert & Barley, 2001; Owen, Wampold, Kopta, Rousmaniere, & Miller, 2016). Anyone who has provided counseling or therapy knows this to be true. One day you're hot, the next you're not.

Over the years, many attempts have been directed toward improving the quality and uniformity of psychotherapy. Standards of training and care have been created and enforced by regulatory bodies and licensing boards. Shared diagnostic systems have been developed and widely disseminated (e.g., *Diagnostic and Statistical Manual of Mental Disorders, International Classification of Diseases*). Entire professional careers and millions in grant funding have been spent constructing a psychological formulary, trusting that applying the correct treatment for a specific disorder will guarantee the best outcome. Although undertaken with good intentions, none of these efforts (as reviewed in Chapter 2) have borne fruit in terms of better or more consistent recovery rates for clients. Indeed, even when therapist competence is held constant and treatments are manualized, significant and meaningful differences in outcome persist (Baldwin & Imel, 2013; Johns et al., 2019).

Consistency of service and uniformity of their products have kept McDonald's at the top of the fast-food market, in not only popularity but also brand value (Statista, 2015). A reasonable person might ask, "How can it be that Mac and Dick McDonald were so amazingly successful while nearly everything *our* profession has done to improve our reach and impact has fallen flat?"

As is readily apparent, meeting a new client presents an entirely different set of challenges than filling an order at McDonald's. There, staff have simply to greet the customer, take their order, and then cook and assemble ready-made ingredients—all of which have previously been checked for consistency and quality. Think of it this way: The only variability a fast-food worker has to sort or manage is what the customer wants to eat. *Welcome to McDonald's. What would you like?* And no matter where you are in the world, the hamburger is essentially the same.

In sharp contrast, in psychotherapy, the ingredients contributing to a successful result vary considerably. Chief among these are what the client brings to the work and what are known as *extratherapeutic events* (Asay & Lambert, 1999; Hubble, Duncan, Miller, & Wampold, 2010). History, premorbid functioning, comorbidity, likability, interpersonal style, existing social support, physical illness, job loss, economic setbacks, and a host of chance events can combine in unpredictable ways to affect the results. Clearly, McDonald's would be far less successful if the ingredients in a Big Mac® or Filet-O-Fish® varied from one sandwich to the next. And yet, despite having no direct control over any of these variables, practitioners must contend with them daily.

How much of outcome is influenced by elements that happen to weave in and out of people's lives while in therapy? According to the evidence, a staggering 93% (Wampold & Imel, 2015)! With so much that is random and unforeseen, it might be difficult to imagine what we could ever do to deliver a more consistent service, to be equally helpful no matter who walks through the door. Fortunately, imagination is not required. The field now has the means to achieve both ends.

Here's the good news. If you've made it to this point in the book and have followed the directions given, you already have everything you need to take the next step. You know how to measure your results. You know how effective you are overall. Close examination of your data may even, as was true for Etta, the psychologist introduced in the case example in Chapter 8, have revealed aspects of your performance that fall short of established benchmarks. What follows next is an evidence-based method for becoming more effectively responsive to the unpredictable and unanticipated (Prescott, Maeschalck, & Miller, 2017; Stiles, 2009). As will eventually be seen, it also will enable you to separate what is random and uncontrollable from the actions you take that reliably affect the outcome of your work in either negative or positive ways. In so doing, your individual targets for deliberate practice (DP) can be identified.

ROUTINE OUTCOME MONITORING

> The more ideas or events or outcomes we average together, the more . . . randomness tends to cancel out.
>
> —Jeffrey S. Rosenthal (2006, p. 41)

In Chapter 7, we introduced researcher Michael Lambert. Recall, he was concerned about deterioration and dropout rates in psychotherapy. He pioneered the development of a process now in use worldwide, known by the generic name *routine outcome monitoring* (ROM; Boswell, Kraus, Miller, & Lambert, 2015; Lambert, 2010a, 2010b). In brief, therapists measure their clients' progress at each session. Whenever the results depart from expected norms, providers are alerted in real time, thereby allowing them to make adjustments or modifications at the time of service delivery. Research to date shows this increased responsiveness to the client's progress improves both retention and outcome (Lambert, 2017; Lambert, Whipple, & Kleinstäuber, 2018; Østergård, Randa, & Hougaard, 2018).

Whether a client is on or off track at any given session can be determined in two ways. The first and simplest is to plot the scores from whatever outcome measure you are using on a graph. After connecting the dots, use the overall slope of the resulting line to assess progress. Is it flat, increasing, or decreasing? Additionally, consider the amount of progress in relationship to the number of visits. In general, most change occurs early in treatment, with studies documenting a steady diminution in the likelihood of improvement over time (J. Brown, Dreis, & Nace, 1999; Lambert, 2010b).

As an example, see the data presented in Figure 9.1. Visual inspection of the client's Outcome Rating Scale (ORS; Miller & Duncan, 2000) scores (depicted by the thick black line) reveals progress is occurring from visit to visit. Indeed, because the amount of change from the first to the seventh meeting exceeds the Reliable Change Index (Bertolino & Miller, 2012; Jacobson & Truax, 1991) for the measure (5 points), the therapist can be confident treatment is contributing to improvement above and beyond the influence of extratherapeutic factors and events. At the same time, the graph makes it easy to see when, during the course of care, increased attention or action may be warranted. The decline in the ORS score at the fourth visit—whether a random occurrence or the result of an error or omission on the therapist's part—requires a response.

With the thin black line, Figure 9.1 also shows the client's Session Rating Scale (SRS; Miller, Duncan, & Johnson, 2000) scores. From the first to the last visit, the slope is positive. Such a trend, as reported in Chapter 7, is associated with better results. Closer examination reveals a drop in SRS scores at the third session. Although small and seemingly insignificant, research shows declines of even a single point are often followed by a deterioration in ORS scores in later visits (Bertolino & Miller, 2012; Miller, Hubble, Chow, & Seidel, 2015; Miller, Hubble, & Duncan, 2007). Once more, monitoring the scores at each session enables the clinician to know when to step in to ensure therapy stays on track. At a minimum, the clinician would want to draw the client's attention to, and ask for help understanding the meaning of, the change.

FIGURE 9.1. Outcome Rating Scale (ORS; Miller & Duncan, 2000) and Session Rating Scale (SRS; Miller, Duncan, & Johnson, 2000) Scores From Seven Sessions of Individual Therapy

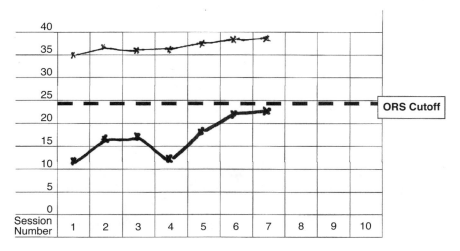

Visual inspection of the client's ORS scores is depicted by the thick black line. The client's SRS scores are depicted by the thin black line.

AUTOMATED DATABASE OUTCOME MANAGEMENT SYSTEMS

In lieu of using paper and pencil to plot scores, as shared in several places in this volume, therapists can use one of the computerized outcome management systems. Beyond the advantage of efficiency, such programs, relying as they do on large, normative samples, pinpoint at-risk cases with greater accuracy and alert the therapist in real time to the potential need for intervention.

Figure 9.2 shows a graph generated by one of the computerized systems supporting Partners for Change Outcome Management System (Miller, Duncan, Sorrell, & Brown, 2005). Three sessions of ORS and SRS scores are displayed. The thick, black line represents the ORS. Starting with the first session, client-specific predictive change trajectories are generated, appearing on the graph as shaded bands. Scores falling in the white zone are on track for a successful outcome, those in the black area are predictive of a negative result, and numbers falling in the gray zone are indeterminate, neither predictive of success or failure.

In this example, the client's scores clearly fall within the black zone, signaling a course of care in jeopardy (i.e., dropout or deterioration). In reality, the therapy has been at risk for a negative outcome since Session 2, as the score was, despite a slight increase on the ORS, in the black zone. Making such a determination would be difficult without access to the empirically derived, color-coded trajectories. SRS scores, represented by the black line, also appear on the graph. Visual inspection shows they, too, are in decline.

The electronic system tracks both scores, alerting the therapist to any meaningful changes. Between the two measures, the therapist would have received multiple notifications to respond to this client's lack of progress and

FIGURE 9.2. "Client Status Report" is a Graphic Display of Outcome Rating Scale (ORS; Miller & Duncan, 2000) and Session Rating Scale (SRS; Miller, Duncan, & Johnson, 2000), and Predictive Trajectories

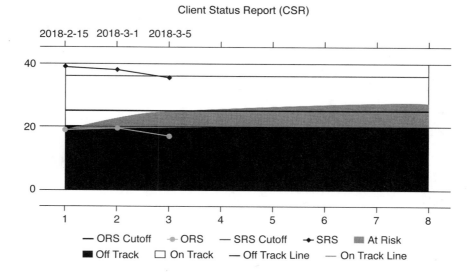

deteriorating scores, including their decreasing satisfaction with the thera-peutic relationship. Furthermore, detailed information about how outcome is related to various patterns and interactions on the ORS and SRS—a clinical process known as *feedback-informed treatment*—can be found in a series of manuals, books, and videos (Bertolino & Miller, 2012; Miller, 2011b, 2011c; Prescott et al., 2017).

While the scores, whether based on paper-and-pencil charting or a computer-generated graph, can signal when a response is warranted, they do not provide instruction on what to do or how best to do it. They also do not differentiate between a deterioration in scores resulting from the impact of some random, extratherapeutic factor or event versus a recurring error made by the therapist. Regardless of cause, it is necessary to solicit feedback from the client of sufficient detail for the clinician either to repair the alliance or make adjustments to the treatment. Whatever one's current abilities, eliciting feedback is a skill that can be refined and significantly strengthened through the discipline of DP.

ETTA ON THE LINE

If you want to go far, go with others.

—African proverb

When we last left Etta,[1] she was feeling discouraged. A small adjustment in how she introduced the outcome and alliance measures had, in time, led to an improvement in her effectiveness. Fewer clients were deteriorating or dropping out. Notwithstanding, 6 months following the last consultation with the test author, her work had stalled. She was no longer getting better results.

After struggling on her own for a while, she reached out to the consultant once again. As before, the four building blocks of DP—individualized learn-ing objectives, a coach, feedback, and successive refinement—informed the consultation.

Her email began, "At first, I thought, 'This is as good as it gets'; you can only squeeze so much juice out of an orange!"

To this the test developer replied, "The way you put it is interesting. Oftentimes, periods of progress are followed by a leveling off, plateauing. It is an entirely normal and frustrating part of deliberate practice." Continu-ing, "A course of diminishing returns sets in and you can 'squeeze' all you want and it's unlikely to yield much more. On the other hand, based on my experience with the instruments, I have a hunch there may be more 'juice' in that orange."

---

[1]Etta is a fictitious case example created from the authors' real-world experience providing consultations. The test developer is one of the authors (SDM).

He ended the email, offering a few possible meeting times and a request that she once again send a screenshot of her most recent performance metrics. He also asked her to transcribe the end of session discussions she had with three clients, past or present, who scored below the clinical cutoff on the SRS.

After catching up with Etta, the consultant began the video conference saying, "Of the three transcripts I have, let's start with Hannah." He continued "Your introduction of the measure is spot on, very thorough, and welcoming. You point out her score is below the clinical cutoff. Then, you make your first request for feedback, asking, 'What can I do differently next time we meet, so you'll feel better about the session?'"

"That's my standard opening question when SRS scores are low," Etta matter-of-factly replied.

"OK. As you see, Hannah responds, saying, 'No, it was fine.'"

"Yeah, she does. She doesn't give me any feedback despite her low score."

"And if you read through the rest of the transcript, that is what happens: No feedback is given. Over the years, though, we've learned that certain lines of inquiry are much more likely than others to invite specific, actionable feedback from clients."

When Etta asked for clarification, he explained, "The best questions, we've discovered, embody a set of common principles. I have them in a handout. Let me send it to you right now" (see Figure 9.3).

"What strikes you about these?" he asked Etta.

"Well," she started, "All of them emphasize what can be seen or heard, kind of like you were watching a video. Also, no judgment is involved."

"Exactly. They focus on getting the facts. What else?"

"Well, they focus on the client, their experience or perceptions."

"That's right," he agreed, "And so, thinking about these principles, take a moment: What first strikes you about *your* opening question?"

"It's definitely vague," Etta responded quickly, "and also evaluative."

"Absolutely. So, let's work with it. How might you change your question?"

FIGURE 9.3. Principles for Eliciting Negative Feedback

PRINCIPLES FOR ELICTING
NEGATIVE FEEDBACK
- Descriptive v. Evaluative
- Observations v. Inferences
- Specific v. General
- Quantities v. Qualities
- Task v. Person-Oriented

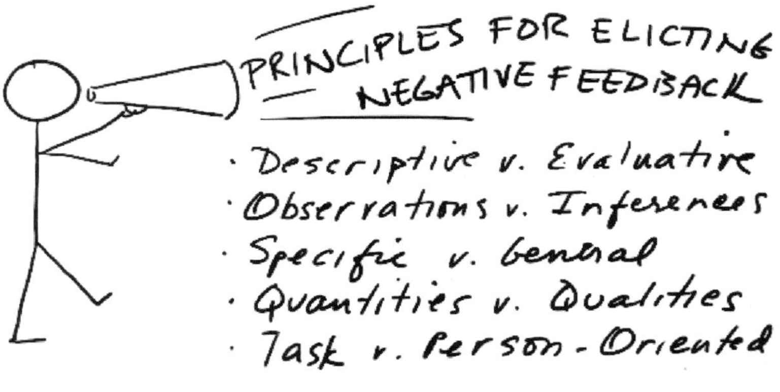

Pausing to think, "Perhaps, I'd ask, 'What specifically would you like to be different next time?'"

"OK. It's no longer evaluative, and it *sounds* more specific."

"But, looking at the principles," she added, "it is still more person than task oriented."

"That's right. The use of personal pronouns, like 'you'—as well as 'I,' 'me,' 'your'—reduces the chance of getting feedback. Albeit indirectly, they put the client in the position of criticizing *you*."

"Right," she said. Exhaling loudly, "This isn't easy!"

"*This*," the consultant replied, "is the essence of deliberate practice. It can be painfully slow. And while you're doing it, focusing on your errors, it can leave you feeling incompetent, like you don't know anything." He emphasized, "*But* that's what happens when you upend what comes naturally and automatically, and work consciously on developing new thoughts and actions."

The two then continued to work at refining how Etta processed her client's scores on the SRS. Although initially difficult, by the end of the hour, the questions she was formulating had evolved considerably. Gone were the vague, evaluative inquires focused on improving the client's experience of the next visit. In their place were more specific, detailed, task-oriented questions focused on the here and now. For example,

- "What would have to happen (more or less often) for the score on the SRS to be a 35 rather than a 34?"

- "Thinking back on the visit, what specific moments come to mind when the score might have been a point or two lower (or higher)? What changed? Caused that?"

- "Anything that did (or didn't happen) during the session today that would make the score on (one of the specific items on the SRS [e.g., understanding, goals and topics, approach or method, overall]) move up a point?"

The consultant ended the video conference, asking Etta to record and reflect on her end-of-session discussions with clients, taking the time to write out questions more in line with the principles on the handout. The two then agreed on a time to meet in a month.

TO SUM UP

Unlike cooking a hamburger, in psychotherapy, the ingredients contributing to a successful result vary considerably. As introduced before, a client's history, premorbid functioning, comorbidity, likability, interpersonal style, existing social support, physical illness, job loss, economic setbacks, and a host of chance events can combine in unpredictable ways to affect the process and outcome of care. ROM enables therapists to become more sensitive and responsive to the vicissitudes of progress *and* the quality of the relationship in any psychotherapy.

WHAT TO DO RIGHT NOW

What we observe is not nature itself, but nature exposed to our method of questioning.

—WERNER HEISENBERG (1958, p. 25)

Mindful of the evidence and information reviewed in this chapter, we invite you to take the following steps:

1. Begin tracking your client's scores on a session-by-session basis, responding in real time whenever the measures you are using indicate outcome or engagement is at risk.

2. Don't be surprised if your initial efforts to elicit feedback fall short. Together, studies and clinical experience show processing measures with clients is a skill that takes time and practice to develop (Brattland et al., 2018). Be deliberate in your efforts. Record and transcribe your work, specifically, the portions related to your introduction and processing of the measures. Reflect on, revise, and evaluate your attempts to improve.

3. Should you begin feeling discouraged, follow Etta's example. Find a coach. Reach out to the authors of articles on ROM. Join an online forum, such as The International Center for Clinical Excellence (see https://www.iccexcellence.com), on which you can meet and work with peers who can provide support and guidance.

In the next chapter, we move beyond using measures merely to improve therapists' responsiveness in the moment. Attention is directed to identifying and modifying recurring patterns in your work that negatively impact effectiveness.

10

How Being Bad Can Make You Better

Success hinges, in powerful and often counterintuitive ways, on how we react to failure.
—MATTHEW SYED (2015, p. 8)

Classical pianist Rachel Hsu enters the auditorium.[1] Among the many pieces she'll perform on this occasion is the Concert Étude no. 3 by Franz Liszt. Un Sospiro (Italian for "sigh"), as the composition is known, is a famously challenging work to play and a pleasure to watch. The hands mirror the sound of the music, moving rapidly up and down the keyboard in an intricate, crisscrossing fashion, which, when done correctly, evokes images of water tumbling over rocks in a small, mountain brook. Experts consider Liszt's Étude no. 3, with its third staff, abundance of notes, and complex fingerwork, exceptionally difficult—a 12 on a scale from 1 to 10.

Clad in a simple black satin dress and red sash, Rachel silently makes her way to the piano. A hush falls over the crowd as she sits and, with a practiced poise, effortlessly adjusts the bench, which offsets her diminutive size. She straightens her back, takes a deep breath, and raises her hands, holding them momentarily above the keys. Then, magic.

To say the audience is stunned would be a gross understatement. Those in attendance are entirely unprepared for what they witness. Six minutes of

---

[1]Portions of this section are from "The Road to Mastery: What's Missing From This Picture," by S. D. Miller and M. A. Hubble, 2011, *Psychotherapy Networker, 35*, pp. 22–31. Copyright 2011 by The Psychotherapy Networker, Inc. Reprinted with permission.

http://dx.doi.org/10.1037/0000191-010
Better Results: Using Deliberate Practice to Improve Therapeutic Effectiveness, by S. D. Miller, M. A. Hubble, and D. Chow

perfection: a combination of music and performance that brings many to tears—an experience made all the more compelling by the fact that the pianist is only 8 years old.

Exceptionally talented children are nothing new, of course. Mozart, whose story was introduced in Chapter 3, is one. Nowadays, similarly gifted kids are a frequent feature on television and social media, wowing audiences with abilities seemingly far beyond their years. In an interview following her performance, Rachel insists she is no natural, "I have to work at it, practicing every day, at least 4 hours, including my birthday and Christmas!" When asked what she possibly could spend so much time each day "working on," she speaks up immediately: "Well, my mistakes, of course! I make a lot of mistakes. . . ." Laughter fills the auditorium in response. Given Rachel's performance, her admission is difficult to accept. Judging by the look on her face, it's clear she's serious.

MISTAKEN ABOUT MISTAKES

> Before we demand more of our data, we need to demand more of ourselves.
> —Nate Silver (2012, p. 9)

The advice to learn from one's mistakes is offered with such regularity, it borders on cliché. It has been said in many different ways across many generations. "Mistakes . . . are the portals of discovery," Irish novelist James Joyce (1922/1946, p. 188) once observed. More recently, actor and television personality Mary Tyler Moore said, "Make mistakes. That's how you grow" ("You Can't Be Brave If You've Only Had Wonderful Things Happen to You," 2017). And, from that timeless sage, "Anonymous," "Never say, 'Oops.' Say, 'Ah, interesting.'"

Given the frequency of its invocation and enduring cultural support, a reasonable person could conclude everyone heeds the recommendation, applying it as much as possible in their daily lives. Evidence shows otherwise. Implementing these simple words of wisdom is beset by a variety of challenges.

Consider the results from one representative neuroimaging study. Briefly, researchers Downar, Bhatt, and Montague (2011) scanned the brains of physicians while they were making treatment decisions in a series of virtual patient encounters. Immediate feedback was given on the accuracy of their selection. Interestingly, when some of the physicians were told they'd made the wrong choice, their brains responded by shutting down, literally ignoring the negative feedback. Simultaneously, specific areas associated with anticipating rewards lit up, suggesting these participants valued being right more than learning from their mistakes. For this group, performance did not improve over successive trials. What's more, experience level only served to compound the problem, with those who had practiced medicine the longest being the most confident of their judgment and the *least* likely to pay attention to, and learn from, their errors.

Hundreds of studies in social psychology and the psychotherapy outcome literature confirm just how difficult it can be to—quoting the lyrics of the once popular children's song "The Roses of Success" (Sherman, Sherman, & Rodgers, 1968)—transform "the ashes of disaster . . . [into] the roses of success" (Gilovich, Griffin, & Kahneman, 2002; Nisbett & Ross, 1980). To begin, the more a mistake conflicts with one's self-image, or hoped for result, the less likely it is to be noticed, remembered, or used to change existing beliefs (Gilovich et al., 2002). Consider a study by Gilovich (1991). In it, people were asked to read the diary of a person who believed dreams were prophetic. Unknown to readers, the researchers had arranged the journal so that half of the accounts were paired with a subsequent, confirmatory event, and the other half, not. When later tested for recall, the participants' memory for dreams that were confirmed was significantly better than those that were not. Said another way, people are less likely to remember experiences that do not confirm their a priori beliefs—a result that has obvious, negative implications for anyone hoping to learn from their mistakes.

More recently, Tappin, van der Leer, and McKay (2017) examined how people weigh evidence when adjusting their beliefs. In the study, participants were asked which candidate they supported in an upcoming election. They were also asked to state, regardless of their personal preference, which one they actually believed would win. Participants were then given a report of polling data that either supported their judgment but was undesirable ("I want *A* but believe *B* will win. The new information confirms my belief") or was contrary to their judgment but desirable ("I want *A* but believe *B* will win. The new information contradicts my belief"). After reading the report, researchers asked participants to once again state which candidate they believed was most likely to win.

Contrary to what one might hope would happen when evidence was provided, the results showed subjects were more likely to incorporate the polling data into the latter assessment when it favored the outcome they desired. Importantly, the effect was independent of the participants' initial belief about who would win, a finding that showed the differential weighting of evidence had less to do with confirming a priori beliefs than with reinforcing the hoped for result (Tappin et al., 2017). Given these and the previous findings, it is not hard to understand why research shows therapists believe they help more people than they do, fail to predict which of their clients will stay the course or drop out, mistake deterioration for progress, and believe they are improving over the course of their careers when they are not.

THE JOY OF MISTAKES

> What'll I start tomorrow?
> —Kurt Vonnegut ("If I'm Not a Writer Then I'm Nothing," 2012)

If learning is the goal, but the barriers to success are ample, what are therapists to do? The solution is simple. First: Don't see what you know, know what you see. As introduced in Chapter 3, familiarity with performing a given task leads to automaticity. Behaviors become routine, requiring less conscious effort. This entirely natural process is both friend and foe. On the one hand, efficiency, proficiency, and confidence increase. On the other, as Ericsson (2006) observed, "People lose conscious control over the production of their actions and are no longer able to make specific intentional adjustments to them" (p. 694). Completely outside of awareness, learning begins to stall, and performance is put at risk of deterioration (Ericsson, 2006; Ericsson & Pool, 2016; Goldberg, Rousmaniere, et al., 2016).

If research from neuroscience and social psychology can provide any guidance, it is this: effective learners focus less attention on what they are doing right than on what they are doing wrong. As Downar et al. (2011) showed, their brains literally "light up" on learning when they've made an error. That is when they are most "jazzed"—precisely the point Rachel made to her disbelieving audience following her performance: "Hardly anyone notices [the mistakes], of course, but I do, *and I remember*" (Miller & Hubble, 2011, p. 25, emphasis in original). A sound of excitement then entered her voice as she described how, with the aid of her teacher, she identifies the specific passages she'll target, slowly playing and replaying each until mastered.

RANDOM VERSUS RECURRING ERRORS

As critical a first step as attending to errors is, it is not sufficient. For learning to take place, it is necessary to distinguish between two types of mistakes: random and recurring. Conservatively speaking, people make about 2,000 decisions—some conscious, most unconscious—per waking hour (Sahakian & LaBuzetta, 2013). That number increases with the degree of focus, complexity, and responsibility involved in the task performed.

Although no formal count has ever been published, most would agree psychotherapy is cognitively demanding. Any given hour will, therefore, contain myriad (a) "coulda, woulda, shouldas" as well as (b) an untold number of in-the-moment adjustments. To elaborate, in the first instance, a mistake is made but is accidental, not part of a recurring pattern. In the second, whether effective or not, an action is taken in response to a unique and unpredictable set of circumstances. Nothing can or should be learned in either case, and neither has any broader meaning than, "Sometimes s _ _ _ happens" or "It just seemed right at the time." Here, routine outcome monitoring (ROM), as introduced in the preceding chapter, can be especially helpful, as this evidence-based methodology enables clinicians to (a) identify and address random errors at the time of service and (b) check the success of whatever responses they make to the "unanticipated" in psychotherapy (cf. Lambert, 2010b; Prescott, Maeschalck, & Miller, 2017).

If responsiveness and mutuality—that is, doing the right thing at the moment, together—are, as some have argued, fundamental to effective care— learning to use ROM effectively could prove an important target for deliberate practice (DP; Stiles, 1988, 2009; Cornelius-White, Kanamori, Murphy, & Tickle, 2018; Coyne, Muir, Westra, Antony, & Constantino, 2018). Indeed, Stiles and Horvath (2017) argued convincingly, "Certain therapists are *more* effective than others . . . *because* [they are] appropriately responsive . . . providing each client with a different, individually tailored treatment" (p. 71; italics added). Adding empirical rigor to these assertions, J. Brown and Cazauvieilh (2019), in recently reported results, found average therapists who are more "engaged"—as measured by frequency with which they logged in to a computerized outcome management system to view their performance results—were significantly more effective than their peers, averaging .19 σ (standard deviation) greater in severity adjusted effect size (see Figure 10.1).

Distressingly, the evidence shows many clinicians, even when presented with feedback indicating treatment is off course, do not respond in any meaningful way. Research by Lutz (2014), for example, found "in-session" discussions with clients only took place 60% of the time (changes to the method or interventions, 30%; arrangement of assistance with other resources, 27%; efforts to enhance the therapeutic relationship, 10%; variations in the intensity or dose of services, 9%; and consultation and supervision, 7%). Bottom line: Make ROM a routine part of your clinical work and professional development.

Consistent with the theme of the present chapter, attention is now turned to using data generated by ROM to separate the impact of random events from patterns of action or inaction that reliably affect the outcome of your work in negative ways. The information generated will, in turn, be used to identify your *zone of proximal development*—the specific areas in which your usually effective care breaks down—and set learning objectives to focus on in developing and executing your individualized DP plan. Returning to the words of 8-year-old pianist, Rachel, "What I focus on when I practice are the parts that are really hard to play right all the time" (R. Hsu, personal communication, October 20, 2010).

FIGURE 10.1. Differences in Severity-Adjusted Effect Sizes (SAES) Between Therapist With High Engagement Versus Therapist in Low Engagement of Their Outcomes

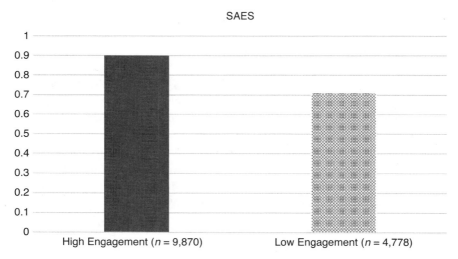

From "Clinician Engagement in Feedback-Informed Treatment (FIT) and Patient Outcomes," by J. Brown and C. Cazauvieilh, 2019. Retrieved from https://acorncollaboration.org/blog/2019/2/12/therapist-engagement. Copyright 2019 by ACORN. Adapted with permission.

FINDING PATTERNS OF THERAPIST EFFECTS

The literary mind can be intentionally prone to the confusion between *noise* and *meaning*, that is, between a randomly constructed arrangement and a precisely intended message.

—Nassim Nicholas Taleb (2004, p. xlii)

Look at Figure 10.2. What do you see? In no time at all, most report a face in profile, one resembling a famous figure from American history. Actually, once seen, it's difficult, if not impossible, to unsee. Try it. Look away momentarily then back again. The face dominates, capturing and holding attention. More, once set in motion, the process can take on a life of its own, leading us to look for more—the head and neck of a goose (or is that the Loch Ness monster?); an anglerfish, mouth wide open; a turkey drumstick; another face, faint by comparison, eerily peering out through the clouds, some might even say warning of a coming calamity (Cheung, 2006). Literally, the sky's the limit.

From an evolutionary perspective, the tendency to find patterns—be it in clouds, polished marble surfaces, burn marks on toast, or tea leaves in a cup—is easy to understand. For our earliest ancestors, seeing eyes in the underbrush, whether real or illusory, had obvious survival value. So, too, would the apparent ability to divine the future in perceived regularities in nature. Whether or not the perceptions or predictions were accurate

FIGURE 10.2. What Do You See?

mattered less than the consequences of being wrong (Shermer, 2008). Survival dictated a high tolerance for errors as the results of *not* believing "something is out there" were so often dire. As researchers Foster and Kokko (2008) pointed out, "Natural selection will favour strategies that make many incorrect causal associations in order to establish those that are essential for survival" (p. 36).

We are hardwired to look for and find patterns. To achieve better results, of course, the valid must be separated from the invalid. Thus, while not denying the "appearance" of the face in the clouds, meteorologists would actively and correctly dispute whether seeing "it" serves any purpose other than being a way to pass the time. Far more important, they would insist, is distinguishing between different types of cloud formations. And in the case of the photo, far from a bad omen, the type shown—cirrus fibratus—is associated with good, stable atmospheric conditions for the near term—essential information for anyone whose life or livelihood depends on accurate weather predictions.

As noted several times in this volume, claims abound regarding the significance of certain "patterns" of clinical work. Like faces in the clouds, they are captivating but have proven to have little predictive validity (e.g., ongoing supervision, training in and adherence to specific treatment approaches/ protocols, professional degree or licensure, years of experience, and various client factors [i.e., diagnosis, resistance, attachment style]). By contrast, the contribution to outcome made by the person of the therapist has, until very recently, largely been ignored. Once research firmly established practitioners reliably vary in their effectiveness (Baldwin & Imel, 2013; Johns, Barkham,

Kellett, & Saxon, 2019), efforts to understand what might account for the differences began in earnest. *Therapist effects* research, as this emerging literature is known, has identified patterns that consistently separate the best from the rest.

FROM REFLEX TO REFLECTION

> The difference between something good and something great is attention to detail.
> —Charles Swindoll (2000)

Before reading further, take out and review the blueprint we asked you to create at the end of Chapter 3, detailing how you do therapy. As each pattern, enumerated shortly, is presented, reflect on your map. How, or does, it take into account the specific issues delineated? Make a note of any ideas that occur to you for potential revisions to the way you conceptualize your work.

Keep in mind: The purpose of identifying which, if any, of the following patterns are present in your work is not to raise your *overall* effectiveness—at least not at present. Learning how to move from average to better results will come. Instead, for now, the objective is to enable you to deliver a *more consistently* effective performance across all your clients. Paraphrasing Imel et al. (2011), the *competent therapist* is one who achieves equivalent outcomes with all clients while also meeting an empirically established norm of effectiveness (p. 296).

To date, research documents therapists vary reliably in effectiveness in six ways. A description of each follows.

1. Client Level of Distress/Severity/Functioning at Intake

A clear and consistent difference between practitioners can be found in their ability to help highly distressed, low-functioning clients. Recall results reviewed previously from Saxon and Barkham (2012), showing significant differences in the recovery rates achieved by individual practitioners. Consistent with what one might expect, the researchers showed a general decline in outcomes as the level of client severity increased. That said, lower levels of client functioning did not impact all clinicians equally. Rather, the clients of less effective clinicians suffered significantly more than those seen by either average or above average practitioners in the sample.

2. Amount of Improvement Over Time

Most clinicians would agree that the outcome of treatment is related to the amount of psychotherapy clients receive. With some notable exceptions (i.e., Battino, 2006; Gingerich & Eisengart, 2000; Talmon, 1990), higher doses are seen as preferable to lower. Nevertheless, such a view is contingent on therapists' having a uniform impact regardless of the length of treatment. The evidence suggests otherwise. In a study using archival data of nearly 17,000 clients and 300 therapists, Erekson, Clayson, Park, and Tass (2018) found significant variation in the amount of change therapists fostered early on in care—a result known to be associated with better outcomes over time. Another, mentioned previously, actually showed therapists tend to decline in effectiveness as their experience in the field increased (Goldberg, Rousmaniere, et al., 2016). Using data from a large, naturalistic data set (n = 5,828 clients, 158 therapists, 50,048 sessions), researchers Goldberg, Hoyt, Nissen-Lie, Nielsen, and Wampold (2018) found a significant interaction between therapist effectiveness and length of treatment. While all demonstrated a substantial, overall tendency to facilitate improvement in clients, the gap between the least and most effective widened as time in treatment increased. In summary, the clients of less effective clinicians stalled, whereas those seeing top performers continued and even accelerated their progress. As the authors put it, "[Unless] one is seeing an effective therapist, . . . simply receiving a larger dose of treatment . . . may not prove worthwhile" (Goldberg et al., 2018, p. 541).

3. Client Culture, Race, Ethnicity

Multiple studies document both between and within therapist differences in outcome along cultural, racial, and ethnic lines (Flückiger et al., 2013; Fuertes et al., 2007; Hayes, McAleavey, Castonguay, & Locke, 2016; Hayes, Owen, & Bieschke, 2015; Imel et al., 2011; Larrison, Schoppelrey, Hack-Ritzo, & Korr, 2011; Worthington, Mobley, Franks, & Tan, 2000). In one representative study, Hayes et al. (2016) found outcomes between the least and most effective therapists differed a full standard deviation when working with racial and ethnic minority clients. Importantly, these results, as well as others, show such variations in effectiveness are *unrelated* to therapist gender, years of experience, self-perceived cultural competence, professional degree, theoretical orientation, or their own race or ethnicity. "*No* therapist is immune," Hayes, Owen, and Nissen-Lie (2017) concluded in their review on the evidence, "from having [cultural] disparities in their caseload" (p. 162; italics added).

4. Gender and Sexual Orientation/Identity

To date, the evidence shows psychotherapy outcomes do not vary in any predictable way based on client gender alone (Hayes et al., 2017; Johns et al., 2019). Owen, Wong, and Rodolfa (2009) were the first to investigate variation at the individual practitioner level, depending on the client's gender. Consistent with the other findings reported here, the absence of main effects belie equivalence when, in fact, significant variability in outcomes exist. As the authors noted, regardless of their own gender, "Some psychotherapists did better with male clients, some . . . with female, and the rest . . . did equally well or equally poor with male and female clients" (Owen et al., 2009, p. 454).

While being the subject of major interest and writing in recent years, much less is known about disparities in outcome owing to client sexual orientation/identity. Not surprisingly, however, results from the one available study of 1,725 clients and 50 therapists by Drinane, Winderman, Roberts, Frierson Freeman, and Wang (2019) once again document significant variability in the effectiveness of individual clinicians based on client sexual identity (sexual minority vs. heterosexual/straight). Specifically, some therapists had sexual minority clients with better outcomes than their heterosexual clients, while, for others, the opposite was true.

5. The Quality of the Therapeutic Alliance

Establishing and maintaining an effective working relationship is another area in which individual clinicians differ in effectiveness. Baldwin, Wampold, and Imel (2007) found a staggering 97% of the difference in client outcomes was attributable to therapist variability in the alliance. Little to none was related to variability in the *client's* connection with the practitioner—findings that led the authors to conclude, "Therapist variability drives the alliance–outcome correlation. . . . [Those] who, on average formed stronger alliances . . . showed significantly better outcomes than therapists who did not" (p. 849).

As introduced in Chapter 7, and illustrated with the story of Etta, a pattern of lower initial alliance scores that improve over time results in significantly better outcomes than those that start and stay high or begin high and decline as time in treatment lengthens (Miller, Hubble, & Duncan, 2007; Owen, Miller, et al., 2016). Such results, it appears, speak to a therapist's ability to create an atmosphere in which their clients feel safe to say what might *not* be working for them so adjustments can be made to better meet their needs.

6. Client Presenting Problem

A number of studies show therapists vary in effectiveness, depending on the problem being treated (Constantino, Boswell, Coyne, Kraus, & Castonguay, 2017; Kraus, Castonguay, Boswell, Nordberg, & Hayes, 2011; Owen, Adelson, Budge, Kopta, & Reese, 2016). Using data gathered by ROM in a real-world clinical setting, Kraus et al. (2016) found individual clinician outcomes, both in general and with specific problems, were remarkably stable over time. That said, 88% of the practitioners studied excelled in at least one problem domain—meaning, of course, they were less effective with others. And indeed, slightly less than half had at least one problem type with which they significantly underperformed. With regard to specific problems, therapist effects—that is differences in outcome between practitioners—were most evident when treating substance abuse (18.28%), quality of life (18.72%), suicidality (12.78%), and depression (11.82%), and were least in mania (1.56%), psychosis (3.71%) panic or anxiety (4.35%), and sexual functioning

(4.44%). While the authors ultimately concluded such differences might be useful for facilitating referrals of clients to therapists with well-matched strengths, the implications for any clinician hoping to achieve more consistent results are obvious: Use your data to identify which, if any, diagnoses or problems might serve as useful targets for deliberate practice (Kraus et al., 2016).

TONY'S TALE OF TELLS: AN EXAMPLE OF BRINGING UP BASELINE

Tony Rousmaniere is a psychologist and researcher who lives and works in Seattle, Washington. Early in his career, he began using ROM in his clinical work. "My overall effectiveness was not bad," he found. "Roughly half of my clients were getting better—some very quickly and dramatically" (Rousmaniere, 2016, p. 10). That meant, of course, 50% were not improving. More, approximately 25% of his clients dropped out, 10% worsened, and in nearly a third of his cases, progress stalled. "It was frustrating," he confessed. "Like most therapists, I got into this field to help people" (Miller, 2017).

Concerned, Tony sought out supervision and training. "My supervisor," he recalls, "was smart, friendly, and approachable [and] . . . had over 3 decades of experience." He also sought out every training opportunity that came his way. "I became a psychotherapy-training groupie . . . filled a stack of lined pads with careful notes and accumulated a large library of books on psychotherapy models, methods, techniques." His plan was as simple as it is common among therapists hoping to improve their performance. With "a toolbox of shiny new tools," he believed he would finally "be able to reach the 50% . . . [he'd] previously failed to help" (Rousmaniere, 2016, p. 22).

Consistent with the research evidence on supervision and training, his plan failed miserably. Observed Tony, "After a year of immersing myself . . . I still had the same problem. . . . What was I missing?" That's when he came across intensive short-term dynamic psychotherapy. "I was convinced," he said, "I had found the key to unlock a new level of therapeutic effectiveness" (Rousmaniere, 2016, p. 25). He dove in head first, buying all the books and attending every workshop he could find. Again, he was disappointed. Despite developing relationships with many "motivated and bright clinicians . . . the impact on . . . clients was more of the same" (p. 25).

It was when Tony came across the work of Scott Miller, he was first introduced to the term *deliberate practice* (Rousmaniere, 2009). As was his custom, he read everything he could put his hands on, paying particular attention to the four ingredients of effective practice: (a) individualized learning objectives, (b) a coach, (c) feedback, and (d) successive refinement.

His first critical decision was finding a coach. Despite having accessed teachers and supervisors in the past, he recognized something was missing in his previous attempts to achieve better results. The one he chose was not only accessible but also an internationally known clinician and supervisor. Having once been a professional musician, he was also deeply familiar with the principles of DP. "Struck by how differently psychotherapy training was conducted,"

Tony says, his coach had "developed his own training regimen that included an intensive process of watching videotapes of his work, getting feedback from experts, and practicing key skills" (Rousmaniere, 2016, p. 33).

Using ROM data as a guide, Tony purposefully selected videos of his work with clients he was not helping. While watching the recordings together, his coach quickly identified a problematic pattern—a tell; in particular, Tony's management of the therapeutic alliance (see item 5 in the list of factors influencing therapist effectiveness in the preceding section, From Reflex to Reflection). Over and over, in one recording then another, the issue recurred. Whenever a client was hesitant or ambivalent, Tony recalled, "I did most of the talking." The coach immediately zoomed in on specific interactions—mere seconds of dialogue—first highlighting the missed opportunity, next teaching why a different response was called for, and having Tony put the feedback to work in role plays using his own words. The process was repeated, "not once or twice but 5 times, 10 times, or more," Tony said, "until it was clear that I had internalized the skill" (Rousmaniere, 2016, p. 39). At the end of the hour, the coach assigned homework. Consistent with the principles of DP, it included solitary video study with behavioral rehearsal addressing the "errors identified in each . . . session." (p. 42).

Tony followed through, spending about 15 minutes at the beginning of each day watching brief segments of sessions with clients whose ROM data indicated they were not making progress, had a poor alliance, or were deteriorating. He would look for the pattern, stop the video, recall the principle he'd been taught for a more effective response, struggle until he was successful formulating an alternative, and repeat. As he reported in his detailed account, *Deliberate Practice for Psychotherapists* (Rousmaniere, 2016), Tony finally reached the performance objective that had previously proven so elusive. His dropout rate declined, and both his alliance and outcome scores improved.

Tony's story illustrates how ROM can aid in professional development, functioning like a sophisticated radar system, identifying "threats" not always visible to naked eye. It also shows the key role a good coach plays in transforming performance pitfalls into opportunities for positive change. Of note,

Tony's choice of coach was not based on convenience or propinquity—the senior clinician who just happens to be down the hall. Risking rejection, he reached for the best, and succeeded. Specifically, his coach also was intimately familiar and experienced with DP. He proved to be a careful observer. Watching videos, he identified Tony's zone of proximal development, the limits of his performance he now needed to move beyond. He gave clear, explicit directions and preferred working on the fundamentals over theoretical discussions. He was corrective rather than critical, an authority not authoritarian, and, instead of trying to create a clone, focused on helping Tony become a better, more effective version of himself.

TO SUM UP

Being bad can make you better. The key is using your data to identify specific areas where your performance falters. Once you've seen a sufficient number of clients, good places to begin looking for professional growth opportunities include differences in effectiveness based on client: (a) level of distress; (b) rate of improvement; (c) culture, race, ethnicity; (d) gender/sexual orientation or identity; (e) engagement in the therapeutic alliance; and (f) presenting problem. Targeting such areas first will enable you to deliver a more consistently effective service.

WHAT TO DO RIGHT NOW

An idea not coupled with action will never get any bigger than the brain cell it occupied.

—ARNOLD H. GLASOW ("QUOTES," n.d.)

The six ways therapists vary reliably in effectiveness identified in this chapter should not be considered exhaustive. Rather, they merely reflect the field's current state of knowledge. Other patterns, and interactions between them, will most certainly be uncovered in the future. Although no specific studies exist at present, it is reasonable to believe individual therapists could vary in effectiveness when (a) working with clients from different socioeconomic backgrounds (rural vs. urban, professional vs. blue collar, rich vs. poor) and age groups (e.g., youths vs. adults, adults vs. the elderly); (b) delivering services in different formats (e.g., individual, group, couple, face-to-face vs. online) or settings (e.g., public vs. private, hospital vs. clinic); and (c) a host of unrelated psychological, interpersonal, environmental, and temporal factors (e.g., attachment style, salary and work conditions, time of day, day of the week).

(continues)

WHAT TO DO RIGHT NOW (*Continued*)

In light of the potentially limitless ways a therapist's performance metrics can be parsed, the question is how best to proceed when identifying individualized learning objectives and establishing a plan for DP. Our counsel is to do the following:

1. Start with the patterns that have been shown empirically to affect outcome. Create a table listing the patterns along the horizontal axis and your performance metrics on the vertical (i.e., effect size, relative effect size, percentage achieving reliable/clinically significant change, deterioration, dropout, average number of sessions, average intake Session Rating Scale; Miller, Duncan, & Johnson, 2000). Examine the numbers in the individual cells to determine under what conditions your effectiveness varies. Of any you find, pick one you feel passionate about or want to address. DP is hard enough. Nothing is gained from compounding difficulty with drudgery. Keep in mind: The more you divide your metrics, the greater the risk of drawing spurious correlations—both seeing a pattern that does not exist and missing one that does. Be conservative.

2. The list we have provided is instructive, but don't ignore your gut/intuition. Again, using a table, consider factors you suspect might interfere with your work. Then, look for differences in your actual data. Perhaps you feel your effectiveness is lower when working with particular kinds of people or presenting problems (mandated vs. voluntary, one motivational stage vs. another, substance abuse vs. mental health). Maybe you prefer delivering services in a particular format or setting (e.g., group vs. individual, clinical vs. in-home, led by one manager/supervisor or another). Whatever it might be, once you have data "in the can," it's possible to confirm, reject, or refine your hunches.

3. Don't be surprised if you don't find any glaring pattern of deficits in your metrics. After all, a virtual mountain of evidence obtained in naturalistic settings documents the majority of practitioners are effective (Baldwin & Imel, 2013; Hill & Castonguay, 2017; Erekson et al., 2018; Johns et al., 2019). As Saxon and Barkham (2012) reminded us in their review of the therapist effects literature, the focus on improving results should not "detract from acknowledging that the average group of therapists . . . [*are*] effective, with a patient recovery rate of 60%" (p. 543; italics added).

At this point, you either will have found a shortcoming in your clinical work to target with DP or not. If you have discovered a deficit, turn the page. If you haven't and instead learned you are delivering a consistently effective service—that is, no reliable variations above or below expected benchmarks in your work—you have a decision to make. Are you happy with your results? As shared in Chapter 7, average outcomes in psychotherapy are on par or better than many medical treatments. It is, therefore, perfectly acceptable to stop here. On the other hand, should you want more, to move from "good enough" to *better results*, turn the page. Regardless of whether your motivation is to smooth out or move beyond your baseline, in the next chapter, we provide a structure for organizing your plan for improvement.

11

What Matters Most for Better Results

Drawing an overly tight relationship between results and decision quality affects our decisions every day, potentially with far-reaching, catastrophic consequences.

—ANNIE DUKE (2018, p. 8)

Let's do a quick thought experiment. Is doing psychotherapy more like playing chess or poker? Pick one or the other. No hedging. Make a choice.

If you chose chess, you are in good company. Since its inception, the field, its luminaries, and researchers have treated psychotherapy as though it can be reduced to a series of tactical moves (called *techniques*) informed by a grand

http://dx.doi.org/10.1037/0000191-011
Better Results: Using Deliberate Practice to Improve Therapeutic Effectiveness, by S. D. Miller, M. A. Hubble, and D. Chow

master plan (i.e., *theory* or *model*). The client usually makes the first move, revealing their position (e.g., *problem*) or strategy (e.g., *psychopathology*). Informed by their training, experience, and treatment model, the therapist responds, then waits for the next move. Although a stalemate can occur, the assumption is that as long as the client remains engaged and the clinician has correctly read the board, neutralizing any obstacles that arise and executing the correct moves (i.e., *treatment plan*), the outcome is all but assured. Checkmate! Problem solved.

Like students learning how to be therapists, chess players spend hours studying strategy. The best even commit entire games of the masters to memory. The eventual goal is to be able to quickly identify the best template or plan of action for any given game (e.g., best practice), thereby emulating the decision making and behavior of players who consistently win. Research on chess actually shows this approach works, with substantial correlations reported between a player's international ranking and the amount of time devoted to serious study (Charness, Tuffiash, Krampe, Reingold, & Vasyukova, 2005; Gobet & Charness, 2018). That said, similar to what the data show about the relationship between practitioner experience and psychotherapy outcomes, the number of hours spent playing chess has actually been shown to be negatively correlated with performance. Once again, experience is no guarantee of effectiveness.

How nice it would be if the effectiveness of psychotherapists could be improved the same way chess players are known to develop, that is, by learning a series of well-studied moves that, when faithfully followed, increases the probability of success. As it is, therapists and their clients, the evidence indicates, believe as much (Eugster & Wampold, 1996; Feifel & Eells, 1963; van Os, Guloksuz, Vijn, Hafkenscheid, & Delespaul, 2019; Wampold, 2001). More, the worldwide movement among professional and regulatory bodies to establish and enforce treatment guidelines—for problem X, do A, problem Y, do B, and so on—is based exclusively on that premise (Chambless, Baker, et al., 1998; Chambless & Hollon, 1998).

Unfortunately, decades of research aimed at identifying what works best for particular problems have been an abysmal failure (Duncan, Miller, Wampold, & Hubble, 2010; Wampold & Imel, 2015). Scores of meta-analytic studies containing head-to-head comparisons of competing therapeutic methods have not found any one to be consistently more effective than another for any presenting problem, complaint, or diagnosis tested (cf. Imel, Wampold, Miller, & Fleming, 2008; Miller, Wampold, & Varhely, 2008; Spielmans, Gatlin, & McFall, 2010; Wampold et al., 2011; Wampold et al., 2017). As noted in Chapter 2, neither clinicians' competence in delivering specific forms of treatment nor their adherence to so-called evidence-based protocols has been "found to be related to patient outcome and indeed . . . estimates of their effects [are] very close to zero" (Webb, DeRubeis, & Barber, 2010, p. 207).

Alas, doing psychotherapy is *not* like playing chess. What about poker? Unlike chess, where all pieces are visible and their placement and movement on the board are the same from one match to the next, critical information is hidden, and key elements of the game are governed by chance. The players must act quickly, in the moment, as evidenced by the fact that the average "rounder" makes between 600 and 1,000 decisions in a typical hour, all with potentially significant financial consequences. Taking time to deliberate is actually considered bad etiquette. What's more, players go out of their way to dissimulate, hiding facial expressions behind sunglasses and assuming postures relative to other players inconsistent with the facts (e.g., bluffing, deliberate distraction, even intimidation). And where making the right move at the right time leads to success in chess, drawing a bad hand in poker doesn't necessarily result in losing, nor does having a good hand ensure taking the pot.

What the foregoing hopefully makes clear is that, forced to choose, poker is by far the better analogy for psychotherapy. To begin with, chance influences the process from start to finish. For most practitioners, their caseload has more in common with cards randomly drawn from a shuffled deck than the predictable, strict structure and uniformity of a chessboard. And while therapists can make sophisticated guesses about the "cards" their clients hold, critical information almost always remains missing or hidden and subject to misjudgment. The feedback received is also inconsistent, delayed at best, and often inaccurate. Among the various similarities noted, perhaps the most troubling is that a clinician can technically do all the right things, make all the right decisions, and still experience a poor outcome.

For all that, the results of both poker and therapy are *not* random. Therapists' outcomes are largely consistent from year to year (Goldberg, Rousmaniere, et al., 2016; Luborsky, McLellan, Diguer, Woody, & Seligman, 1997; Luborsky, McLellan, Woody, O'Brien, & Auerbach, 1985; Owen et al., 2019). Additionally, some poker players, as is true of the "supershrinks" introduced in Chapter 7, rise to the top, clearly better than others, returning to the table to win one tournament after another.

Doing so, as simple as it sounds, is the result of making better bets over the long run, knowing that the outcome of any particular hand does not affect the overall probabilities of the game. Thus, losing to a royal flush—the most unlikely (.000154%), yet strongest hand possible—does not mean a player should fold whenever they draw a mere pair in the future. Indeed, with a cumulative probability of nearly 50%, two cards of the same rank will win the round 27% of the time. Whatever influence chance or luck exerts at any given moment, the best poker players hew to the probabilities that help them win in the end.

In a similar way, researchers have identified a group of factors associated with the outcome of psychotherapy. Like the probability of various hands in poker, the percentagewise contribution each makes to effectiveness is well established. To be sure, knowing the degree to which any particular one affects the results does not mitigate, much less eliminate, the luck, chance, and randomness inherent in the work—a reality most effectively managed, as described in Chapter 9, by using routine outcome monitoring to increase responsiveness to individual client presentation, needs, and progress (Cornelius-White, Kanamori, Murphy, & Tickle, 2018; Coyne, Muir, Westra, Antony, & Constantino, 2018; Lambert, 2017; Østergård, Randa, & Hougaard, 2018; Stiles, 1988, 2009)—so much as enable clinicians to make better bets about how, and on what, to invest their professional development time.

PLAYING THE 'PERCENTAGES' FOR BETTER RESULTS

In the land of the blind, the one-eyed man is king.
—Michael Lewis (Duchon & Burns, 2008)

Consider the Venn diagram pictured in Figure 11.1, representing five factors accounting for variability in the outcome of psychotherapy. In order of the percentage contribution each makes, they are: client/extratherapeutic (80%–87%), alliance/therapeutic relationship (5%–8%), the therapist (4%–9%), hope and expectancy (including allegiance 4%), and structure (including model and technique < 1%). While the assignment of fixed numbers can lend the impression the factors are independent and discrete, the truth, as hopefully captured by the visual rendering, is they are interdependent and fluid. In actual clinical interactions with clients, as Hubble, Duncan, Miller, and Wampold (2010) summarized, "they cause and are caused by each

FIGURE 11.1. Factors Accounting for the Variability in the Outcome of Psychotherapy

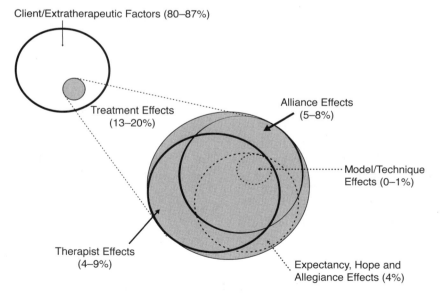

Figure is not to scale. Adapted from *The Heart and Soul of Change: Delivering What Works in Therapy* (2nd ed., p. 366), by B. L. Duncan, S. D. Miller, B. E. Wampold, and M. A. Hubble (Eds.), 2010, Washington, DC: American Psychological Association. Copyright 2010 by the American Psychological Association.

other, exerting their benefits through their joint and inseparable emergence over the course of therapy" (p. 35).

For the purpose of understanding the contribution each can make to potentiating the chances deliberate practice (DP) will be successful, the factors are discussed in turn. Once presented, a worksheet called the *Taxonomy of Deliberate Practice Activities* (TDPA, Chow & Miller, 2015) is introduced. Whether attempting to push beyond average or address a specific shortcoming or deficit pattern in your work, completing the TDPA (a) shows you how the factors currently contribute to your results; (b) helps you identify which, when targeted by DP, are likely to exert the greatest influence on your subsequent performance; and (c) provides direction for operationalizing each factor and structuring your DP activities.

Once more, retrieve the "How I Do Therapy" blueprint we asked you to create (see Chapter 3). As you review the five factors, consider how each contributes to your current effectiveness and the unique ways you operationalize them in your therapeutic encounters. Doing so will be of no small help when you later move on to the TDPA.

Client and Other Extratherapeutic Factors

Coming in first place, accounting for a hefty 80% to 87% of the variability in psychotherapy outcome, are factors that are part of the client or the client's life circumstances that either promote or hinder recovery. They include the client's strengths, life history, premorbid functioning, and even chance events. As examples, the client can get a job or lose one, have a supportive family and social network or none at all, or come to treatment severely compromised or just facing a bad time in life. They make up the sum total of what the client brings to the therapy room and what influences their lives on the outside.

The Alliance and Therapeutic Relationship

The next class of factors weighs in with 5% to 8% of successful outcome variance. This category represents a wide range of relationally oriented behaviors found in all therapies regardless of the practitioner's theoretical orientation. Empathy, caring, warmth, acceptance, congruence, encouragement, affirmation, and consensus building are but a few. Second to client and extratherapeutic factors, these elements are probably responsible for most of the gains clients experience.

The Therapist

No two therapists are alike, a fact that, it turns out, has a decisive impact on the effectiveness of psychotherapy. Decades of research confirms who the therapist is matters. Much of the effect, as reported in the previous chapter, stems from the individual practitioner's unique ability to establish and maintain the therapeutic relationship (cf. Baldwin, Wampold, & Imel, 2007). When personality, life experience, and all else that makes a person unique are added to the mix, the individual doing therapy accounts for between 4% and 9% of outcome variance.

Hope and Expectancy

Coming in at 4% is the portion of improvement resulting from the client's knowledge of being in treatment and their favorable assessment and acceptance of the therapist's clinical rationale and related techniques. Expectancy rests on the idea that both client and therapist believe—referred to, in the case of the practitioner, as *allegiance effects*—in the restorative power of the approach and rituals employed (Dragioti, Dimoliatis, Fountoulakis, & Evangelou, 2015; Munder, Brütsch, Leonhart, Gerger, & Barth, 2013; Wampold & Imel, 2015). Hubble, Duncan, and Miller (1999) added, the impact this class of factors exerts on outcome is "not thought to derive specifically from a given treatment procedure; they come from the positive and hopeful expectations that accompany the use and implementation of the method" (p. 10).

Structure

All therapies have a start and finish; all sessions, a beginning, middle, and end. The contents of the work—the nature of the conversations, interpretation of what the client says and does, and the use of strategies or techniques—are inescapably linked to and influenced by the treater's theoretical persuasion. The number of books, research publications, workshops, and training of every stripe attests to the importance of treatment models in professional discourse. So, too, does research showing practitioners believe "the expertness of their therapeutic technique . . . lead[s] to successful outcomes" (Wampold, 2001, p. 29). And yet, the evidence shows model and technique account for, at most, 1% of outcome variance.

As regards effectiveness, such findings indicate the particular method used is far less important to success than the work having a reliable structure and focus. Studies dating back more than 35 years show "one of the best predictors of negative outcome in psychotherapy is a *lack* of focus and structure . . . an error that occur[s] with a surprising degree of frequency . . . [and has] a greater impact on outcome than the personal qualities of either the therapist or client" (Miller, Duncan, & Hubble, 1995, p. 184; see Mohl, 1995, and Sachs, Young, & Miller, 1983).

TO SUM UP

Psychotherapy is more like poker than chess. Chance plays a significant role in the outcome. At the same time, the results of both endeavors are *not* random. The most effective players and therapists attend to the probabilities that enable the best outcomes in the long run. Like the chances of drawing various hands in poker, the percentage-wise contribution of a group of factors predictive of psychotherapy outcome is well established. While not eliminating the luck and randomness inherent in the therapeutic work, knowing the degree to which any particular one affects the results can enable clinicians to make better bets about how, and on what, to invest their professional development time.

WHAT TO DO RIGHT NOW

The true beginning of scientific activity consists . . . in describing phenomena and then in proceeding to group, classify and correlate them.
—SIGMUND FREUD (1953, p. 60)

You are now ready to begin identifying and classifying aspects of your clinical performance likely to have the most leverage for improving your results. Start by making a paper copy of the TDPA found in Appendix D, or download a free, electronic version from the web.[1] As coaching is central to effective DP—one of the four building blocks—a version of the tool is available for your supervisor or coach to complete (see Appendix C). Step-by-step instructions are provided on the first page of both documents.

To get the most out of completing the TDPA, your responses must be informed by your actual work with clients. Therefore, if in your use and analysis of your performance metrics you have identified a particular problematic pattern or deficit (e.g., high dropout, low effect size, less effectiveness with particular presenting problems, cultural backgrounds, levels of severity), pull and review your notes (or recordings) prior to beginning. On the other hand, should your results document a stable, average (or even above average) performance across clients, contexts, and circumstances, you can either draw a *random* selection of clients from your files or sample from those you've met within the past month.

Other recommendations:

1. After finishing the TDPA, take a moment to reflect on your "How I Do Therapy" blueprint. Consider which therapeutic factors are already represented and supported in your work and those that, perhaps, have not received your full attention. What does this then suggest to you about what you want to change?

(continues)

[1]https://scott-d-miller-ph-d.myshopify.com/collections/performance-metrics/products/performance-metrics-licenses-for-the-ors-and-srs

WHAT TO DO RIGHT NOW (*Continued*)

2. Complete the TDPA first on your own before consulting with a coach or supervisor. Doing so will help you select the person—whether by reputation, word of mouth, or your own research—with the skills for assisting you to achieve your specific learning objectives. Once you have found the right coach, have them complete the worksheet (after watching you work live or on video). Use any differences to foster a discussion about refining or sharpening your goals for DP.

3. Take your time. Successful DP is not a sprint. If you begin feeling overwhelmed, it likely means you are taking on too much, too soon. Keep in mind: The purpose of the TDPA is not to show you how little you know but how many possibilities exist for new learning and growth. As you are faced with opportunities to improve your work, a sense of humility may arise. This is perfectly acceptable, if not desirable. In truth, research documents that professional self-doubt is associated with better decision making, work performance, leadership skills, greater self-control and tolerance, stronger alliance formation, and superior outcomes (Kesebir, 2014; Nissen-Lie, Monsen, & Rønnestad, 2010; Nissen-Lie et al., 2017).

In the next chapter, a complete, in-depth, case example is provided of how a clinician—using their performance metrics and "How I Do Therapy" blueprint in combination with the TDPA, all in consultation with a coach—can identify specific learning objectives and prepare and execute a DP plan.

12

A Study in Deliberate Practice

A theory must be tempered with reality.

—JAWAHARLAL NEHRU (1954, p. 235)

What topics interest clinicians? Pick up a research journal, attend a continuing education event, or examine the syllabus from many graduate school courses, and you'll see that the hottest topics seem to be (a) diagnoses/presenting problems (e.g., the popular *Diagnostic and Statistical Manual of Mental Disorders* codes, trauma), (b) treatment methods (i.e., approaches touted as effective for specific problems or diagnoses), and perhaps (c) the brain (i.e., the neurological basis of clinical problems and treatment methods).

Survey practitioners, and the answers are entirely different. That's exactly what Giorgio Tasca and colleagues (2014) did, publishing their results in the journal *Psychotherapy*. Here's what they found. Regardless of age or theoretical orientation, the top three topics of interest among practicing clinicians were (a) the therapeutic relationship, (b) therapist factors, and (c) professional development. With only a moment of reflection, we see the wisdom of, and connection among, these three interests.

From last to first, large, multinational studies document the central importance professional development plays in the identity and satisfaction of clinicians (Orlinsky & Rønnestad, 2005; Rønnestad, Orlinsky, Schröder, Skovholt, & Willutzki, 2019). As much as is true for clients, therapists know growth is a very personal undertaking, requiring a focus on one's self—the identification

http://dx.doi.org/10.1037/0000191-012
Better Results: Using Deliberate Practice to Improve Therapeutic Effectiveness, by S. D. Miller, M. A. Hubble, and D. Chow

and acceptance of flaws and fallibility being an early step. "All of the significant battles," humanistic psychologist Sheldon Kopp (1972) observed in his classic book *If You Meet the Buddha on the Road, Kill Him!*, "are waged within the self" (p. 224). And, clearly, as relationship is listed as the number one topic of interest, therapists realize their personal work is often in service of helping them offer, create, and sustain therapeutic alliances. For all that, a recent study found between 40% and 47% of graduate programs in psychology make no reference to relationship skills in their course syllabi, program descriptions, or list of training competencies (Miller, 2018b).

Given how little attention is focused on the therapeutic relationship in graduate and continuing education training, it is not surprising how often the "relationship" is identified as the focus of deliberate practice (DP) plans—even, as the following example illustrates, when a clinician's performance metrics appear to suggest nothing is amiss.

OUT OF NOTHING, SOMETHING

Bad times have a scientific value. These are occasions a good learner would not miss.

—Ralph Waldo Emerson (1860, p. cviii)

Everett[1] is a licensed clinical social worker who works at a community mental health agency in the Midwest of the United States. In anticipation of changing Joint Commission standards, upper management sponsored training in the Partners for Change Outcome Management System (PCOMS; Miller, Duncan, Sorrell, & Brown, 2005) and then made it an official part of all clinical work starting early 2017. Although skeptical at first and worried the process might make reaching the agency's already demanding productivity requirements more difficult, Everett nevertheless complied. In short order, he found it took little time, and the results he achieved were affirming. Twice a month, he attended supervision sessions with a senior staff member. There, he was able to discuss cases identified by the computerized outcome management system as at risk. He was pleased to be able to check his clients' progress using the tools and see the positive impact of changes he made in his approach based on the feedback.

Everett's performance metrics can be found in Table 12.1. A brief review of the numbers reveals his data meet established benchmarks (see Chapter 7). The average intake Outcome Rating Scale (Miller & Duncan, 2000) indicates he is working with clients who are slightly more distressed than the norm. His Session Rating Scale (SRS; Miller, Duncan, & Johnson, 2000) scores reveal he is soliciting feedback regarding the quality of the alliance. With regard to dropout, he is doing particularly well, beating the benchmark by slightly more than 40%.

---

[1]Everett is a fictitious case example based on the authors' collective experience.

TABLE 12.1. Everett's Performance Metrics

Data points	Active	Inactive
Clients	65	71
Sessions	325	421
Average sessions	4.8	6.3
Average treatment length	3.2	4.4
Average intake ORS	17.6	18.1
Average intake SRS	33	37
Percentage reaching reliable change	67%	64%
Percentage reaching clinically significant change	45%	44%
Effect size	.75	.78
Relative effect size	−.01	−.01
Dropout	12.6%	12%
Deterioration	8.6%	9.1%

Note. ORS = Outcome Rating Scale (Miller & Duncan, 2000); SRS = Session Rating Scale (Miller, Duncan, & Johnson, 2000).

When the PCOMS trainer later returned to the agency, Everett volunteered his results for review as part of a follow-up training on how to use the performance indices to inform and improve clinical work. Surprised and encouraged by his results and discussion, he approached the consultant at the end of the day, asking about the possibility of private consultation. Despite his solid results, he expressed a desire to improve. The trainer agreed and suggested Everett download, complete, and send the Taxonomy of Deliberate Practice Activities (TDPA) worksheets (Chow & Miller, 2015; see Appendix D) before their first meeting.

The First Consultation

Connecting by video conferencing software, the two reviewed Everett's answers to the TDPA. On the consolidation page, he had identified a "stretch goal" taken directly, per instructions, from his ratings in the "Alliance" section of the worksheet. Taking into account his overall positive performance data, he believed his best chances for moving from "good" to "better" could be found in learning how to use the measures to further enhance his responsiveness to clients. When the consultant noticed several items in the "Structure" section were blank, a conversation ensued, leading to the emergence of a different performance profile and learning objective.

"I notice a number of these items have not been filled out," the trainer began.

"Oh, yeah, that's because those relate to the first session," Everett responded matter-of-factly. "That's when I'm doing intakes. When the client returns the second time, that's when I start therapy."

"So, you're not completing the measures the first time you meet people?"

"No, no," he said, "I think that's the way everybody at the agency is doing it. That's the way we've been told to do it."

"Oh, okay. Um, how was . . . when was. . . . Scratch that. Who decided that?"

"I remember us all talking after the first training and deciding, together with the implementation team. Since some of the people we do intakes on might end up working with someone else at the center, or even be sent to another agency," he proceeded, "it would be a waste of time to do the measures at first appointments." [*Note*. Research and experience document greater success in implementing routine outcome monitoring when a team comprising supervisors, practicing clinicians, and managers oversees the implementation process, using feedback from line therapists piloting the tools to solve any problems with its use and overcome objections and obstacles (Bertolino & Miller, 2012)].

"What percentage," the consultant began, "do you suppose continues with you after the first visit? That you decide, once you've completed the 'intake', is appropriate to meet with you for therapy?"

When Everett replied he was unsure, the trainer suggested pulling the files and computing the numbers by hand before continuing with consultation.

The Second Consultation

Sure enough, when the two connected online a week later, Everett's calculations confirmed the importance of addressing items not originally completed on the TDPA. Turns out, the majority of people he met for a first session, 82%, ended up seeing him for therapy. When the dropout rate of this group was calculated, Everett was surprised by the number who did not return: a figure 2.5 times larger than the rate reported in his overall stats (approximately 12%). In fact, after running the numbers, the mode, rather than the mean number of sessions attended, more accurately represented his work. Turns out, with the people who he agreed to treat himself, most attended a single visit.

"I'm floored," he said, finishing his sentence with an "ugh" for emphasis.

"Isn't data amazing?" the trainer stepped in. "And while it might not feel very good right now, it can help us narrow down what to address and identify an objective that will help you get where you want to be."

Together, the two returned to the TDPA, taking time to complete all of the items, in particular, those bearing on how Everett began and ended his first sessions. From the consultant's point of view, it was important for Everett to change his mindset, to stop making a distinction between intake and therapy.

"Think of it this way," he suggested. "Regardless of policy and procedure, it's the *client* who decides when therapy starts; and for them, that's the first time they meet you.

"Don't get me wrong. I know the requirements about documentation. They're crazy, really. At the same time, though, it's clear, given our discovery here, you've got to do something different, structure that initial meeting differently. And here's where the data and research findings give us guidance. As you heard me say at the initial training, the quality of the client's participation is the single best predictor of treatment outcome. So, right from the get-go, we've got to get people engaged."

"I'm open," Everett immediately replied. "Where to start?"

The trainer suggested beginning to use the Outcome Rating Scale (Miller & Duncan, 2000) and SRS (Miller et al., 2000) at the first visit. An initial DP plan and follow-up consultations were organized around using the scales to start and end the session. Similar to the earlier example of Etta, Everett also spent time with the consultant, learning how to elicit critical feedback.

As is hopefully evident, Everett's work with the consultant makes use of all four building blocks of DP (see Figure 4.1). To begin, wanting to achieve better results, he sought out a coach. Close examination of his performance using the TDPA revealed a problematic pattern in his work. Initial learning objectives were established (i.e., implementing routine outcome monitoring in first sessions and soliciting negative feedback), designed to improve his outcomes (e.g., decrease his dropout rate). Ongoing review, feedback, and refinement of his performance followed.

Progress Revisited

Within a couple of months, the percentage of clients dropping out following the first visit declined but not dramatically so. When Everett expressed dissatisfaction with his rate of progress, the trainer suggested revisiting his learning objectives. Returning to the TDPA, they focused on another item left blank on the "Structure" section, specifically, how Everett maintained the organization and focus of his work from session to session.

"Goal consensus is a critical component of an effective therapeutic alliance," the consultant instructed. "It structures the work, tells you where you are going, and helps create a focus for discussion from one appointment to the next." Following a brief pause, "Now, the good news is, because many of the clients who continue with you get better, we can assume they feel you understand and are working on what they want: their goals. While this may sound kind of simple, a first step, then, would be to take what you already do that works and introduce it in your initial visits."

"That makes sense . . . but . . .," his voice trailing off, "we're up to our eyeballs in paperwork, stuff that has to be done the first time I meet with a new client. And now, if I add the measures, too, I'm certain to run over."

At this juncture, the consultant recommended several steps. The first was for Everett to conduct a *time study* of initial sessions. Dating back to the period between World Wars I and II and the industrialization of the American workforce, the purpose of this type of research is to "establish a time for a qualified worker to perform specified work under stated conditions and at a defined rate of working" (Whitmore, n.d.).

The process begins, he explained, by compiling a detailed list of every activity to be completed by the end of the first visit. Next, estimates are made of the time each task takes the average clinician to finish. For this, Everett was encouraged to seek management's permission to do an anonymous survey of his peers using an online platform. When done, he could then compare his performance with what is typical in the agency. If taking longer than his peers, the consultant agreed to make suggestions for how to improve time allocation in first sessions. On the other hand, if the study found documentation requirements exceeded the time available, the consultant would present the results to leadership so adjustments could be made in either the intake protocol or time allotted for its completion. Either way, the process would help establish realistic targets (e.g., learning objectives) for DP.

The second recommendation the consultant made was for Everett to develop a "How I Do Therapy" blueprint, a detailed map of how he works (see Chapter 3).

"What do you mean?" he asked.

"Think of it this way: In time, our work becomes routinized and automatic. What once took a great deal of thought and concentrated attention becomes habitual. You do it without even thinking. It's kind of like riding a bike. When you first start, you are watching your every move, completely absorbed in the task, having to think about and consciously control every action."

"Interesting you'd use that example. I've just been teaching my daughter to ride, and I can see that. I couldn't really tell her how to do it. I just held on and told her to pedal!"

"Right," the consultant said. "You really notice this when you are trying to teach someone to do something you already do well, and also when you want to improve or make a change in what you're already doing. The first step is becoming conscious again of all your actions."

"Okay, I can do that."

"Now, go slow, Everett," the consultant advised, a hint of mischief in his voice. "It's going to take time. People I've worked with before have said a good way to do this is to devote some time following each session and ask yourself, 'Why did I do what I did?'" Taking a moment to reflect, "Not for the purpose of finding fault but to understand your thought process, how you decide what to do from moment to moment. Make a lot of notes before you try to organize them into an overall map."

The final suggestion was for Everett to organize a sample of transcripts (or recordings) of session segments devoted to establishing initial goal consensus. These, the consultant advised, should be taken from interviews with clients who, following the first session, dropped out, deteriorated, or continued in treatment without benefit. Together, the two agreed to reconnect in a month to evaluate the results of the time study, review his map, and determine whether there was enough case material to review.

Several Months Later

The consultant was impressed with the amount of work Everett had completed by their next meeting: multiple transcripts from first and later sessions as well as initial results from the time study and map of his clinical performance.

"Looks like all you've being doing is working!" he began.

"I can't really explain it, but . . . this whole thing has actually been energizing," Everett replied. "And not just me. A couple of my colleagues have joined in, too. We pulled the survey responses together and have been meeting once a week to discuss DP."

"Wow, that's great. So, what do you find?"

"Well, interestingly, in cataloging all the stuff that needs to be completed by the first visit, we found a number of redundancies."

"Say some more."

"The same questions are being asked in different ways in different parts of the record. . . . Not only that, forms, it seems, are constantly being added but only rarely integrated into the total record. So, you have to keep going back and forth between different docs and web pages, which eats up tons of time."

"Okay, sounds like this is a job for your implementation team, the group overseeing the adoption of PCOMS," the trainer commented.

"Yep, already done," Everett answered. "They're reviewing the report now."

"Good. But let me ask, based on my experience working with other agencies. I'm wondering: Can any of the questions you routinely ask be completed by clients *before* you meet with them, in the waiting area or prior to the first visit?"

When Everett indicated he didn't know and wouldn't have the authority to make a decision anyway, the consultant again suggested he and his colleagues discuss the idea with the implementation team.

The trainer then asked, "And what did you find out about how you are using *your* time?"

"I'm pretty compulsive," he quickly replied. "I want to get everything done in that first visit, so it's off my desk."

Responding with a laugh, "Are you saying you spend more time than your coworkers on certain tasks?"

"Guilty," Everett responded, returning the laugh. "I spend a lot more time, specifically on the treatment plan."

"And, just to be clear, that needs to be done by the end of the first visit?"

"Well, yes and no."

Truth was, for Everett, the answer was yes; for the agency, it was no. In fact, for many of their contracts, clinicians had considerable latitude regarding the submission of the treatment plan.

"So, let's take a look at a transcript, Everett, and see how the first meeting unfolds and what, if any, impact the pressure you feel about having to complete the treatment plan might have on establishing the relationship."

Together, they carefully reviewed one of the transcripts. It was immediately apparent to both that not only was Everett doing most of the talking, but the interaction was also more transactional than therapeutic in nature, as though he was taking a loan application at a bank. Back and forth the exchange went, with the client soon learning to wait to be prompted rather than volunteering information. Additionally, when the client shared more than was required to answer the question asked, Everett interrupted, a pattern that only increased as time in the session grew shorter.

"Painful . . .," Everett remarked. "I guess, I wouldn't come back to me either."

"Yeah, well, tell you what," a warm chuckle in the trainer's voice, "let's put the self-loathing on the shelf for the moment. We can always revisit that later if you want. Deal?"

"Deal."

"Okay, let's take a look at what's going on here. It's clear to me that, despite how it ends up sounding, your intentions are good. You want to get through what's required so you can attend to your client."

"Yes, I do."

"It's an occupational hazard. I'm reminded of some research about physicians. They face many of the same struggles we do. They're burdened by paperwork and have waiting rooms full of patients. Feeling the heat, they wind up interrupting. Actually," he added, "studies show [for more information, see Singh Ospina et al., 2019] patients speak for around 11 seconds before being interrupted, and most of the time, any real dialogue ceases. Of course, the doctors think they are doing the right thing. They think they are getting to what most matters: the patient's problem and the treatment."

"I know," Everett replied. "I've felt that way myself at the doctor's office."

"But here's what's interesting, though. It doesn't work. The studies that have been done show that patients who feel interrupted are less likely to comply with treatment recommendations, and, because they did not feel heard, more likely to call back or schedule subsequent appointments. So, while the physicians think they are being efficient, they are actually making more work for themselves, eventually having to spend *more* time than if they had simply listened in the first place, not to mention the fact that treatment is delayed."

"I get it," Everett said. "But what to do?"

"Well, that's what deliberate practice is all about. It's going to take time and a fair bit of thought and planning. In principle, what we need to figure out is how you'll establish and maintain a therapeutic relationship during that first visit."

"Absolutely."

"Your data clearly indicate you can. And now that you've got your map and you know you don't have to complete the entire treatment plan by the end of the first visit, it's time to pull it all together. So, I suggest sitting down and deliberately planning out how you'll integrate the two." Consider," he said, "what has to be done, the amount of time each task takes, and sort what you will do during the first visit, mindful of the actions you take when doing therapy that facilitate a partnership."

"Okay, I'm ready to start."

"That's great. But, as corny as this may sound, think of this as a journey, not a destination. Your job isn't to *finish* the task. The more you revisit and refine your plan, the more effective it will be in the end. That's what we've learned experts across the whole gamut of human performance do. They don't settle. They're constantly monitoring their performance and, with feedback in hand, making and testing small adjustments."

Stuck Again

By the time Everett and the consultant met 6 weeks later, the implementation team at the agency had completed an initial review of the documentation requirements and were considering options for reducing and consolidating the forms and information gathered. An experiment was in the works aimed at testing the efficiency and effectiveness of having clients arrive early for their first scheduled appointment to complete larger portions of initial paperwork in the waiting area. Finally, there was talk about bringing in an expert on *concurrent/collaborative documentation*—a structured process of completing paperwork together with clients, which some studies suggest improves trust, transparency, adherence, and engagement—to review the current system and potentially train staff at the agency (cf. DiCarlo, 2018; McLaney, Strathern, Johnson, & Allen-Ackley, 2010; Stanhope, Ingoglia, Schmelter, & Marcus, 2013).

"It's all good," Everett said, after recounting the latest developments at the agency.

Sensing some hesitancy, the consultant replied, "Is there a 'but' in there?"

"Well, yeah, it's . . .," exhaling, "about me."

"Okay, so what's up?"

"I was working, you know, as we talked about, on integrating my map, 'How I Do Therapy,' with stuff that has to be done the first time I meet a client, and I realized, it's me."

Tentatively, "I'm not sure I follow . . ."

"Well, um, as I was going through my map, I-it seemed, I discovered that it, while we *do* have a lot to do during that visit, it wasn't the actual documentation that was holding me up."

"Okay . . . ?" the trainer's voice rising.

"I don't see how I can do therapy . . . The way I work, for me, it requires that I-I have to have the plan completed before I can get started. So, that's why I've been working so hard to get the treatment plan finished during that first visit. I-I don't know how else to do it . . . but then, that leaves me right where we started."

"I get it. How can you start therapy if you don't know what you're treating?"

"Yeah," Everett said, relieved.

"Makes sense," the consultant quickly responded. "Let me see if I can help a bit here." Clicking about on his desktop, he found and displayed a file containing a graphic representation of factors associated with the outcome of psychotherapy (see Figure 6.4).

"Take a look," the consultant directed. "These are factors affecting the outcome of the work we do. I don't expect any of these are going to be a surprise to you, except look at the tallest one."

"Goal consensus and collaboration . . ."

"It makes a *large* contribution, the largest actually. More than empathy. More than positive regard. More than congruence."

"I see that, yeah . . ."

"Now, look all the way to the right . . . adherence to protocol, competence, treatment techniques . . ."

"Almost nothing . . ."

"Comparatively speaking, that's right. So, what's my point? My point is to stop waiting around to *do* therapy. Think of therapy as a verb instead a noun. You're not there to 'do a treatment.' Your job is to *be* therapeutic. And that happens, you are actually helping people, when you take time to convey genuine understanding and interest. Just doing that is helpful . . . way more than whatever technique or treatment you eventually do." Adding, "And, giving people the opportunity to really think and dream about what they want, how they want their lives to be better or different, given what the data show here, is *not* something you do before starting therapy." With emphasis, "It *is* therapy. In fact, given the historically low number of times people see a therapist—here, and across the world, around five or six visits—I'd argue, helping them sort what's meaningful and important accounts for a large part of the impact of our work. How many times . . . what's your average number of sessions, again?"

"Um, right around six . . ."

"Yeah, well, think about that. If you look at the individual graphs and your overall performance metrics, it's clear many of clients are well on their way *before* much in the way of 'treatment' has happened, often improving significantly in the first couple of visits. What could account for that?"

"Hmm," Everett replied.

"Being with you, the caring you offer, it's remoralizing. Add to that, an interest in and an exploration of what people want, what's important to them, and you've got the beginnings of hope and, in time, the restoration of a sense of meaning and purpose . . . possibility. Make sense?"

Everett took a moment to think before restating what he understood.

"That's it, you've got it," the consultant confirmed, adding, "Now, I recognize translating this into action in the room with clients is going to take some work." Clicking around once more on his desktop, he displayed a new image (see Figure 12.1).

"So, what we're working on is keeping your clients engaged in therapy *after* the first visit, preventing them from dropping out."

"Exactly," Everett acknowledged.

"So, your objective is to keep them seated in your office." Pointing to the screen: "Thinking of the therapeutic alliance as a three-legged stool emphasizes this idea of engagement, participation. A big part of our work is keeping clients comfortably seated, so to speak, for the duration of the work. The three legs, what gives it support, holds it up, are (1) mutually and collaboratively determined goals, meaning or purpose—in other words, what the client wants from being there; (2) agreement on the means or

FIGURE 12.1. Components of the Therapeutic Alliance

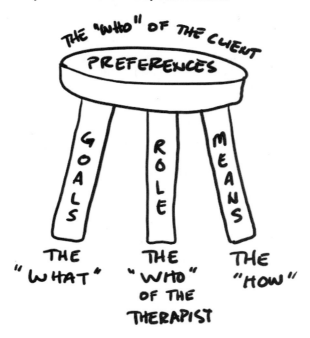

methods to be used for reaching their goals; and (3) the client's view of your role in the process—how you need to act to be experienced as warm, caring, empathic, genuine, and respectful. In all three cases, you can see, it's the client's experience that matters, not what we think. Last but not least, is the seat or cushion: client preferences. It's who they are, what they bring to the visit—their background, culture, values, and worldview—and, specifically, our ability to see them as they wish to be seen. When all these pieces fit together, you have a stable bond, a kind of glue that holds the relationship together."

"I understand everything you've said," pausing momentarily, "but it's still pretty 20,000 foot for me."

"I can appreciate that," the consultant replied, "and I can give you some materials to read that flesh out the stool analogy after we finish today. . . . But, for now, I think what we should do, to make it more real, bring it down to ground level, is to apply the ideas to your work. We can do that by, again, looking through transcripts of your work" [for more information about the alliance stool, see Bertolino & Miller, 2012; Prescott, Maeschalck, & Miller, 2017].

The consultation ended with Everett agreeing to review the transcripts he'd already gathered and then pinpoint segments of first and later sessions in which he saw himself working collaboratively to achieve consensus on clients' goals for treatment.

Experience Redux

Slightly more than a month passed before the two reconnected via video conference. As was the case in previous consultations, Everett had done his homework between visits.

"I've been working at being more present," he began, "during first sessions. Purposefully giving the process, you know, time. Being less rushed. Not trying to get it all done at once."

"That's great . . . and?" pausing.

"Well, it's too early to tell if it's having any impact on my results . . ."

"Right."

"But I have been keeping detailed notes. Actually, I created a kind of rating scale."

Interested, "Really?"

"Yeah. I have my map. I have the stool. And, at the end of each first session, I've been rating myself on a scale from 1 to 5, kind of like an SRS, but for me. 'How did I do?' 'Did I explore what the client wanted?' 'Did they feel heard?' 'Did I respond in a way that fit, reflected their preferences?'"

"Brilliant!" the consultant responded.

"Thanks. I've been thinking about brainstorming when the scores are lower, what I could do different. And I've been writing that stuff out, what I come up with." With a laugh, "I have to say, it's a little bit like being back in grad school, having to think through everything I do."

"It is *just* like grad school or any other thing else when you're starting out. You're acutely aware of every action and decision. It's called, the *centipede effect.* I learned the rhyme when I was a kid: A centipede was happy— quite!/Until a toad in fun/Said, 'Pray, which leg moves after which?'/This raised her doubts to such a pitch,/She fell exhausted in the ditch,/Not knowing how to run."

Everett chuckled as the trainer pulled up another diagram on his desktop (see Figure 12.2).

"You may have heard the terms *System I* and *System II thinking*? It's from the work of psychologist Daniel Kahneman [see Kahneman, 2011]. The two concepts fit really nicely with deliberate practice. What we do on a daily basis becomes familiar, routine. We operate more and more on impressions and intuition in daily activities. It *has* to be that way. It makes us efficient. Otherwise, we wouldn't be able to function."

He continued, "If we want to learn something new, though, or improve, like when you were teaching your daughter to ride a bike, System I is no good. It's about performing, doing, not learning or changing. So, by measuring and reviewing your work, looking for errors and opportunities for change, we've been pushing you into System II, making a plan and consciously and effortfully working to implement it. And it's going to feel slow, like you're plodding, a rank beginner." Pointing, "As the arrows at the bottom show, eventually, with practice, the new and novel becomes familiar and

FIGURE 12.2. System I and System II Thinking

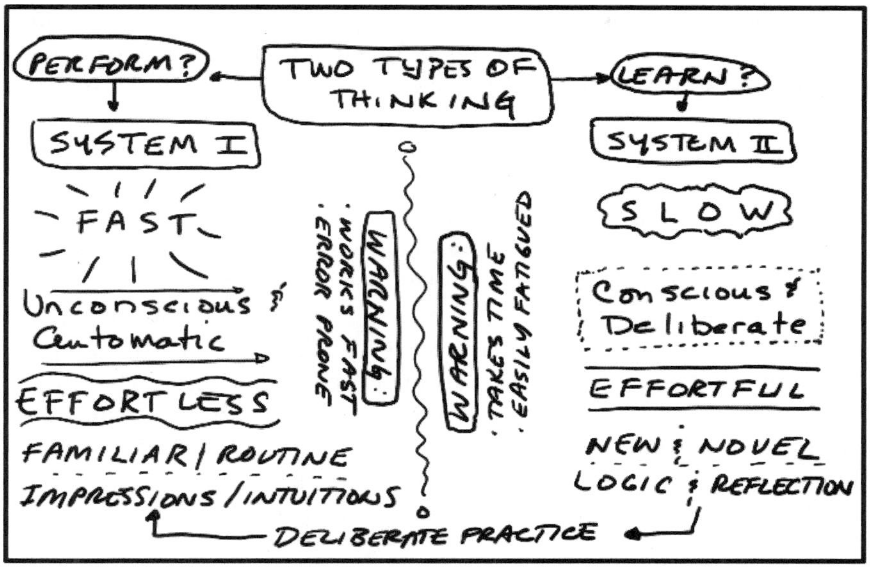

Data from Kahneman (2011).

routine—done without much thought. We then sail along until our next learning challenge."

"Well," Everett said, "I'm definitely in that System II, centipede state of mind right now. I've got a lot of data here and need some help making sense of it."

With that, the two began analyzing Everett's transcripts, looking for connections between his own and the clients' ratings of the session.

"Nothing jumps out at me, honestly," the consultant observed. "A fair bit of the time, you're on the same page with each other. Occasionally, you rate it lower, but then your client's marks are fine . . . and when they are low, you do a great job of soliciting feedback. And in terms of reaching goal consensus . . .," his voice trailing off. "I don't know. I can't see anything that might be connected to dropping out. . . ."

"What? Wait . . ." Everett quickly jumped in: "Are these . . . these are all supposed to be, we are wanting to look at . . . just those cases that dropped out?"

"Yeah," the trainer replied.

"Oh, no. This time, I've, uh, it wasn't clear to me last time we spoke that's what you wanted, so I typed up examples of both . . . people who stayed and those who left."

"Okay, I probably wasn't clear. Yes, we're looking for patterns of errors. I'm sorry for the confusion. So, do you know which ones are which?"

"I do."

"Let's sort them, then."

Breakthrough

In short order, a pattern became visible. Although slight, in cases that failed to return, the clients' ratings on the SRS tended to be lower. For the most part, Everett's own ratings and postsession notes indicated he missed this crucial feedback.

"Look at this," the consultant began, pointing to the decline of a single point on a couple of the clients' first session SRS scores. "I call this, quoting my grand-mother, 'Damning with faint praise.' It's subtle, making it hard to see and rec-ognize its significance. But, we know from research that such changes, even though small, are reliably associated with poorer outcomes." He continued, "So, I think we're on to something here. Let's go back and look for clues in the transcripts, in particular, the sections you've highlighted about goal setting."

"I'm into 'SMART' [specific, measurable, achievable, relevant, and time bound; see Doran, 1981] goals," Everett explained, when the consultant suggested—referring back to the alliance stool—means and goals were fre-quently being conflated in his interaction with clients.

"With this one, the client with the alcohol problem, the goal you two agree on is stopping drinking."

"Right."

"But, that is *not* a goal."

"Huh? Well . . .," Everett responded, a note of confusion in his voice, "that's what we put in the . . . that fits with the treatment plan. It's a SMART goal. It lets me track progress," he explained. "It's what I agree to work on with the client. It's specific, measurable, attainable—of course, with a bunch of small steps in between—um, and it's relevant, and time based . . ."

Interrupting, "Sorry, Everett, let me stop you here. I understand what you are saying, believe me. And I know about SMART goals. But stopping drinking, or going to AA [Alcoholics Anonymous] meetings, exercising . . . all those things you're putting on the treatment plan, whether you can state them in SMART terms or not, they're not goals. They are means. Stopping drinking is a means. The goal is what the person gets as a result of doing that."

Tentatively, "And what would that be?"

"I don't know," the consultant matter-of-factly responded. "It's going to be different for each client. But the point is finding out what's meaningful and important to them. So, if you ask, 'What do you want from coming to therapy?' and the client responds, 'I need to stop drinking,' or whatever—'I won't be depressed,' 'I won't have panic attacks,' 'I'd stop fighting with my partner'—it's a good place to start but not a goal. You need to ask, 'And what then?' What will be different in your life, once that's happened.' And flesh that out."

"This is mindblowing," Everett responded, chuckling. "I've gotta think this through. So, you're saying, SMART goals are wrong."

"No, not exactly. SMART goals are . . . one way of structuring the work. And, as the TDPA makes clear, you've got to change how you structure your work, particularly in those initial visits. More, in these cases, your actual work with clients, working that way is not helping. The *clients* are saying it's not."

"By dropping out . . ."

"No. Well, yes, eventually, but they're saying it right in the moment with their SRS scores. Not to confuse matters, but, I find the whole 'got to set goals' before we can do anything meaningful a rather limited and limiting perspective, especially as regards therapy. Let me give you an example. When I went to college, I was an accounting major." With a laugh, "I can't quite believe it now, but it's true. Everything changed, though, when I met this one professor in an undergrad psych class. Regardless of how SMART-ly we'd negotiated my college goals, thank goodness my advisor didn't push me to stick to the original 'plan,' the one we'd worked out together the first time we met. It would have been wrong for me. Looking back, I can see myself dropping out of college if I'd stayed in accounting."

Together, Everett and the trainer practiced identifying and separating means and ends, as well as methods for adding detail and vividness to clients' descriptions of how they wanted their lives to be different. Along the way, care was taken to emphasize the principle behind the practice: Rather than a destination, goals are best viewed as aspirations with multiple end points qualifying as success.

The impact of Everett's DP was immediate. His retention rate following first sessions increased, this time, significantly. Eventually, changes in his performance metrics became visible, with his overall dropout rate declining by nearly 30%, and the percentages achieving reliable and clinically significant improvement steadily climbing. The two continued to work together, at first, every couple of months, and then once a quarter, monitoring and fine-tuning Everett's performance.

TO SUM UP

The evidence is incontrovertible: Therapists want better results. It is critical to their identity and career satisfaction. Traditionally, emphasis has been placed on learning content. Therapists are told, "Master this subject," "Learn this new method," "Adhere to this standard of care," and improvement is assured. Ask clinicians what they want to learn, and the answers are entirely different and consistent with what the evidence indicates will lead to growth and development. Emphasis is placed on the process, closely examining how one works and changing the actual "doing" of therapy.

WHAT [NOT] TO DO RIGHT NOW

Almost all absurdity of conduct arises from the imitation of those whom we cannot resemble.

—SAMUEL JOHNSON (1751, p. 278)

Unlike the endings of previous chapters, this one concludes with what *not* to do now versus what to do. We are beings who learn by imitation. It starts early and continues throughout life. Through observation and play, children learn how to act and communicate. As adults, it is one of the principal ways we acquire new knowledge and skills. Without being able to copy the actions and behaviors of others, tradition and even culture would not endure from one generation to the next.

While imitation is essential for achieving proficiency in any particular performance domain, it is the enemy of excellence. To realize better results, your DP must focus on what you need to address. Every practitioner's journey will be different—a fact that explains why, as reviewed in Chapter 2, adopting new treatment models, attending continuing education events, and participating in supervision have failed to improve the outcomes.

What you should *not* do right now is:

- Decide "what" to practice based on Everett's, Tony's (see Chapter 10), or Etta's (see Chapters 8 and 9) stories or, for that matter, anyone else's example. Do the work. Mine your data. Complete the TDPA. Identify and then work on learning objectives emerging from a careful analysis of *your* performance.

- Look for shortcuts. Promises of "new and improved" are frequent. They are also persuasive, especially when considering how much more commitment and time DP requires than most other professional development or continuing education activities. Eventually, as top performers report, engaging in DP becomes inherently satisfying (Colvin, 2009).

- Go it alone. All, or nearly all, of those who rise to the top, have help: a network of people, places, resources, and circumstances supporting their pursuit of better results (Chow, 2016b; Miller & Hubble, 2011). Chief among these is a coach whose job (see the qualities identified in Chapter 10) is to help you become a more effective version of yourself: helping you observe and monitor what you do, giving critical feedback, assisting you in the development of your DP plan, and serving as an anchor when the going gets tough.

V

HOW TO DELIBERATELY PRACTICE

13

"Yeah, But What Am *I* Supposed to Do?"

We must adjust to changing times and still hold to unchanging principles.
—JIMMY CARTER (THE WHITE HOUSE, n.d.)

If you've been reading the chapters in order and completing the recommended steps along the way, then you will recognize that everything you need to know about how to achieve better results through deliberate practice (DP) is summarized in Figure 13.1.

Let's recap what you've done so far. You have

- created a detailed blueprint for how you do therapy,
- adopted and begun using a routine outcome monitoring system to measure your results,
- used real-time feedback to improve your responsiveness to individual clients,
- mined your performance metrics in search of problem patterns,
- engaged the services of a coach and, together, completed the Taxonomy of Deliberate Practice Activities worksheets (TDPA; Chow & Miller, 2015), and
- identified a specific learning objective to address with DP.

At this stage, even with your hard work and determination, don't be surprised if you find yourself saying, "Yeah, that's all fine and good, but . . . what am I supposed to do?"

How do we know you might be thinking this? It's a comment we've heard many times at the end of workshops and in private consultations on DP.

---

http://dx.doi.org/10.1037/0000191-013
Better Results: Using Deliberate Practice to Improve Therapeutic Effectiveness, by S. D. Miller, M. A. Hubble, and D. Chow

141

FIGURE 13.1. The Deliberate Practice Decision Tree

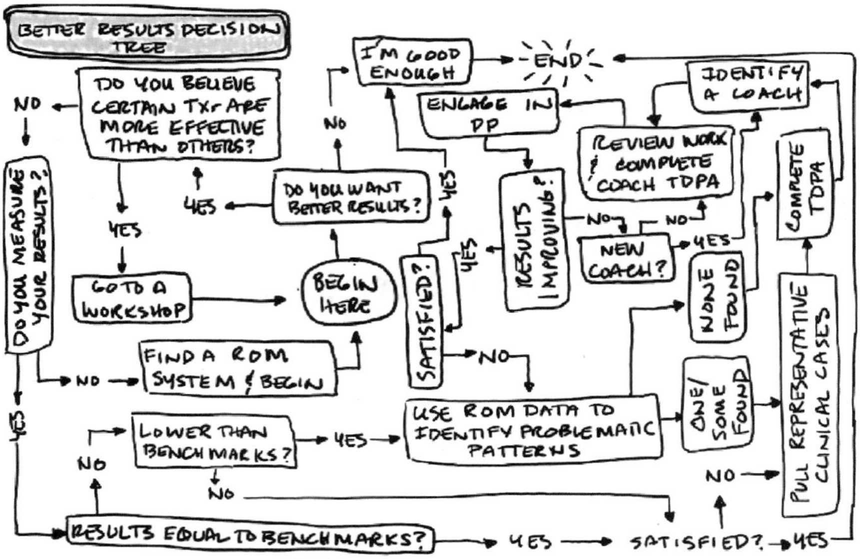

DP = deliberate practice; ROM = routine outcome monitoring; TDPA = Taxonomy of Deliberate Practice Activities worksheets (Chow & Miller, 2015); TXs = treatments.

It's also one we've encountered when doing research (to be described shortly) in which explicit instructions about what to do were provided, or so we thought. Then the same or similar questions came up again. Said in different ways, at different times, "Tell me what to work on, and I will do it." "Okay, so what book should I read?" "Is there a video I can watch of someone doing this the right way?" "How about 'master' therapists? Can I learn from them?" "What about peer support?" "When's your next workshop?" And so on.

We had similar questions ourselves when we first began our research into DP. Despite diving deep into the expertise literature, we found nothing really applicable or specific enough to replicate in our own efforts to become better therapists. By contrast, in such pursuits as golf, chess, and even surgery, what had to be practiced—the mechanics of a good performance—was easy to see and reproduce. So, we did a study, surveying clinicians about how they went about practicing to improve their therapeutic skills (Chow et al., 2015). Participants were asked how much time they devoted to, and the frequency with which they engaged in, various activities. They were also polled about their perception of the relevance and amount of cognitive effort each required. Importantly, we had access to these clinicians' outcome data, allowing us to test *which* approaches to DP, if any, worked best.

The analysis of the data revealed therapists rated four out of 25 possible activities as *highly relevant*—that is, central, or key, for improving their clinical skills. These included (a) reviewing difficult/challenging cases alone, (b) attending training workshops for specific models of therapy, (c) mentally recalling and reflecting on past sessions, and (d) mentally reflecting on and planning what to do in future sessions. Importantly, however, while these four activities rose to the top, later analyses showed none was related in any substantive way to outcome, nor were the two activities rated as requiring significantly more cognitive effort (i.e., attending training workshops for specific models of therapy and clinical supervision of difficult/challenging cases and/or cases with no improvement). In fact, out of the 25 possible practice activities, no single one contributed uniquely to better results (Chow et al., 2015).

Although this was initially frustrating, we would, in time, see how our findings were entirely consistent with those reported in the expertise and expert performance literature. Across a wide range of human endeavors, with the exception of the amount of time devoted to practice, better results were never made possible by simply aping what top performers did. Individual differences mattered. Bottom line: Everyone had to find what worked for them. That was the main finding from our survey. Think about it: Finding that no one activity was best meant *all* could potentially work to improve results. The old adage applies: "Be what you is 'cause if you be what you ain't, you ain't what you is."

Human nature being what it is, the temptation to imitate is often too great to resist. Thus, millions are spent each year on videos and courses promising to teach how to swing a golf club like a pro, master the backhand of an award-winning tennis player, or use the treatment techniques of the latest therapeutic method touted as achieving superior outcomes. The results of this approach to improving performance, reviewed throughout this volume, speak for themselves: *It does not work.*

Imitation may be a good way to get started, but research shows learners able to extract and operationalize principles associated with effective performance fare better in the long run (P. C. Brown, Roediger, & McDaniel, 2014). Indeed, novices tend to be *example learners*, limited to collecting and replicating what they have personally seen or experienced. Given their tendency to be distracted by irrelevant or superficial details, this approach, as reviewed in Chapter 3, risks mistaking form and style for substance. *Rule learners*, on the other hand, look across examples in an effort to identify similarities and differences that allow them to transfer know-how to other performance contexts and circumstances (Gick & Holyoak, 1983; McDaniel, Cahill, Robbins, & Wiener, 2014). More, focusing on the principles of, rather than resemblance to, an effective performance has the added advantage of allowing individuals to operationalize the effective elements in ways unique to the people involved— among other variables, their background, culture, biology and temperament— and contexts in which they find themselves (e.g., inpatient vs. outpatient, public vs. private, individual vs. group, certain client characteristics and demographics vs. others).

Still, you may be wondering, what this would look like in actual practice? How in the world can one learn principles, that is, move from mere mimicry to a higher order of conceptualizing what matters most in therapy and then, using these principles, to inform our clinical actions (Chow, 2017b)? To answer these questions, we turn our attention to a project that began right around the time we finished the survey (Chow et al., 2015) just reported.

FROM IMITATION TO EMBODIMENT

> Imitation cannot go above its model.
> —Ralph Waldo Emerson ("Divinity School Address," n.d.)

By the time we started surveying practitioners about their practice habits, we'd been studying top-performing therapists for several years. We knew from the literature that much of their superior effectiveness was directly linked to how they managed the therapeutic relationship. Indeed, as first reported in Chapter 7 (Baldwin, Berkeljon, Atkins, Olsen, & Nielsen, 2009), their abilities in this area accounted for 97% of the difference between the best and the rest! One additional study (T. Anderson, Ogles, Patterson, Lambert, & Vermeersch, 2009) published that same year confirmed and extended these findings. As will be seen, it also served as a key source of inspiration for our own project testing principle-based DP.

Briefly, T. Anderson et al. (2009) recruited a group of clinicians to participate in a study of facilitative interpersonal skills (FIS). In it, participants were asked to respond to a series of video simulations "'as if' they were the therapist in the situation" (T. Anderson et al., 2009, p. 759). Practitioners watched eight scenarios, each representing a different difficult situation complicated by a client's anger, dependency, passivity, confusion, or need to control the interaction. The participants' baseline levels of effectiveness had already been established via their use of routine outcome monitoring, thereby enabling the researchers to look for correlations between performance on the FIS task and the clinician's real-world outcomes.

When the study was complete and the data analyzed, a clear picture emerged. Regardless of the scenario or the client's interpersonal presentation, the practitioners with the best outcomes obtained the highest scores on the measure used to assess the quality of their therapeutic responses. In all, the investigators found the more effective the therapist, the more capable they were of responding collaboratively and empathically, and the less likely they were to create distance or offend (T. Anderson et al., 2009).

On reading the study, we immediately wondered whether it might be possible to design training that would help clinicians develop the deeper, broader, and, at the same time, more accessible nuanced relationship abilities the most effective practitioners possessed. In short, could we teach to the test? Similar to T. Anderson et al. (2009), we (Chow et al., 2019) began by developing a series of short videos (60 seconds or less), each depicting a challenging therapeutic event (e.g., report of suicidal intent, a threat to leave or terminate therapy, displeasure with the therapist) conveyed in a different manner (e.g., anger, hopelessness, reluctance, blaming).

In a pilot study known as the difficult conversations in therapy project (DCT; Chow et al., 2019), we gave practitioners a brief description of the client depicted in the video they were about to watch. One vignette, for instance, featured a client with a diagnosis of borderline personality disorder angrily expressing dissatisfaction with the therapist. The protocol called for watching the same video four times. Following each viewing, detailed, individualized feedback was provided based on an assessment of the participant's responses using the same standardized measure employed by T. Anderson et al. (2009).

Shortly into the DCT, two findings emerged that would ultimately lead to the development of a principle-based approach to DP. First, across all participants, and regardless of the scenario, strong thematic similarities emerged in the feedback. Second, in instances in which specific instruction about what to say was given, subjects tended to parrot the words in the next trial, merely repeating what they'd been told and missing the underlying intent or thrust of the feedback (Chow et al., 2019).

These findings gave us pause. Mindful of the emerging similarities and hoping to discourage mimicry and stock responses (e.g., "What I hear you saying is . . ." or "So, you are feeling . . ."), a change was introduced in the protocol (Chow et al., 2019). In the place of specific, detailed feedback, a series of cue cards were prepared, each highlighting a known principle of alliance formation and repair. Once done, we sorted the principles into three tiers organized along a continuum, with establishing or restoring a connection or bond with the client on the one end and engaging or reengaging the client in therapeutic work on the other.

Figure 13.2 shows the initial results were promising, with 90% of therapists gradually improving their FIS as they were exposed to principle-based feedback over repeated trials (Miller, Hubble, Chow, & Seidel, 2015). As can be seen, little improvement was observed for the group as a whole between the 1st and 2nd viewing of the video. During that time, participants were simply instructed to reflect on and attempt to improve their response, a finding supporting the conclusion that the feedback provided in later trials was responsible for the gains. When, in the fifth and final trial, a new video featuring a different client and presenting circumstance was introduced, data showed the participants generalized their prior learning to the novel situation.

The initial DCT study[1] has since been replicated in a larger randomized controlled trial using the same tiered, principle-based feedback (Chow et al., 2019). The study also featured three additional opportunities for successive refinement—thus, eight in total—with particular interest directed

---

[1] The DCT pilot study results were first reported in Miller, Hubble, Chow, and Seidel (2015).

FIGURE 13.2. Facilitative Interpersonal Skills Scores Over 5 Trials in the Difficult Conversations in Therapy Pilot Study

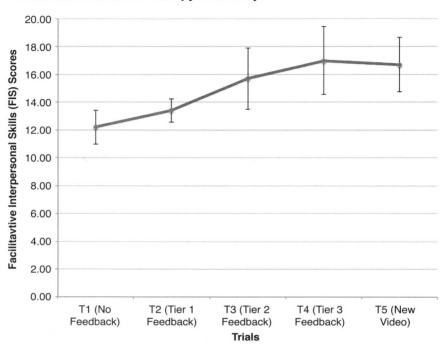

Difficult conversations in therapy pilot study results. T = trial. Adapted from "Beyond Measures and Monitoring: Realizing the Potential of Feedback-Informed Treatment," by S. D. Miller, M. A. Hubble, D. Chow, and J. Seidel, 2015, *Psychotherapy, 52*, p. 454. Copyright 2015 by the American Psychological Association.

toward assessing whether additional exposure to principle-based feedback supports generalization (Chow et al., 2019). Unlike in the pilot, a group engaged in self-reflection *without* feedback was added as a separate control condition.

Reviewing the results (Chow et al., 2019; see Figure 13.3), we see the scores of therapists in the feedback group made steady gains. On the other hand, those in the control condition—consistent with Trials 1 and 2 of the pilot (i.e., no feedback provided)—experienced no overall improvement. A small increase in the scores of both groups can be seen at Trial 5. At that juncture, a new vignette had been introduced. In subsequent trials, the scores of those receiving feedback appeared to generalize to the novel scenario and, until the eighth and final trial, either continued to improve or were maintained. On the other hand, the increase in scores of therapists in the control condition proved temporary, more likely a sign of heightened concentration and attention due to novelty rather than generalization.

Later interviews with participants in the feedback condition helped us understand what they believed led to their improved performance (Chow

FIGURE 13.3. Facilitative Interpersonal Skills Scores Over 8 Trials of the Difficult Conversations in Therapy Clinical Trial

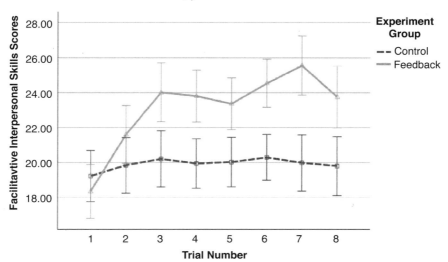

Difficult conversations in therapy results. Error bars represent 95% confidence intervals. T = trial. Adapted from *Improving Therapists' Ability Through Deliberate Practice: The Difficult Conversations in Therapy (DCT) Randomized Clinical Trial*, by D. Chow, S. Lu, S. D. Miller, T. Kwek, A. Jones, and G. Tan, 2019. Manuscript in preparation.

et al., 2019). In the particular, they told us prioritizing principles over content enabled them to be more creative, generating responses consistent with their own style and personality as well as adapting in the moment to their individual client's temperament and circumstances. Indeed, several specifically mentioned how, following their participation in the study, principles rather than stock phrases or treatment techniques immediately came to mind when confronted with challenging and novel conversational moments in their clinical work.

One last finding from the project deserves mention. Intriguingly, despite measured improvement of clinicians in the feedback condition, on average, they did not think they had improved, and several of them reported less confidence in their ability over successive trials (Chow et al., 2019). The confidence ratings of participants in the control condition, by contrast, did not change from start to finish. While such findings may, at first blush, seem paradoxical, they are entirely consistent with research on top-performing clinicians. As reported by Nissen-Lie and Rønnestad (2016), multiple large-scale studies document

> Professional Self-Doubt (PSD) in practice (e.g., therapist-endorsed items such as lacking confidence that they might have beneficial effects on clients; feeling unsure how best to deal effectively with a client) [is] strongly and positively linked to therapy process and outcomes. Therapists higher on Professional Self-Doubt showed stronger therapeutic alliance, as rated by the clients and, even more importantly, greater client-rated therapeutic gains (e.g., Nissen-Lie, Monsen, & Rønnestad, 2010; Nissen-Lie, Monsen, Ulleberg, & Rønnestad, 2013). (p. 7)

It would seem feedback undermined automaticity, and thereby confidence, ultimately improving therapist ability to attend to the nuances in the clinical presentations.

If curious about the nature of the feedback shared, and how it might inform and improve your own work, take the time to respond to the case scenario presented in the next section. It is taken directly from those used in the original DCT study.

PUTTING PRINCIPLE-BASED FEEDBACK TO WORK

The true method of knowledge is experiment.
—William Blake (Blake, 1788)

A small but growing body of evidence suggests taking notes (as well as completing some types of assignments) by hand has certain advantages over typing into a computer (Mueller & Oppenheimer, 2014). When doing the latter, people tend to write down as much as they can, limited only by the speed their fingers move over the keyboard. By contrast, working longhand requires selectivity, forcing the writer to process the material and distill its essence rather than take verbatim notes or complete tasks in a rote fashion. While writers and typers ultimately do not differ in their recall of facts covered in a lecture or gleaned from an assignment, writers demonstrate a deeper understanding of, and have superior outcomes when later called on to apply, the concepts involved (May, 2014).

In the next paragraph, a transcript from one of the vignettes used in the original DCT study (Chow et al., 2019) is presented. The process is admittedly artificial. A real therapeutic encounter would, of course, be characterized by shorter, back-and-forth exchanges. In this case, to get the most out of this exercise, be as generative and thorough in your response as possible. Given the research just cited, we strongly recommend completing the task by hand. Be sure to leave several blank rows in between each line of written text, so, following feedback, modifications can be made to your responses without having to rewrite it entirely.

One note of advice: Don't give in to the temptation to jump ahead or read through what follows from start to finish in a single sitting. Done right, DP is cognitively demanding, requiring time and reflection to transform information into actions that are personally meaningful and effective.

As soon as you have a pen and legal pad (or lined notebook paper) in hand, feel free to proceed.

Step 1

Consistent with the study protocol, we begin with background information about the client. Read through it once, then continue directly to the client's remarks:

> Annie[2] is a 24-year-old Singaporean woman. She was referred to you by her psychiatrist to work on problems with anger and self-harming behaviors. Although she strongly disagrees with it, her diagnosis at the time of referral was borderline personality disorder. The following statement was made at the beginning of the third visit. In prior sessions, Annie spent much of the time relating how others had failed her. For example, she recently had a falling-out with a close female friend after she showed up late for their planned outing—a sign, she believed, of her friend's not valuing her or their relationship. At various times during the preceding two visits, Annie showed subtle signs of anger and impatience toward you.

Please write your response to the following in as much detail as possible and in a manner consistent with your personal style without returning to the background information:

ANNIE: [First sighing, then speaking quickly and without pause] You know what? I'm just not comfortable with your sessions. Every time when I come here, I feel worse after that. It's not supposed to be like that, right? I'm supposed to feel better after that, but I don't, I feel worse. I mean, I've been coming here for an entire month, and all you do is just sit and nod. You just sit there in your chair and nod at me.

---

[2] Annie is a fictional client portrayed by an actress in the training video *"Angry Annie" Difficult Conversations in Therapy Project Video #1*, by D. Chow, 2016, retrieved from https://www.youtube.com/watch?v=pgJj288Xw_g&feature=youtu.be. Copyright 2016 by Daryl Chow and Sharon Lu. Transcript printed with permission.

When I cry, like, you know, you don't, there's no response from you. You just continue sitting there. Like, I don't even know whether you really care about me. Do you really care? I mean, like, I thought it would be worthwhile changing therapists, you know? But you are exactly the same as my ex-therapist, exactly the same. You just tell me the things I already know. So, what's the point of me coming here, right? What's the point? I mean, I think this is just useless.

Reply to Annie now. Do not reread the background information or her statement. Once done, set your written response aside and take a 5-minute break.

Step 2

Begin by rereading Annie's background information, remarks, and your reply. Reflect on how you might improve what you've written to strengthen its therapeutic impact. Make any revisions to your written response before reading further.

For comparison purposes, here's a response from one of the participants in the original study (Chow et al., 2019). It is not included because it is representative of how clinicians responded but, rather, as an example of what one practitioner initially said:

STUDY PARTICIPANT: Annie, what I hear you saying is that you're very upset and angry and that you see me as responding in ways that you didn't expect and haven't found helpful. From what you've told me before, there seems to be some similarity in how you are feeling about me and what's happened between you and your friends. Perhaps we should look at that more closely. Can you see the connection?

Per the study protocol, the participant was given time to reflect on and attempt to improve their initial response after viewing the video a second time, resulting in the following reply:

STUDY PARTICIPANT: Annie, I can see you are upset and angry. Obviously, and from what you've said, I've not responded in the way you hoped. Given that this has happened before, with your friends and prior therapist, and the pain it's causing you, perhaps it's worth taking a look at more closely?

Take a moment to compare and contrast the therapeutic responses before and after self-reflection, and answer the following questions:

- Do the two strike you as significantly or meaningfully different?
- Is the latter better than the former? If so, why? If not, why not?

Now, consider your own responses. Is one better than the other? Did the time you took to reflect and revise help? If the available evidence can be trusted, the answer to both questions likely is, "No"—that is, at least when responses are scored using a standardized measure of FIS. If your assessment is different, take time to identify how the two differ and why you believe one is superior to the other.

Step 3

With your revised response in hand, consider the following principle-based feedback. Did you

- Identify both the *explicit and implicit emotion* expressed by Annie? Frequently, clinicians identify or emphasize one or the other, less often, both. The combination tends to heighten clients' feeling heard and understood, a key aspect of empathy (Elliott, Watson, Goldman, & Greenberg, 2004; Greenberg, 2002; Norcross & Wampold, 2011b).

- Explicitly acknowledge the *target of the emotions* expressed by Annie? Acknowledging who the client is referring to adds immediacy, thereby reducing interpersonal distance (cf. C. E. Hill, Knox, & Pinto-Coelho, 2018).

- Make a verbal attempt to *relate compassionately*? Doing so simultaneously demonstrates tenderness and vulnerability, and can facilitate client self-compassion (cf. Galili-Weinstock et al., 2018; Sommers-Spijkerman, Trompetter, Schreurs, & Bohlmeijer, 2018).

Now, please reread the background information and Annie's statement. Following that, revise your response in light of the preceding three principles. Do so before reading further.

Once more, as an example, here's how the participant previously cited altered their response following feedback (Chow et al., 2019):

STUDY PARTICIPANT: Annie, I can feel just how angry [*explicit emotion*] you are with me [*target of emotion*]. But even more, your disappointment [*implicit emotion*], having come here for help and left feeling dismissed [*implicit emotion*], and, in response to your crying, with me just sitting and nodding. Were I in your shoes, given what's happened here and in your life, I, too, would be wondering if my therapist cared, and if I should really continue [*compassionate attempt to relate*].

Step 4

At this point, you have read Annie's background information and statement three times. You've revised your response following a period of reflection, and then again, after reviewing the first tier of principle-based feedback. Before proceeding, take a moment to consider how confident you are about your interpersonal abilities. Is it the same as when you started? More? Less? Regardless, note any specific reasons that come to mind as to why you feel the way you do.

Next, review your current answer in light of the five principles that follow. As these fall in the second tier, they should be considered subordinate to the prior feedback principles. Keep in mind, the purpose of this activity is to increase the likelihood of Annie's feeling heard, understood, and respected.

In your response, do you

- *Disarm by agreement?* Listening for, acknowledging, and agreeing with what the client is right about can reduce withdrawal and invite reciprocity in the interaction (cf. Eubanks, Muran, & Safran, 2018; Spencer, Goode, Penix, Trusty, & Swift, 2019).

- *Take ownership?* Studies confirm the negative impact of any therapist behavior perceived as hostile, pejorative, critical, rejecting, or blaming (Binder & Strupp, 1997; Lambert & Barley, 2002). By contrast, accepting responsibility not only works to de-escalate intense emotions but also begins the process of reestablishing trust.

- Frame the rupture as *a critical juncture in therapy*? Doing so can normalize and even positively reframe relational difficulties while simultaneously serving to reconnect the work to the client's goals (Eubanks et al., 2018).

- Reconnect with, or begin to renegotiate, the *client's goals for therapy*? As reported in Chapter 12, goal consensus is a key aspect of the therapeutic relationship and strongly related to outcome (Tryon & Winograd, 2011).

- Suggest *alternatives or new directions for the future*? Facilitating a collaborative relationship is a key part of alliance formation and repair (Norcross, 2011; Safran & Muran, 2000).

Here's the response of the study participant following the second tier of feedback:

STUDY PARTICIPANT: Annie, I can feel just how angry [*explicit emotion*] you are with me [*target of emotion*]. You are right [*disarm by agreement*] to feel disappointed [*implicit emotion*], having come here for help and left feeling dismissed [*implicit emotion*], and, in response to your crying, with me just sitting and nodding. I really did fail you [*taking ownership*] and would, were I in your shoes, and given what's happened here and in your life, be wondering if my therapist cared and if and why I should really continue [*compassionate attempt to relate*]. What you've said here, and the fact that you took a chance and did say it, I think is very important [*frame rupture as a critical juncture*], a step in the right direction. Could we, or are you in a place where you'd feel comfortable enough with me starting over, or at least looking at [*suggest new direction for the future*] what would be most helpful to you [*reconnecting with the client's goals*]?

Step 5

Clinicians, as reported in Chapter 10, make thousands of decisions and offer hundreds of responses in a given therapy hour. Here, we have devoted a significant amount of time to writing out, reflecting, and revising a single reply! In completing this process, participants in the trials spent several hours getting to this point. Most reported feeling exhausted by this time, or earlier, and needing a break. Recall the study of violinists and pianists published by Ericsson, Krampe, and Tesch-Römer (1993). It showed that the most skilled not only devoted more time to practice but also to rest, specifically taking more naps than either average or the least capable musicians. Such periods were critical, the researchers concluded, to enable "individuals to recover and thereby maintain a steady state [of concentrated focus and practice] from day to day" (p. 371). Bottom line: If you are feeling physically or mentally fatigued, you are likely engaged in DP and may benefit from taking a break.

Once refreshed, please read the background information and Annie's statement one last time in light of the next group of principles. While doing so, keep in mind as these fall in the third tier of feedback, they should be considered last in terms of import and significance:

- Point out *recurring therapy themes.* Care should be taken to ensure understanding is experienced by the client *before* attempts are made to intervene therapeutically as the latter, if experienced as confrontational, has been shown to be "ineffective, perhaps even hurtful, in psychotherapy" (Norcross & Wampold, 2011a, p. 101).

- Directly express *respect and care for the client.* Be mindful any such sentiments must be experienced by the client as genuine in addition to being congruent with the clinician's actual feelings and behavior (Kolden, Wang, Austin, Chang, & Klein, 2018; Nienhuis et al., 2018; Norcross & Wampold, 2011a).

The response of the study participant following the third and final tier of feedback was as follows:

STUDY PARTICIPANT: Annie, I can feel just how angry [*explicit emotion*] you are with me [*target of emotion*]. You are right [*disarm by agreement*] to feel disappointed [*implicit emotion*], having come here for help and left feeling dismissed [*implicit emotion*], and, in response to your crying, with me just sitting and nodding. I really did fail you [*taking ownership*] and would, were I in your shoes, and given what's happened here and in your life, be wondering if my therapist cared and if and why I should really continue [*compassionate attempt to relate*]. What you've said here, and the fact that you took a chance and did say it, I think is very important [*frame rupture as a critical juncture*], a step in the right direction. Could we, or are you in a place where you'd feel comfortable enough with me—because I do care about you and really respect and admire the courage it took to come back and speak up for yourself [*direct expression of care or respect*]—to start over, or at least look together at what would be most helpful to you [*reconnecting with the client's goals*]?

To appreciate the breadth and quality of the change in participant's response over time, here is the original:

STUDY PARTICIPANT: Annie, I can see you are upset and angry [*identify the explicit emotion*]. Obviously, and from what you've said, I've not responded in the way you hoped. Given that this has happened before, with your friends and prior therapist, and the pain it's causing you, perhaps it's worth taking a look at more closely [*point out recurring therapy themes*]?

Before finishing, take a moment to identify what stands out most in the revised response in terms of establishing, maintaining, and repairing the therapeutic relationship with Annie. What about your response? Did it change and evolve? If so, in what specific ways? If not, why?

TO SUM UP

At this stage, if you have been following the recommendations in each chapter, you have accomplished much. The question remains how to translate the information into specific practice activities that will improve your individual performance. Human nature being what it is, the temptation to imitate will be strong. The field offers a never-ending supply of books, videos, and trainings promising shortcuts or "tricks." Resist. In the long run, research shows learners able to extract and operationalize *principles* associated with effective performance fare better. Those who merely copy can expect to remain average.

WHAT TO DO RIGHT NOW

It's like a finger pointing away to the moon. Don't concentrate on the finger or you will miss all that heavenly glory.

—BRUCE LEE (LEE & LITTLE, 2000, p. 92)

WHAT TO DO RIGHT NOW (*Continued*)

Were you a participant in either the first or follow-up DCT project, the next step in the process would be applying what you'd learned to a new scenario: one featuring a different client, problem, and interpersonal presentation. In lieu of that, make a plan:

1. How will you recall, practice, and keep track of your use of the specific principles presented in this chapter in your future work?

2. Identify empirically supported principles in whatever domain your specific learning objective falls on the TDPA. Consult the research literature. Speak to experts. Connect with a community of practitioners who share your drive, values, and ambitions.

Regardless of your answers to these two questions, we've found that those who eventually succeed in achieving better results differ in how they organize and structure their DP. It is to those strategies that we turn in the next chapter.

14

Designing a System of Deliberate Practice

Only practice on the days that you eat.

—SHINICHI SUZUKI, MUSIC EDUCATION PIONEER
(BIGLER & LLOYD-WATTS, 1979, p. 29)

Do you make resolutions? Between a third and 50% of people make them at some point during any given year. Among the top three are losing weight; setting aside more time for self, family, and friends; and adopting a more healthy lifestyle (e.g., stopping smoking, reducing drinking, losing weight, increasing physical activity). Vows to improve one's financial standing by organizing a budget, reining in spending, and paying down debt are also popular. Most do very well in keeping their commitments—that is, at least, for a few weeks (approximately 71%). Within a month, however, a very different picture emerges. By that time, less than half (approximately 43%) have maintained their initial momentum, a figure that drops to between 8% and 12% within 3 to 6 months (J. Griffiths, 2018; Norcross, Mrykalo, & Blagys, 2002).

Much is made in the self-improvement and therapy literature about the importance of setting goals. Thus, *Forbes* magazine contributor Dan Diamond (2013) advised setting "small, attainable goals . . . bounded by rational, achievable metrics . . . [and] shar[ing] [them] . . . with family and friends . . . to build accountability." And to those who become discouraged (or get off track) along the way, all that is needed is to "keep believing you can do it."

http://dx.doi.org/10.1037/0000191-014
Better Results: Using Deliberate Practice to Improve Therapeutic Effectiveness, by S. D. Miller, M. A. Hubble, and D. Chow

Then, he argued, "your journey to self-improvement will become a self-fulfilling prophecy."

All good, right? Except as anyone who has made a New Year's resolution knows, belief and willpower are insufficient for success. "Like water," award-winning American football coach Bill Walsh ("The Score Takes Care of Itself—Bill Walsh," n.d.) once observed, ". . . individuals will seek lower ground" (i.e., our best intentions will almost always give way to what seem, at the moment, more pressing matters, such as seeing the next client, catching up on progress notes, replying to e-mail, consulting on a case with a colleague, helping a child with their homework). Could there be another way?

SYSTEMS VERSUS GOALS

"If you study people who succeed," famed *Dilbert* creator Scott Adams (2013) wrote in his autobiography *How to Fail at Everything and Still Win Big*, "you will see most of them follow systems, *not goals*" (p. 33; italics added). While the latter provide focus, they are—even when accompanied by generous amounts of desire and self-belief—not the same as a having a way of working—a routine—and can actually be quite demotivating. The problem, Adams explained, is that "goal people exist in a state of continuous pre-success failure at best. . . . Systems people succeed every time they apply their systems, in the sense that they did what they intended to do. . . . That's a big difference in terms of maintaining your personal energy in the right direction" (p. 32).

So, what might the components of a successful deliberate practice (DP) "system" be?

INTEGRATION OF DELIBERATE PRACTICE INTO YOUR DAILY ROUTINE

[Great creative minds] think like artists but work like accountants.
—David Brooks (2014)

Interview well-known authors about *how* they write, and they mostly give the same answer. Indeed, their reply is so common, it borders on the hackneyed. To wit, make writing a habit. "I write every day," Ernest Hemingway once said, and then "try to live through until the next day when you hit it again" (Plimpton, 1958). Wait for inspiration, opportunity, or the right conditions, E. B White once observed, "[and you] will die without putting a word on paper" (White, 2011, p. 209). Khaled Hosseini offered similar advice: "Write whether you feel like it or not" (Charney, 2017), as did Maya Angelou: "Nothing will work unless you do" (Curry, 2014). "The important thing," Haruki Murakami advises, is "the repetition itself," with many of the bestselling authors completing less than a page of writing per day (Wray, 2004).

DP is not an activity that can be left to chance or choice. Rather, to be effective, it must be *the* default option, a part of your day that is engaged in without forethought or planning—much the same as making coffee in the morning or going to work. As a way of helping make your DP a habit, we propose a framework known by the acronym ARPS, standing for (a) automated structure, (b) reference point, (c) playful experimentation, and (d) support. Each is discussed in turn, as follows.

A: Automated Structure

As the stories of the famous authors illustrate, DP needs to be a regular part of your daily routine. Simply stated, thinking *whether* you'll do it ensures you *won't*. The when, where, and what must be a foregone conclusion, decided long ahead of time, and requiring no conscious decision making (Foer, 2011). On this score, like saving for retirement, investing a small amount of time on a regular basis is far more effective than periodic binges. Research shows the former facilitates gradual growth and improvement—in part, by minimizing the size and impact of the failures that are an inherent part of successive refinement—the latter, at best, transitory changes in performance and often self-defeating exhaustion (Ericsson, Krampe, & Tesch-Römer, 1993).

In terms of creating an automated structure for your DP, we suggest you *think algorithmically*—in other words, create a set of simple and clear instructions, and carry them out without modification in a prescribed manner. Here are a few suggestions:

- *Schedule it.* DP is cognitively depleting. As a result, the available evidence indicates short bursts of intense work (20–45 minutes) followed by rest (5–15 minutes) are the most effective, with the capacity for maintaining focus and concentration growing with time and experience (see Figure 14.1; Ericsson et al., 1993). We know from personal experience how tight schedules and limited time can make the temptation to skip resting difficult to resist. Don't. Research shows *not* taking the time to recover from intense periods of concentration and practice interferes with both motivation and learning (Loehr & Schwartz, 2005). What constitutes rest? Short naps are a favorite among top performers in other fields (e.g., musicians [Ericsson et al., 1993]). That said, meditating, going for a walk, engaging in mindless chores, and daydreaming also qualify (Chow, 2018a).

Prevent your "best intentions" being swept away by other obligations and distractions: Plan to practice at the same time on the same days. Make sure these periods stand out in your calendar for yourself and anyone who

FIGURE 14.1. Facilitating Learning and Motivation by Engaging in Short Periods of Intense Deliberate Practice With Rest in Between

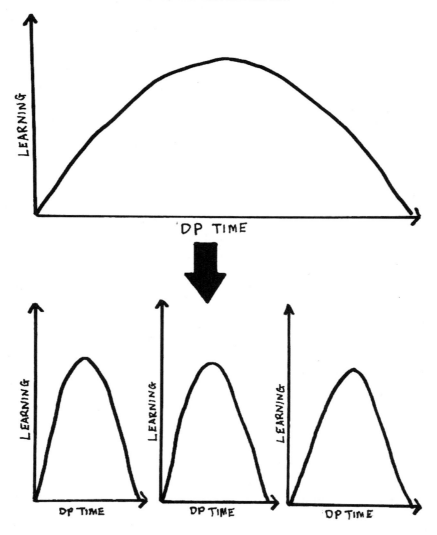

could impact your schedule (Newport, 2016). A variety of electronic applications and websites are available that can help with planning, scheduling, and breaking down DP time into optimal practice and rest periods (e.g., Be Focused Pro [see https://apps.apple.com/us/app/be-focused-pro-focus-timer/id953426154], Gestimer [see http://maddin.io/gestimer/]). Known popularly as the Pomodoro Technique®—after the tomato-shaped Italian cooking timer—the chief benefit of such products is they automate time management, thereby reducing the impact of disruptions, both internal and external, on one's focus and flow.

- *Protect the environment.* DP is the "endangered species" of professional life. For it to survive, the surrounding environment must be protected from intrusions and intruders. Safeguard your time and attention by shutting your door, turning off your phone (or message notifications), and disconnecting from the Internet.

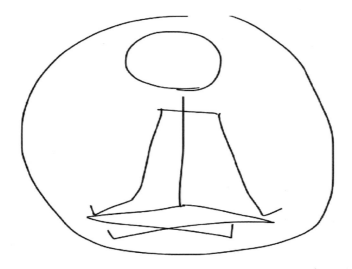

Imagine what you might accomplish if the first order of business each morning was DP, instead of checking your email and social media feed? Surveys show, on average, people reach for their phone at 7:31 a.m. and then spend more than three and a quarter hours per day actively using the device (Woollaston, 2014)! Perhaps most distressing is the finding that many confess to using it without realizing they are, with an astonishing two thirds admitting to logging into social media sites without thinking. Should you fall into that category, consider using an application that will silence, stop, or redirect your electronic devices for specified times (e.g., Freedom; https://freedom.to/). Newport (2019) provides other tips for improving your relationship with technology.

- *Create a "blackbox."* Air travel hasn't always been as safe as it is today. According to Wikipedia ("Aviation Safety," n.d.), "by 1980, fatal accidents per million flights decreased 16 fold . . . and fatalities per trillion revenue passenger kilometers decreased 54 fold." While many factors are responsible, one of the chief contributors was the introduction of the blackbox (Syed, 2015). Comprising two pieces of equipment, the device keeps a record of all conversations in the cockpit as well as an array of specific aircraft performance parameters—88 in total, including time of day, engine functioning, altitude, speed, and flap position (Tilley, 2015). The data stored provide investigators, and the industry as a whole, with information critical for learning and improvement following aviation accidents.

Given the advances the blackbox has made possible in aviation, it makes sense for practitioners to have something similar at their disposal—an "always on" device that can be consulted when a critical incident occurs in treatment, or when routine outcome monitoring data indicate a lack of progress or problems in the relationship. Any resistance to routinely recording clinical work does not, at least according to the latest evidence, come from clients (Briggie, Hilsenroth, Conway, Muran, & Jackson, 2016). Indeed, when a clear rationale is presented, their confidence in us and the treatment increases. As it is, no fancy equipment is needed. Inexpensive, pocket-sized, high-definition recording devices are widely available, including sophisticated applications on most mobile phones. Besides obtaining written consent from clients, it is important to check and adhere to any applicable ethical standards and privacy statutes (see Briggie et al., 2016, for sample consent forms).

One other item to consider adding to your "therapy blackbox" is a log of your weekly learnings and mistakes (Chow, 2014b, 2017a, 2018b). Start by setting aside a specific time at the end of each week to reflect on your work. Revisit your calendar to remind you of the people you met. Then, in 100 words or less, write down one thing you did well, specifically, a positive event your actions either contributed to or directly caused. Alternately, record an idea, strategy, or principle you learned from sources outside the therapy room (e.g., reading, watching a video, consulting with a colleague or supervisor). Next, do the same for a mistake made during the week.

From experience, we know this process—even for the most self-assured practitioners—can quickly become overwhelming. Stick to identifying one success and one error. If trying to recall an entire week's worth of work is too challenging, try jotting down a Twitter-length note (140 characters or less, although, at this time of writing, Twitter has now doubled the limit) of any learnings and errors made while seeing clients. Use your reflection time to first organize your collection into themes and then make connections with your individualized learning objective as identified in the "Taxonomy of Deliberate Practice Activities" worksheets (TDPA; Chow & Miller, 2015).

A simple calculation proves just how much information can be generated in this manner. Within the space of a single month, you will have harvested four of each type—a number that will grow to between 160 and 192 in a year! Ongoing review can, as illustrated in Figure 14.2, enable you to identify

FIGURE 14.2. The Iterative Process of Learning From Successes and Mistakes

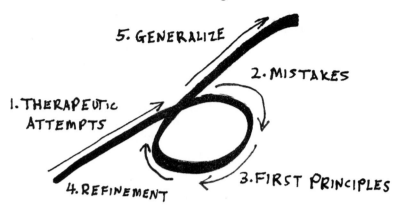

From "First Principles: The 5-Step Process for Deep and Accelerated Learning in Therapy" [Blog post], by D. Chow, 2017. Retrieved from https://darylchow.com/frontiers/first-principles-5-steps/. Copyright 2017 by Daryl Chow. Reprinted with permission.

principles that, when refined over time and with practice, become generalizable across clients and contexts (Chow, 2017c).

One caveat before moving on to the next part in the ARPS framework. Recall: Data presented in Chapter 4 showing treatment methods contribute negligibly to outcome. As such, unless your professional development goals fall within the "structure" portion of the TDPA—and the items related to methods and techniques, in particular—avoid categorizing "failing to follow a specific treatment protocol" as a mistake.

R: Reference Point

Scuba divers are trained to establish a reference point (e.g., the shore, boat, anchor line, bottom topography, compass heading) prior to descending below the surface of the water. It's part of a 5-point system all learn during certification (Gibb, 2019). Doing so ensures they end up where they are supposed to be, headed in the direction they want to go—two objectives that can be challenging given local dive conditions (e.g., low visibility, strong currents) and the spatial disorientation that can occur under water.

Establishing a reference point is the second component of an effective DP system. Its purpose is to keep us from getting lost as we work at and explore the edge of our current abilities. Experience reveals diffusion of effort is one of the most common challenges encountered along the way. The key is to *think directionally*, maintaining focus by adopting a binocular perspective. Some practical tips include:

- *Keep one eye on your data.* As presented in Chapter 10, research shows the more you check your results, the better your outcomes will be over time (J. Brown & Cazauvieilh, 2019). For this reason, make reviewing your performance metrics a routine part of your DP. Additionally, use measures with all your clients, graphing and discussing the results at every session.

Ensure your supervisor or coach has access to your individual client as well as aggregated data when discussing cases and designing, evaluating, and refining your DP plan.

- *Keep your other eye on your individualized learning objective.* If you haven't yet established an individualized learning objective, do so now. Once done, write it on a Post-it® note and stick it to your desktop monitor. Better yet, take a photo and use it as the wallpaper on your mobile phone. Because the "consolidation" page of the TDPA contains your top three learning objectives, print out a copy and hang it in a prominent location. Make what you are working on right now, visible.

Maintaining a *binocular vision*—one's eye on performance, the other on development—allows you to both monitor your professional development efforts and their impact on your effectiveness (see Figure 14.3).

P: Playful Experimentations

Reading the broader DP literature can invite discouragement. Why? Put bluntly, doing it doesn't sound *fun*—at all. In fact, K. Anders Ericsson, the psychologist and researcher who first coined the term, clearly states as much, saying, "Unlike play, deliberate practice is not inherently motivating; and unlike work, it does not lead to immediate social and monetary rewards . . . and [actually] generates costs" (Ericsson & Charness, 1994, p. 738). While the evidence suggests that, in time, the process can become self-reinforcing— a virtuous cycle of identifying and overcoming errors, setting and achieving small performance objectives—the same data show its slow, difficult nature causes many to give up long before they reap rewards (Ceci, Barnett, & Kanaya, 2003; Colvin, 2009; Miller & Hubble, 2011).

The antidote to the drudgery of deliberateness is to embrace a spirit of playfulness. Therefore, regardless of your specific learning objective, when

FIGURE 14.3. Binocular Vision on Performance and Development

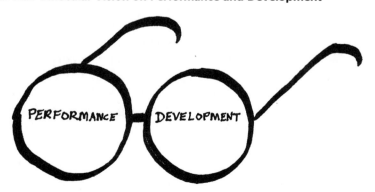

From "Reigniting Clinical Supervision: An In-Depth Online Course," by D. Chow, 2018. Retrieved from https://darylchow.com/courses/. Copyright 2018 by Daryl Chow. Reprinted with permission.

designing and executing your DP exercises, think like a child. Instead of trying to "get it right," experiment; instead of focusing on performing, play. Doing so, S. Brown and Vaughan (2009) noted in their seminal work on the subject, adds vividness to learning, helping us remain "open to serendipity, enjoying the unexpected, [and] embracing a little risk" (p. 173).

Of course, play can take many forms. With this in mind, the following suggestions should be considered neither definitive nor exhaustive. Their common purpose is facilitate continued engagement in the hard work of DP.

- *Engage in lateral learning.* Not all learning needs to take place directly. Lewis Hamilton, one of only five Formula 1 racers to hold four world titles, maintains his fine motor skills by playing the guitar. More, for as long as he can remember, he's loved music. Former San Antonio Spurs forward Tim Duncan stayed energized and engaged in learning when he was off the court by playing basketball videogames and the fantasy role-playing game Dungeons & Dragons (Hardwood and Hollywood Staff, 2018).

  While working to achieve better results, seek out activities that support, stimulate, and inspire your DP. Possibilities include reading books (both fiction and nonfiction), seeing a movie, attending or participating in sporting events, playing musical instrument, learning a language, or playing a part in a public performance (e.g., musical, play, stand-up, storytelling). One practitioner created rhymes that captured their weekly learnings and mistakes, sometimes singing them to the melodies of popular tunes. We've since borrowed that idea and used it at workshops. The energy it engenders—both nervous and creative—is remarkable, as are the results, with some songs becoming earworms referred to over and again at subsequent points during trainings.

- *Call on your "ideal" identity.* Contrary to what many believe, research indicates we feel at our most authentic when our actions are consistent with our ideal rather than actual self (Gan & Chen, 2017). Take some time to describe that person. Be thorough and playful. What character traits do they possess? How do they act? Make decisions? What do they do under stress? Who do you know—friend, family member, colleague, public figure, or even a superhero—who embodies such traits and attributes? How do they dress? What kinds of symbols or artifacts could serve as reminders of their ideals? Most important, perhaps, with whatever challenge or difficulty you are facing at the moment with a client or therapeutic encounter, think: *What would my ideal self do?*

- *Try the "it's never too late to have a good session" technique.* From your blackbox, retrieve a recording of a session that didn't go well. The best choice is the one you find yourself ruminating about on the way home from the office. With your individualized learning objective in hand, listen until you find that moment you wish you could do over. Maybe it's the way you started the visit or a comment you made that missed the mark. Whatever it might be, pause the recording at that point. Now, imagine what you could have said instead. Better yet, imagine two or three alternative responses, writing each out long hand. Now, respond to each as though you were your client. Consider what they might say and how you would, in turn, reply. Keep a record of whatever you learn in your weekly log.

- *Arrange a "surprise party."* Research on top-performing therapists indicates they are more likely to experience surprise in response to client feedback than their less effective peers (Chow, 2014a). Such a response, it appears, is an indication of their openness to being corrected, specifically, a willingness to consider another's point of view even when doing so contradicts their expectations. Given the impact surprise can have on identifying learning opportunities, we recommend the following activity:

  Step 1. Per usual, have the client complete a standardized alliance measure at the end of the visit (e.g., Session Rating Scale; Miller, Duncan, & Johnson, 2000).

  Step 2. At the same time, complete the measure yourself, as though you were the client, attempting to guess as accurately as possible how they experienced the session.

  Step 3. Compare and contrast the scores, paying particular attention to what you missed and why?

  The same activity can be used with whatever outcome measure you employ to track progress. Based on observation alone, complete the tool, guessing whether and in what ways the client is better or worse than in prior sessions. Note what surprises you as well as how and what you might attend to in the future to make more accurate assessments. Recall the nurses in the "infected babies project" reviewed in Chapter 7? Surprise (and dismay), followed by careful observation, is what led to their ability to discern the presence of a disease process *before* confirmation by medical testing, and even when tests returned false negatives.

- *"Test to learn," don't "learn for the test."* Testing, writer Annie Murphy Paul (2015) observed, has traditionally been treated "as a kind of dipstick that we insert into a student's head, an indicator that tells us how high the level of knowledge has risen." Doing so, she asserted in a provocative article published in *Scientific American,* ignores a century of both empirical research and experience on the subject of learning. If the objective is understanding, such data make clear tests should not be treated as periodic assessments of facts but opportunities for strengthening and consolidating memory. Studies show that *retrieval practice*—repeatedly bringing information to mind via regular tests, quizzes, and concept mapping—improves not only recall but also the ability to apply knowledge to novel situations and contexts (Paul, 2015). If you've completed the tasks recommended in *Better Results* as you've been reading—in particular, the "How I Do Therapy" blueprint and TDPA—you're already familiar with concept mapping. Make reviewing and updating these two documents a routine part of your DP. To facilitate what researchers call *deep learning*, test your recall of important concepts and practices on a regular basis. For example, try to answer the following questions right now:

- What is your effect size? Relative effect size?

- What percentage of your clients are achieving reliable change this week? How about clinically significant change? Are these metrics improving or staying the same from month to month? Why?

- What is the cutoff on the Outcome Rating Scale (Miller & Duncan, 2000) and Session Rating Scale (Miller et al., 2000)? Why are these indices important?

- What were your weekly learnings and mistakes last week? And the week before?

- What is the first tier of feedback for improving facilitative interpersonal skills? Second? Third? Why should you attend to the first tier before moving on to others?

- What do the letters in the acronym *ARPS* stand for? What is the definition of each? How are they operationalized in DP?

You can automate this process by using any of the digital flashcard applications widely available online (e.g., AnkiApp [see https://www.ankiapp.com], Cram [see https://www.cram.com]). If you are using digital note-taking applications (e.g., Simplenote [see https://www.simplenote.com], Evernote [see https://www.evernote.com]), you can simply scroll through your notes, randomly pick one, look at the header without looking at the details, and test your recall. If you prefer pen and paper, cover with a hand whatever notes you take and see what you can recall when only the first line or heading is exposed. Do the same with this book. Turn to any page. After briefly glimpsing the content or a single line of text you've underlined, try and recall what's next. After doing so, reveal the entire highlighted portion, paying particular attention to what you missed. End by creating a map of important concepts or summary of vital principles. Be prepared to be amazed by both what you remember and have forgotten. By the way, having a sense of familiarity that lacks specificity in terms of facts and meaning is the same as not understanding or remembering.

S: Support

Watching a top performer, be it in sports, music, or therapy, is much like looking into a bright light. Their abilities are so impressive, their execution so flawless, one can be blinded to the complex and interlocking network of people, resources, and circumstances that make their achievements possible. Indeed, for all her dedication to DP, Rachel Hsu—the 8-year-old classical pianist we met in Chapter 10—would not possess the showstopping skill or stage presence had she not enjoyed the dedicated support of important people in her life. Her two parents "devote[d] a massive amount of time, energy, and resources to nurture and advance her abilities. Moreover, she happen[ed] to live in a location that afford[ed] her opportunities to attend world-class concerts, participate in high-level competitions, and take advantage of unsurpassed professional instruction" (Miller & Hubble, 2011, p. 26).

Turning to psychotherapy, the need for supportive people and circumstances is no less critical. Achieving better results through DP requires *thinking communally*. The more thought and consideration you give to *who* will support you in your efforts to improve and *what* people, resources, and opportunities are available in your community, the more successful you are likely to be. One fact is certain: Going it alone almost always leads to giving up.

Suggestions follow for helping you pull together a team to support your system of DP:

1. *Form a "scenius" community:* "I was [previously] encouraged to believe that there were a few great figures like Picasso and Kandinsky, Rembrandt and Giotto . . . who sort-of appeared out of nowhere," said acclaimed ambient musician and producer Brian Eno (2009). "I discovered that . . . what really happened was that there was sometimes very fertile scenes involving lots and lots of people." Breaking from the traditional focus on individual "genius," he coined the term *scenius* (from the word *scene*) to emphasize the collaborative, communal nature of creativity. Success, he argued, results from what he called an ecology of talent (Chow, 2016b).

   Think "big and beyond" when considering who you will include in your DP scene. Who will you talk with about your passion and struggle to improve? In what circles and contexts is DP being discussed? Although critical to success, don't limit yourself to the support of local, like-minded practitioners. Cultivate a committee of mentors—theorists, researchers, and practitioners whose work appeals and inspires you. Most are only a call or an e-mail away. Hint: Focus less on their outputs (e.g., methods, techniques, performance) than their inputs (e.g., what they are reading, how they work, their practice routines).

2. *Find a coach with the "right stuff."* As noted in Chapter 4, coaches are one of the four fundamental elements of effective DP. In the stories of practitioners related throughout the book, references have been made to the qualities of those most likely to help you achieve better results. To summarize, the "right" coach is

   - an authority, not authoritarian;

   - focused on helping you become a better version of you rather than a clone of them;

- clear about what you want help with;
- willing to analyze your game rather than get you to play theirs;

one who will:

- identify and keep you in your zone of proximal development;
- teach the fundamentals; and
- give short, clear, and actionable directions.
- able to distinguish between challenges resulting from you and those arising from the coaching,
- more corrective than critical, and
- focused more on the process involved in improving than the adoption of techniques or tricks.

One last quality deserves mention. The coach with the "right stuff" is typically able to help with both performance *and* development (Chow, 2018d). Consider Table 14.1. On the left, are the aspects associated with coaching for performance. Traditional supervision falls into this category. A challenging therapeutic encounter or case is presented. Suggestions are made for addressing that particular situation or client. It's not unlike using a GPS. Directions are provided on step-by-step, case-by-case basis so that you get your desired location. Coaching for development, by contrast, is focused on the bigger picture, its purpose to improve your overall knowledge of the area and navigational skills. While coaching for development can lead to improved performance, the research reviewed in Chapter 2 makes clear the door does not swing the other way (i.e., supervision does not lead to professional development).

TO SUM UP

Structure is required for creativity.
—Twyla Tharp ("Creativity Is Not Just for Artists," 2015)

Table 14.2 pulls together the material covered in this chapter. It highlights the principal components of a successful DP system, the mind-set required for each, and specific guidance for putting what needs to be done into practice.

TABLE 14.1. Coaching for Performance Versus Coaching for Development

Coaching for performance	Coaching for development
Micro	Macro
Traditional case-by-case discussion	Establishing an ongoing learning and development plan
Improving the outcomes of specific cases	Improving therapist's overall effectiveness
Focus is on the client	Focus is on the therapist

TABLE 14.2. The ARPS System of Deliberate Practice

System	Think . . .	Description
Automated structure	Algorithmically	Schedule it
		Protect the DP environment
		Create a blackbox
Reference point	Directionally	Keep one eye on your outcome data
		Keep the other eye on your current learning objectives (see TDPA)
Playful experimentation	Like a child	Engage in lateral learning
		Call on your ideal identity
		The "it's never too late to have a good session" technique
		Arrange a surprise party
		Test to learn, don't learn for the test
Support	Communally	Form a scenius community
		Seek out separate coaches for performance and development

Note. ARPS = automated structure, reference point, playful experimentation, support; DP = deliberate practice; TDPA = "Taxonomy of Deliberate Practice Activities" worksheets (Chow & Miller, 2015).

WHAT TO DO RIGHT NOW

Nothing more needs be said except, "Make it so." Before ending, one final, important thought. Turn the page. . . .

15

Epilogue

A book should serve as an axe for the frozen sea within us.
—FRANZ KAFKA (IN EPIGRAPH IN SEXTON, 1962)

"I can't be a perfect therapist," says clinician Wendy Amey. "No matter one's experience or training, it's an imperfect practice." Amey is one of the first practitioners we encountered at the outset of our research into excellence. She is literally "Therapist Zero," our point of reference—the person whose way of working showed us how deliberate practice could be applied to psychotherapy (Miller & Hubble, 2011).

By the time we first met, Wendy had been gathering outcome and alliance data about her practice for years. Her results were impressive. Nevertheless, our initial contacts left us feeling underwhelmed. Given that she worked with victims of the most severe types of trauma, we expected *more*—more confidence, more certainty, a more convincing presence commensurate with her results. "Is this it?" we wondered. "What are we missing?" Wendy was nothing like the charismatic master therapists we'd come to know in books, videos, our own supervision experiences, and on the workshop circuit.

Portions of this epilogue are from "The Road to Mastery: What's Missing From This Picture," by S. D. Miller and M. A. Hubble, 2011, *Psychotherapy Networker, 35*, pp. 22–31. Copyright 2011 by The Psychotherapy Networker, Inc. Reprinted with permission.

http://dx.doi.org/10.1037/0000191-015
Better Results: Using Deliberate Practice to Improve Therapeutic Effectiveness, by S. D. Miller, M. A. Hubble, and D. Chow

"I don't see myself as a brilliant therapist," Amey insisted, when asked to account for her superior effectiveness, "my brain doesn't work that fast, and my memory is really quite limited. Other people always seem to have better ability than me. I have to struggle to keep up." And, as though to prove the fact, she told us of once being referred for an assessment of a learning disorder. Her constant questioning and struggle to learn whatever material she was being taught had apparently led some to think she was cognitively impaired. She was not. In fact, tests showed her to be well above average.

Eventually, our feelings of confusion gave way to admiration and respect. At the time, we found it difficult to put into words. Her entire way of being, how she looked at herself, how she approached her work and the world were different. In effect, she was always arriving, never giving herself credit for having arrived. "Being limited," she explained, "means I have to try harder, to work harder than most do. You see, what comes easily to others, takes time for me. If I had their ability, I probably wouldn't need to work as hard as I do."

As we delved more deeply into the expertise literature, we discovered Wendy could not have been more right for the wrong reason. Her fierce unwillingness to settle and her belief that better results were possible paralleled the mind-set of top performers across a wide range of endeavors. "Even if you always do your best," she said in one interview, "it won't always be good enough for this client, at this time and place." For Wendy, nothing was more obvious. However good one might be, there was always room for improvement.

That said, attributing her hard work and dedication to a *lack* of innate ability was, without a doubt, incorrect; in fact, that *was* her ability—dare we say, it was her "superpower." Research reviewed in this volume now confirms what came naturally to Wendy: Professional self-doubt is associated with better decision making, work performance, leadership skills, greater self-control and tolerance, stronger alliance formation, and superior outcomes. "If you aren't invested in looking superior," she matter-of-factly explained, "then why not admit you don't know, and ask?" (Miller & Hubble, 2011, p. 60).

And so, as we come to the end of the book, we find that the disquiet we felt on first meeting Wendy has given way to a contented uncertainty. We wonder:

- Has the material presented worked for you?
- Are you engaged? Putting the ideas into practice?
- What more do you need to get going or stay on track?
- Where can we improve?

After years of neglect, the study of the individual therapist—their strengths, weaknesses, impact on outcome, and methods for optimizing professional growth and development—is in full swing. Since the publication of our first article on the subject in 2007, deliberate practice has also become a hot topic in psychotherapy outcome research (Miller, Hubble, & Duncan, 2007). Still, much remains unknown and subject to future exploration and discovery. We harbor no illusions of having offered the final word. We're excited about, and look forward to, the revisions and refinements sure to come in light of new findings. Should you have ideas, feedback, research—anything—we'd appreciate your sharing them with us directly or via our social networking platform: The International Center for Clinical Excellence (https://www.iccexcellence.com).

Of this, no doubt exists: Our field's traditional methods for achieving better results have fallen short. As the people we work with and the culture in which we live are constantly changing, so must we. The time is now.[1]

---

[1]As our gift to you for completing this book, go to http://www.betterresultsbook.com/gifts to download a special set of resources.

Reliable and Clinically Significant Change Chart for the Outcome Rating Scale

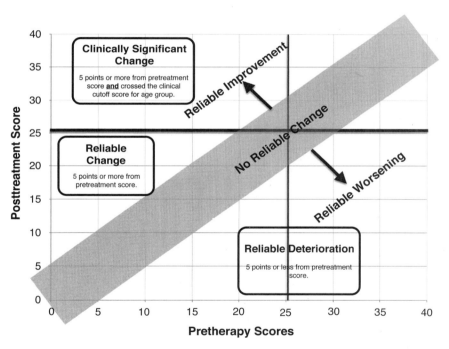

Note. Data from Miller and Duncan (2004). Copyright 2020 by Scott D. Miller, Mark A. Hubble, and Daryl Chow. Reprinted with permission.

Calculating a Standard Deviation

Given the widespread availability of online calculators, few would calculate a standard deviation (σ) by hand. That said, here is the formula for calculating it:

$$\sigma = \sqrt{\frac{1}{N}\sum_{i=1}^{N}(x_i - \mu)^2}$$

σ = standard deviation; N = the number of data points; x_i = each of the values of the data; μ = the mean of all the values.

The $i = 1$ in the summation indicates the starting index. For example, suppose your outcome measures (Outcome Rating Scale [ORS]; Miller & Duncan, 2000) for the first sessions are 15, 16, 17, 18, 19; then, $i = 1$ would be 15, and $i = 2$ would be 16, and so on. Hence, the summation notation simply means to take each of the first-session ORS measures minus the mean, and then square it—that is, $(x_i - \mu)^2$ on each value through N.

In the following example, N is 5 because there are five ORS measures in this data set.

$$\mu = (15+16+17+18+19)/5 = 17,$$

$$\sigma = \sqrt{(15-17)^2 + (16-17)^2 + (17-17)^2 + (18-17)^2 + (19+17)^2/5},$$

$$\sigma = \sqrt{4+1+0+1+4/5} = 1.58.$$

A simpler way to calculate standard deviation is to use a spreadsheet (Microsoft Excel or Google Sheets). Here are the steps:

1. Input all of your first-session outcome measures (e.g., ORS) in a column (e.g., B2 to B65).

2. Go to the bottom of that column (keep a few rows blank, so that if you use a filter to sort your data, it will not affect your computations at the bottom) and key in the following in the bottom cell:

=STDDEV(B2:B65)

Alternatively, you can use an online calculator, such as https://www.calculator. net/standard-deviation-calculator.html.

APPENDIX C

Taxonomy of Deliberate Practice Activities in Psychotherapy— Supervisor/Coach Version (Version 5.1)

Daryl Chow, PhD and Scott D. Miller, PhD (© 2015, 2017, 2019)

Your Name: _____   **Supervisee's Name:** _____

Date: _____

Objectives

- To develop clear and concrete learning objectives specific to the clinical population your supervisee works with in order to promote professional development

- To establish a baseline of learning goals for your supervisee and to evaluate professional growth routinely (i.e., monthly) in concert with routine outcome monitoring (ROM) practices

Overview

There are five broad domains for deliberate practice in psychotherapy:

Instructions

1. **Know Your Supervisee's Work:**
   Review your supervisee's audio/video recordings of a few cases.

2. **Rate:**
   Go through the list of activities, then rate each of them according to your own appraisal of how your supervisee performed in each of the domains.

3. **Describe:**
   Make an effort to provide notes in the last column to add richness and detail to your ratings.

4. **Prioritize:**
   Go through the ENTIRE list again, and identify the **Top 3 Activities across all domains*** you believe will have a significant impact on improving your supervisee's ability to engage and help their clients. After you have identified your top 3 activities, select **one** to work on at a given time.

5. **Compare and Contrast:**
   Compare the ratings and the identified Top 3 Rankings with your supervisee's ratings. Come to a consensus and use this as a platform for designing a clear learning objective.

6. **Consolidate:**
   Discuss the **Consolidation** section (see last page) with your supervisee.

7. **Plan:**
   Develop a routine for reviewing the Taxonomy of Deliberate Practice Activities in Psychotherapy (TDPA) periodically (i.e., every month). Expect learning objectives to change and evolve as you make progress.

Note.* Please select the TOP 3 ACTIVITIES across the entire list (e.g., not necessarily within each of the domains). The three do not have to be the lowest scored item. Complete the **Consolidation section (see last page) to help clarify your supervisee's professional development plan.

TABLE C.1. The Structure Domain of Deliberate Practice Activities

Themes	Activities	Current Rating (0–10)	Select and Rank the TOP 3 Activities to Work On*	Notes
	How do you start a first session?			
	How do you start subsequent sessions?			
	How do you close a session?			
	How do you formally elicit detailed and nuanced feedback at each session?			
Structure	How do you integrate the use of feedback measures into your way of working?			
	How do you change your way of working in response to client feedback (e.g., the method, the frequency/dose, the provider)?			
	How do you prepare for a planned closure of therapy?			

(continues)

TABLE C.1. The Structure Domain of Deliberate Practice Activities *(Continued)*

Themes	Activities	Current Rating (0–10)	Select and Rank the TOP 3 Activities to Work On*	Notes
	How do you share with your client that your work together is unfolding as it should so they know progress is being made toward the resolution of their problem/concern?			
	How do you maintain the organization and focus in your work from session to session?			
	How do you ensure the accuracy and timing of your therapeutic interventions?			
	How do the methods, techniques, and activities within and outside of formal sessions flow logically from your theory/model for helping clients?			
	Others (please describe specifically to structuring the session):			

*Note. Please select the TOP 3 ACTIVITIES across the entire list (e.g., not necessarily within each of the domains). The three do not have to be the lowest scored item.

TABLE C.2. The Hope and Expectancy Domain of Deliberate Practice Activities

Themes	Activities	Current Rating (0–10)	Select and Rank the TOP 3 Activities to Work On*	Notes
	How do you induct clients into therapy?			
	A. How do you inform them about what to expect from one session to the next?			
	B. How do you explain your respective roles (e.g., client, therapist)?			
Hope & Expectancy	How does the explanation you offer for your client's distress engender hope and expectation for change?			
	How do you persuade the client to have a favorable assessment and acceptance of your clinical rationale and related techniques?			
	How do you adapt your treatment rationale to foster client engagement and hope?			

(continues)

TABLE C.2. The Hope and Expectancy Domain of Deliberate Practice Activities (*Continued*)

Themes	Activities	Current Rating (0–10)	Select and Rank the TOP 3 Activities to Work On*	Notes
	How do you communicate a hopeful and optimistic stance toward your client and their problem/concerns?			
	How do you convey a sense of confidence and belief in you and your treatment approach?			
	Others (please describe specifically to hope and expectancy):			

Note. Please select the TOP 3 ACTIVITIES across the entire list (e.g., not necessarily within each of the domains). The three do not have to be the lowest scored item.

TABLE C.3. The Alliance Domain of Deliberate Practice Activities

Themes	Activities	Current Rating (0–10)	Select and Rank the TOP 3 Activities to Work On*	Notes
Alliance: Effective Focus	How do you establish goal consensus in the first/subsequent sessions?			
	How do you help a client who has no clear goals in therapy?			
	How do you mobilize a client's willingness to engage in a therapeutic process/activity?			
	How do you encourage your client to confront, experience or deal with difficult topics or problems?			
Alliance: The Impact Factor	How do you explicitly convey warmth, understanding, and acceptance toward your client?			
	How do you promote emotional engagement/safety?			

(continues)

TABLE C.3. The Alliance Domain of Deliberate Practice Activities *(Continued)*

Themes	Activities	Current Rating (0–10)	Select and Rank the TOP 3 Activities to Work On*	Notes
	How do you foster a sense of mutuality with your client (e.g., responsiveness, feelings, expectations, reciprocity)?			
	How do you explicitly communicate empathic attunement?			
	How do you deepen your client's emotional experiencing?			
Alliance: Motivation	How do you assess and work with a client's readiness for change?			
	How do you increase homework compliance?			

Alliance: Difficulties		
How do you deal with ruptures in the alliance?		
How do you deal with an angry client?		
How do you deal with a client who is feeling hopeless?		
How do you deal with strong and difficult emotions arising in the session?		
How do you manage a client who is at high risk of suicide?		
How do you manage a client mandated for treatment?		
Others (please describe specifically to alliance factors):		

Note. Please select the TOP 3 ACTIVITIES across the entire list (e.g., not necessarily within each of the domains). The three do not have to be the lowest scored item.

TABLE C.4. The Client Factors Domain of Deliberate Practice Activities

Themes	Activities	Current Rating (0–10)	Select and Rank the TOP 3 Activities to Work On*	Notes
	How do you incorporate your client's strengths, abilities, and resources into care?			
	How do you incorporate your client's values, beliefs, and cultural systems into care?			
Client Factors	How do you actively utilize chance events (positive and negative) to influence participation and progress?			
	How do you incorporate or build the client's social support network?			
	Others (please describe specifically to client factors):			

*Note. Please select the TOP 3 ACTIVITIES across the entire list (e.g., not necessarily within each of the domains). The three do not have to be the lowest scored item.

TABLE C.5. The Therapist Domain of Deliberate Practice Activities

Themes	Activities	Current Rating (0–10)	Select and Rank the TOP 3 Activities to Work On*	Notes
	How do you regulate your anxiety when encountering a difficult interaction with a client?			
	How do you manage negative feelings toward your client?			
Therapist: The Use of the Self	How do you maintain appropriate boundaries and roles with your clients (e.g., not letting personal emotions or life events bleed into/affect your clinical work)?			
	How do you remain reflective versus reactive in session with clients?			
	How do you utilize self-disclosure?			

(continues)

TABLE C.5. The Therapist Domain of Deliberate Practice Activities (*Continued*)

Themes	Activities	Current Rating (0–10)	Select and Rank the TOP 3 Activities to Work On*	Notes
	How do you integrate your life experiences into your personal clinical style?			
	How do you operationalize empirically supported principles of effective clinical work in a way unique to you as a person?			
	How do you find the right words at the right time or in the right situation?			
Therapist: Outside of Sessions	How do you engage in solitary deliberate practice *outside* of sessions in your typical work week?			
	Others (please describe specifically to therapist factors):			

*Note. Please select the TOP 3 ACTIVITIES across the entire list (e.g., not necessarily within each of the domains). The three do not have to be the lowest scored item.

CONSOLIDATION

Instructions

1. The **Top 3 Activities** to work on from the taxonomy are your supervisee's **Stretch Goals.** They are the objectives at the margin of your "zone of proximal development." List them in order of priority. Once listed, choose **ONE** to focus on in your supervisee's deliberate practice. Recall: To improve results, your supervisee's one identified stretch goal must be associated with treatment outcome. Consult the research evidence to confirm (see https:// darylchow.com/frontiers/what-are-the-perennial-pillars-for-psychotherapists/ for some examples).

2. Discrepancies are likely to exist between the goals you and your supervisees identify and are a good place to begin dialogue. Choosing and refining learning objectives are parts of an iterative process. Revise until agreement is reached that fits your supervisee's interests and your coach or supervisor's knowledge and skills.

3. Help your supervisees state their chosen stretch goal in **SMART** terms (**S**pecific, **M**easurable, **A**ttainable, **R**elevant, a **T**ime Line) to assist them in identifying concrete activities they can engage in to reach the stretch goal.

4. Review your supervisee's stretch and SMART goals on an ongoing basis, setting aside a specific date and time to review their progress. Check for impact on their performance metrics.

Current Date: _____

Review Date: _____

TABLE C.6. Consolidation of Stretch and Smart Goals

Serial Number	STRETCH GOAL (Your Supervisee's current identified Top 3 Activities to Work On)	SMART GOAL (Specific, Measurable, Attainable, Relevant, a Time Line)	Review and Reflect
1			
2			
3			

APPENDIX D

Taxonomy of Deliberate Practice Activities in Psychotherapy— Therapist Version

Daryl Chow, PhD and Scott D. Miller, PhD (© 2015, 2017, 2019)

Your Name: _____   **Your Supervisor/**
Date: _____   **Coach's Name:** _____

Objectives

- To develop clear and concrete learning objectives specific to the clinical population you work with in order to promote professional development

- To establish a baseline of learning goals and to evaluate professional growth routinely (i.e., monthly) in concert with routine outcome monitoring (ROM) practices

Overview

There are five broad domains for deliberate practice in psychotherapy:

Structure	Hope & Expectancy	Working Alliance	Client Factors	Therapist Factors

Instructions

1. **Know Your Work:**
   Recall as vividly as possible your clients in the last typical work week (extend to the past two work weeks, if necessary). To aid with your recall, review audio/video recordings of your sessions.

2. **Rate:**
   Go through the list of activities, then rate each of them according to your own appraisal of how you performed in each of the domains.

3. **Describe:**
   Make an effort to provide notes in the last column to add richness and detail to your ratings.

4. **Prioritize:**
   Go through the ENTIRE list again, and identify the **Top 3 Activities across all domains*** you believe will have a significant impact on improving your ability to engage and help your clients. After you have identified your Top 3 Activities, select **one** to work on at a given time.

5. **Compare and Contrast:**
   Enlist a supervisor/coach—or someone who knows your clinical practice well—to complete the Supervisor version of this form. Cross compare the ratings and Top 3 areas. Work together to identify and design a single learning objective.

6. **Consolidate:**
   Complete the **Consolidation** section (see last page).

7. **Plan:**
   Develop a routine for reviewing the Taxonomy of Deliberate Practice Activities in Psychotherapy (TDPA) periodically (i.e., every month). Expect learning objectives to change and evolve as you make progress.

---

*Note. Please select the TOP 3 ACTIVITIES across the entire list (e.g., not necessarily within each of the domains). The three do not have to be the lowest scored item. Complete the **Consolidation** section (see last page) to help clarify your professional development plan.

TABLE D.1. The Structure Domain of Deliberate Practice Activities

Themes	Activities	Current Rating (0–10)	Select and Rank the TOP 3 Activities to Work On*	Notes
	How do you start a first session?			
	How do you start subsequent sessions?			
	How do you close a session?			
	How do you formally elicit detailed and nuanced feedback at each session?			
Structure	How do you integrate the use of feedback measures into your way of working?			
	How do you change your way of working in response to client feedback (e.g., the method, the frequency/dose, the provider)?			
	How do you prepare for a planned closure of therapy?			

(continues)

TABLE D.1. The Structure Domain of Deliberate Practice Activities (*Continued*)

Themes	Activities	Current Rating (0–10)	Select and Rank the TOP 3 Activities to Work On*	Notes
	How do you share with your client that your work together is unfolding as it should so they know progress is being made toward the resolution of their problem/concern?			
	How do you maintain the organization and focus in your work from session to session?			
	How do you ensure the accuracy and timing of your therapeutic interventions?			
	How do the methods, techniques, and activities within and outside of formal sessions flow logically from your theory/model for helping clients?			
	Others (please describe specifically to structuring the session):			

*Note. Please select the TOP 3 ACTIVITIES across the entire list (e.g., not necessarily within each of the domains). The three do not have to be the lowest scored item.

TABLE D.2. The Hope and Expectancy Domain of Deliberate Practice Activities

Themes	Activities	Current Rating (0–10)	Select and Rank the TOP 3 Activities to Work On*	Notes
	How do you induct clients into therapy?			
	A. How do you inform them about what to expect from one session to the next?			
	B. How do you explain your respective roles (e.g., client, therapist)?			
Hope & Expectancy	How does the explanation you offer for your client's distress engender hope and expectation for change?			
	How do you persuade the client to have a favorable assessment and acceptance of your clinical rationale and related techniques?			
	How do you adapt your treatment rationale to foster client engagement and hope?			

(continues)

TABLE D.2. The Hope and Expectancy Domain of Deliberate Practice Activities *(Continued)*

Themes	Activities	Current Rating (0–10)	Select and Rank the TOP 3 Activities to Work On*	Notes
	How do you communicate a hopeful and optimistic stance toward your client and their problem/concerns?			
	How do you convey a sense of confidence and belief in you and your treatment approach?			
	Others (please describe specifically to hope and expectancy):			

Note. Please select the TOP 3 ACTIVITIES across the entire list (e.g., not necessarily within each of the domains). The three do not have to be the lowest scored item.

TABLE D.3. The Alliance Domain of Deliberate Practice Activities

Themes	Activities	Current Rating (0–10)	Select and Rank the TOP 3 Activities to Work On*	Notes
Alliance: Effective Focus	How do you establish goal consensus in the first/subsequent sessions?			
	How do you help a client who has no clear goals in therapy?			
	How do you mobilize a client's willingness to engage in a therapeutic process/activity?			
	How do you encourage your client to confront, experience or deal with difficult topics or problems?			
Alliance: The Impact Factor	How do you explicitly convey warmth, understanding, and acceptance toward your client?			
	How do you promote emotional engagement/safety?			

(continues)

TABLE D.3. The Alliance Domain of Deliberate Practice Activities *(Continued)*

Themes	Activities	Current Rating (0–10)	Select and Rank the TOP 3 Activities to Work On*	Notes
	How do you foster a sense of mutuality with your client (e.g., responsiveness, feelings, expectations, reciprocity)?			
	How do you explicitly communicate empathic attunement?			
	How do you deepen your client's emotional experiencing?			
Alliance: Motivation	How do you assess and work with a client's readiness for change?			
	How do you increase homework compliance?			

Alliance: Difficulties		
How do you deal with ruptures in the alliance?		
How do you deal with an angry client?		
How do you deal with a client who is feeling hopeless?		
How do you deal with strong and difficult emotions arising in the session?		
How do you manage a client who is at high risk of suicide?		
How do you manage a client mandated for treatment?		
Others (please describe specifically to alliance factors):		

Note. Please select the TOP 3 ACTIVITIES across the entire list (e.g., not necessarily within each of the domains). The three do not have to be the lowest scored item.

TABLE D.4. The Client Factors Domain of Deliberate Practice Activities

Themes	Activities	Current Rating (0–10)	Select and Rank the TOP 3 Activities to Work On*	Notes
Client Factors	How do you incorporate your client's strengths, abilities, and resources into care?			
	How do you incorporate your client's values, beliefs, and cultural systems into care?			
	How do you actively utilize chance events (positive and negative) to influence participation and progress?			
	How do you incorporate or build the client's social support network?			
	Others (please describe specifically to client factors):			

*Note. Please select the TOP 3 ACTIVITIES across the entire list (e.g., not necessarily within each of the domains). The three do not have to be the lowest scored item.

TABLE D.5. The Therapist Domain of Deliberate Practice Activities

Themes	Activities	Current Rating (0–10)	Select and Rank the TOP 3 Activities to Work On*	Notes
	How do you regulate your anxiety when encountering a difficult interaction with a client?			
	How do you manage negative feelings toward your client?			
Therapist: The Use of the Self	How do you maintain appropriate boundaries and roles with your clients (e.g., not letting personal emotions or life events bleed into/affect your clinical work)?			
	How do you remain reflective versus reactive in session with clients?			
	How do you utilize self-disclosure?			

(continues)

TABLE D.5. The Therapist Domain of Deliberate Practice Activities *(Continued)*

Themes	Activities	Current Rating (0–10)	Select and Rank the TOP 3 Activities to Work On*	Notes
	How do you integrate your life experiences into your personal clinical style?			
	How do you operationalize empirically supported principles of effective clinical work in a way unique to you as a person?			
	How do you find the right words at the right time or in the right situation?			
Therapist: Outside of Sessions	How do you engage in solitary deliberate practice *outside of* sessions in your typical work week?			
	Others (please describe specifically to therapist factors):			

*Note. Please select the TOP 3 ACTIVITIES across the entire list (e.g., not necessarily within each of the domains). The three do not have to be the lowest scored item.

CONSOLIDATION

Instructions

1. The **Top 3 Activities** to work on from the taxonomy are your **Stretch Goals.** They are the objectives at the margin of your "zone of proximal development." List them in order of priority. Once listed, choose **ONE** to focus on in deliberate practice. Recall: To improve results, your one identified stretch goal must be associated with treatment outcome. Consult the research evidence to confirm (see https://darylchow.com/frontiers/what-are-the-perennial-pillars-for-psychotherapists/ for some examples).

2. Discrepancies are likely to exist between the goals you and your coach identify, and are a good place to begin dialogue. Choosing and refining learning objectives are parts of an iterative process. Revise until agreement is reached that fits your interests and your coach or supervisor's knowledge and skills.

3. State your chosen stretch goal in **SMART** terms (**S**pecific, **M**easurable, **A**ttainable, **R**elevant, a **T**ime Line) to assist you in identifying concrete activities you can engage in to reach the stretch goal.

4. Review your stretch and SMART goals on an ongoing basis, setting aside a specific date and time to review your progress. Check for impact on your performance metrics.

Current Date: _____   Review Date: _____

TABLE D.6. Consolidation of Stretch and Smart Goals

Serial Number	STRETCH GOAL (Your current identified Top 3 Activities to Work On)	SMART GOAL (Specific, Measurable, Attainable, Relevant, a Time Line)	Review and Reflect
1			
2			
3			

APPENDIX E

Troubleshooting Tips

Over the past decade, we've introduced deliberate practice (DP) to hundreds of agencies and thousands of practitioners around the world. As with any endeavor, challenges and setbacks invariably occur. In Table E.1, we have identified the 10 most common problems in implementing DP. To use the guide below, first identify the difficulty you are experiencing from the list on the left. Troubleshooting tips are provided in the center column, references to pertinent chapters or pages in the book in the right.

TABLE E.1. Deliberate Practice Troubleshooting Guide

Problem	Tips	Reference
"I would like to jump into doing DP, but I've yet to establish a baseline performance."	In a word, "don't." Wait until you have established a reliable baseline. Sixty cases is recommended. Analyzing your results with insufficient data wastes time and effort, and can lead to erroneous conclusions. Patience is key.	Chapters 6, 7
"I'm on board with the FIT approach and DP, but my clinical supervisor [agency or setting] isn't."	Share relevant reading materials with your supervisor and colleagues.	Chapter 4
	Organize a group of like-minded peers who meet regularly to discuss and support one another in FIT and DP.	Reread the case example of Tony in Chapter 10
	Find a coach outside of your current work setting.	
"Using measures on an ongoing basis interrupts the flow of my sessions with clients and adds little to my work over and above what I already know."	Don't kid yourself. The data clearly show clinicians' judgment is significantly enhanced by routinely measuring the progress and the quality of the alliance. Of course, it takes time for the process to become second nature.	Chapter 2
	Recall: Self-reflection alone is not sufficient for improving performance. A well-designed learning objective and feedback, coaching, and refinement over time via ongoing practice are required.	Chapter 13

(continues)

TABLE E.1. Deliberate Practice Troubleshooting Guide (*Continued*)

Problem	Tips	Reference
"I lack discipline and time for DP."	Don't depend on willpower. Successful DP requires the ongoing support of others and a system.	Chapters 4, 14
"I choke whenever I go to try something new I've learned from the book in my practice [e.g., administer the measures, ask for feedback)."	Recall the difference between learning and performing. Choking happens when we are asked to perform a task that falls in our panic zone, where expectations exceed ability.	See Individualized Learning Objectives section in Chapter 4.
"Oh, my. I have so many areas I could work on and improve."	First, take a deep breath! It's easy to feel overwhelmed when first starting the DP process. Use the TDPA worksheets to identify one key area to work on that has the leverage to improve your results. Last, don't proceed alone. Seek out a coach. Organize a group of like-minded peers. Use the virtual community available on The International Center for Clinical Excellence website (see https://www.iccexcellence.com).	Chapter 10, Appendix D
"I'm overwhelmed with a heavy caseload and simply don't have time to administer the scales and track the outcomes of all my clients."	Use one of the many available outcome management systems to automate the administration of the scales and manage data aggregation.	Chapter 9
"I've heard I can improve my mastery of a specific therapeutic approach."	To achieve better results, our DP must be a *gradual refinement* of our existing abilities. This does not necessarily mean acquiring new tools. Rather, improvements results from (a) identifying **where** you are (i.e., your baseline of effectiveness), (b) figuring out **what** you need to practice that has leverage in terms of improving your outcomes, and (c) designing and engaging in a plan for **how** you will work on what you need to improve.	Chapter 2
	It goes without saying that you want to invest your time on aspects of your performance that will lead to better results. On this score, recall: The particular approach a clinician uses contributes a negligible amount to outcome.	See Applying Deliberate Practice to Mastering Treatment Models section in Chapter 4
	Starting by checking your performance data and reviewing your TDPA to determine whether a focus on structure and technique is likely to prove beneficial.	Chapter 9, Appendix D

TABLE E.1. Deliberate Practice Troubleshooting Guide (*Continued*)

Problem	Tips	Reference
"I've applied all of the strategies in this book, but my efforts are not translating into better results."	Only two possible explanations exist for this problem. The first, and most likely, is you've not given the process enough time. DP results in slow, gradual improvement, most often occurring over a period of years, not months.	Chapter 13
	The other potential cause can be that the particular area or objective you've chosen to address has little or no leverage on outcome. Start by making sure your individualized learning objective is well defined and connected to a problematic pattern or deficit observable in your baseline performance data. In addition, review your DP efforts with your coach to ensure they are both specific enough and targeted to your particular performance objective.	Chapter 14
"My baseline performance data indicate that I am already achieving above average results. What should I do now?"	DP, research shows, is important not only for the acquisition of superior performance but also for its maintenance (Ericsson, 2009; Krampe & Ericsson, 1996).	Appendix D
	Go through your outcome data and identify 10 to 20 clients who have made significant gains. Look for patterns in you, your clients, and the work that might be responsible. Do the same with a similar number of clients with poor outcomes. Write down what stands out. Next, with the information in hand, review your TDPA for maintenance and improvement possibilities.	

Note. DP = deliberate practice; FIT = feedback-informed treatment; TDPA = "Taxonomy of Deliberate Practice Activities" (Chow & Miller, 2015).

REFERENCES

Adams, S. (2013). *How to fail at almost everything and still win big: Kind of the story of my life*. New York, NY: Penguin Random House.

American Psychiatric Association. (1952). *Diagnostic and statistical manual of mental disorders*. Washington, DC: American Psychiatric Association Mental Health Service.

American Psychiatric Association. (1987). *Diagnostic and statistical manual of mental disorders* (3rd ed., rev.). Washington, DC: Author.

American Psychiatric Association. (2010). *Practice guideline or the treatment for patients with eating disorders* (3rd ed.). Retrieved from https://psychiatryonline. org/pb/assets/raw/sitewide/practice_guidelines/guidelines/eatingdisorders.pdf

American Psychiatric Association. (2013). *Diagnostic and statistical manual of mental disorders* (5th ed.). Arlington, VA: Author.

Amirault, R. J., & Branson, R. K. (2006). *Educators and expertise: A brief history of theories and models*. In K. A. Ericsson, N. Charness, P. J. Feltovich, & R. R. Hoffmann (Eds.), *The Cambridge handbook of expertise and expert performance* (pp. 69–86). Cambridge, England: Cambridge University Press. http://dx.doi.org/10.1017/CBO9780511816796.005

Anderson, K. N. (2016). Premature termination of outpatient psychotherapy: Predictors, reasons, and outcomes. *Dissertation Abstracts International: Section B. Sciences and Engineering, 76*(9-B[E]).

Anderson, T., Crowley, M. E. J., Himawan, L., Holmberg, J. K., & Uhlin, B. D. (2016). Therapist facilitative interpersonal skills and training status: A randomized clinical trial on alliance and outcome. *Psychotherapy Research, 26,* 511–529. http://dx.doi.org/10.1080/10503307.2015.1049671

Anderson, T., Ogles, B. M., Patterson, C. L., Lambert, M. J., & Vermeersch, D. A. (2009). Therapist effects: Facilitative interpersonal skills as a predictor of therapist success. *Journal of Clinical Psychology, 65,* 755–768. http://dx.doi.org/10.1002/jclp.20583

Asay, T. P., & Lambert, M. J. (1999). The empirical case for the common factors in therapy: Quantitative findings. In M. A. Hubble, B. L. Duncan, & S. D. Miller (Eds.), *The heart and soul of change: What works in therapy* (pp. 23–55). Washington, DC: American Psychological Association. http://dx.doi.org/10.1037/11132-001

Averbukh, M., Brown, S., & Chase, B. (2015, October 22). *Baseball pay and performance*. Retrieved from https://www.coursehero.com/file/30946791/baseball.pdf/

Aviation safety. (n.d.). In *Wikipedia*. Retrieved January 29, 2020, from https://en.wikipedia.org/wiki/Aviation_safety

Bachelor, A., & Horvath, A. (1999). The therapeutic relationship. In M. A. Hubble, B. L. Duncan, & S. D. Miller (Eds.), *The heart and soul of change: What works in therapy* (pp. 133–178). Washington, DC: American Psychological Association.

Baer, D. (2014). New study destroys Malcom Gladwell's 10,000 hour rule. *Business Insider*. Retrieved from http://www.businessinsider.com/new-study-destroys-malcolm-gladwells-10000-rule2014-7

Baidya, S. (2014, April 13). *20 facts about burgers*. Retrieved from https://factslegend.org/20-facts-burgers/

Baldwin, S. A., Berkeljon, A., Atkins, D. C., Olsen, J. A., & Nielsen, S. L. (2009). Rates of change in naturalistic psychotherapy: Contrasting dose-effect and good-enough level models of change. *Journal of Consulting and Clinical Psychology, 77*, 203–211. http://dx.doi.org/10.1037/a0015235

Baldwin, S. A., & Imel, Z. E. (2013). Therapist effects: Findings and methods. In M. J. Lambert (Ed.), *Bergin and Garfield's handbook of psychotherapy and behavior change* (6th ed., pp. 259–297). New York, NY: Wiley.

Baldwin, S. A., Wampold, B. E., & Imel, Z. E. (2007). Untangling the alliance-outcome correlation: Exploring the relative importance of therapist and patient variability in the alliance. *Journal of Consulting and Clinical Psychology, 75*, 842–852. http://dx.doi.org/10.1037/0022-006X.75.6.842

Barber, J. P., Gallop, R., Crits-Christoph, P., Frank, A., Thase, M. E., Weiss, R. D., & Gibbons, M. B. (2006). The role of therapist adherence, therapist competence, and alliance in predicting outcome of individual drug counseling: Results from the National Institute Drug Abuse Collaborative Cocaine Treatment Study. *Psychotherapy Research, 16*, 229–240. http://dx.doi.org/10.1080/10503300500288951

Bargmann, S., & Robinson, B. (2012). Manual 2—Feedback-informed clinical work: The basics. In B. Bertolino & S. D. Miller (Eds.), *The ICCE manuals on feedback-informed treatment (FIT)*. Chicago, IL: International Center for Clinical Excellence.

Baring-Gould, W. S. (Ed.). (1967). *The annotated Sherlock Holmes: Vol. 1. A scandal in Bohemia*. New York, NY: Wings Books.

Bathgate, K. E., Bagley, J. R., Jo, E., Talmadge, R. J., Tobias, I. S., Brown, L. E., . . . Galpin, A. J. (2018). Muscle health and performance in monozygotic twins with 30 years of discordant exercise habits. *European Journal of Applied Physiology, 118*, 2097–2110. http://dx.doi.org/10.1007/s00421-018-3943-7

Battino, R. (2006). *Expectation: The very brief therapy book*. Carmarthen, Wales: Crown House.

Beck, A. T., Ward, C. H., Mendelson, M., Mock, J., & Erbaugh, J. (1961). An inventory for measuring depression. *Archives of General Psychiatry, 4*, 561–571. http://dx.doi.org/10.1001/archpsyc.1961.01710120031004

Berrington, K. (2017, May 31). *Marilyn Monroe quotes*. Retrieved from https://www.vogue.co.uk/gallery/marilyn-monroe-best-quotes

Bertolino, B., & Miller, S. D. (Eds.). (2012). *ICCE manuals on feedback-informed treatment* (FIT; Vols. 1–6). Chicago, IL: International Center for Clinical Excellence.

Bertrand, S. K. (2017). *A thousand miles: Collected haiku.* Bloomington, IN: Xlibris.

Beutler, L. E., & Harwood, T. M. (2000). *Prescriptive psychotherapy: A practical guide to systematic treatment selection.* New York, NY: Oxford University Press. http://dx.doi.org/10.1093/med:psych/9780195136692.001.0001

Bickman, L., Kelley, S. D., & Athay, M. (2012). The technology of measurement feedback systems. *Couple & Family Psychology, 1,* 274–284. http://dx.doi.org/10.1037/a0031022

Bickman, L., Rosof-Williams, J., Salzer, M. S., Summerfelt, W., Noser, K., Wilson, S. J., & Karver, M. S. (2000). What information do clinicians value for monitoring adolescent client progress and outcomes? *Professional Psychology: Research and Practice, 31,* 70–74. http://dx.doi.org/10.1037/0735-7028.31.1.70

Bigler, C. L., & Lloyd-Watts, V. (1979). *Studying Suzuki® piano—More than music: A handbook for teachers, parents, and students.* Secaucus, NJ: Summy-Burchard Music.

Bike, D. H., Norcross, J. C., & Schatz, D. M. (2009). Processes and outcomes of psychotherapists' personal therapy: Replication and extension 20 years later. *Psychotherapy: Theory, Research, Practice, Training, 46,* 19–31. http://dx.doi.org/10.1037/a0015139

Bilalić, M., & Campitelli, G. (2018). Studies of the activation and structural changes of the brain associated with expertise. In K. A. Ericsson, R. R. Hoffman, A. Kozbelt, & M. A. Williams (Eds.), *The Cambridge handbook of expertise and expert performance* (2nd ed., pp. 233–254). Cambridge, England: Cambridge University Press. http://dx.doi.org/10.1017/9781316480748.014

Binder, J. L., & Strupp, H. H. (1997). "Negative process": A recurrently discovered and underestimated facet of therapeutic process and outcome in the individual psychotherapy of adults. *Clinical Psychology: Science and Practice, 4,* 121–139. http://dx.doi.org/10.1111/j.1468-2850.1997.tb00105.x

Blake, W. (1788). *All religions are one: The voice of one crying in the wilderness.* Retrieved from https://wwnorton.com/college/english/nael/noa/pdf/blake_All_Religions_Are_One.pdf

Bohart, A. C., & Wade, W. G. (2013). The client in psychotherapy. In M. J. Lambert (Ed.), *Bergin and Garfield's handbook of psychotherapy and behavior change* (6th ed., pp. 219–257). Hoboken, NJ: Wiley.

Bonett, D. G. (2007). Transforming odd ratios into correlations for meta-analytic research. *American Psychologist, 62,* 254–255. http://dx.doi.org/10.1037/0003-066X.62.3.254

Bordin, E. S. (1979). The generalizability of the psychoanalytic concept of the working alliance. *Psychotherapy: Theory, Research & Practice, 16,* 252–260. http://dx.doi.org/10.1037/h0085885

Boswell, J. F., Kraus, D. R., Miller, S. D., & Lambert, M. J. (2015). Implementing routine outcome monitoring in clinical practice: Benefits, challenges, and solutions. *Psychotherapy Research, 25,* 6–19. http://dx.doi.org/10.1080/10503307.2013.817696 (Corrigendum published 2015, *Psychotherapy Research, 25,* p. iii. http://dx.doi.org/10.1080/10503307.2014.942531)

Branch, J. (2009, March 3). For free throws, 50 years of practice is no help. *The New York Times*. Retrieved from https://www.nytimes.com/2009/03/04/sports/basketball/04freethrow.html

Branson, A., Shafran, R., & Myles, P. (2015). Investigating the relationship between competence and patient outcome with CBT. *Behaviour Research and Therapy, 68*, 19–26. http://dx.doi.org/10.1016/j.brat.2015.03.002

Brattland, H., Koksvik, J. M., Burkeland, O., Gråwe, R. W., Klöckner, C., Linaker, O. M., . . . Iversen, V. C. (2018). The effects of routine outcome monitoring (ROM) on therapy outcomes in the course of an implementation process: A randomized clinical trial. *Journal of Counseling Psychology, 65*, 641–652. http://dx.doi.org/10.1037/cou0000286

Braun, J. J., & Linder, D. E. (1979). *Psychology today: An introduction* (4th ed.). New York, NY: Random House.

Briggie, A. M., Hilsenroth, M. J., Conway, F., Muran, J. C., & Jackson, J. M. (2016). Patient comfort with audio or video recording of their psychotherapy sessions: Relation to symptomatology, treatment refusal, duration, and outcome. *Professional Psychology: Research and Practice, 47*, 66–76. http://dx.doi.org/10.1037/a0040063

Brooks, D. (2014, September 25). The good order [Opinion]. *The New York Times*. Retrieved from https://www.nytimes.com/2014/09/26/opinion/david-brooks-routine-creativity-and-president-obamas-un-speech.html?_r=0

Brown, J., & Cazauvieilh, C. (2019, February 12). *Clinician engagement in feedback informed treatment (FIT) and patient outcomes*. Retrieved from https://acorncollaboration.org/blog/2019/2/12/therapist-engagement

Brown, J., Dreis, S., & Nace, D. K. (1999). What really makes a difference in psychotherapy outcome? Why does managed care want to know? In M. A. Hubble, B. L. Duncan, & S. D. Miller (Eds.), *The heart and soul of change: What works in therapy* (pp. 389–406). Washington, DC: American Psychological Association. http://dx.doi.org/10.1037/11132-012

Brown, P. C., Roediger, H. L., & McDaniel, M. A. (2014). *Make it stick: The science of successful learning*. Cambridge, MA: Belknap Press of Harvard University Press. http://dx.doi.org/10.4159/9780674419377

Brown, S., & Vaughan, C. (2009). *Play: How it shapes the brain, opens the imagination, and invigorates the soul*. New York, NY: Penguin.

Bureau of Labor Statistics, U.S. Department of Labor. (n.d.). *Occupational outlook handbook: Psychologists*. Retrieved from https://www.bls.gov/ooh/life-physical-and-social-science/psychologists.htm

Butterworth, B. (2018). Mathematical expertise. In K. A. Ericsson, R. R. Hoffman, A. Kozbelt, & A. M. Williams (Eds.), *The Cambridge handbook of expertise and expert performance* (2nd ed., pp. 616–633). Cambridge, England: Cambridge University Press. http://dx.doi.org/10.1017/9781316480748.032

Buunk, B. P., & Van Yperen, N. W. (1991). Referential comparisons, relational comparisons, and exchange orientation: Their relation to marital satisfaction. *Personality and Social Psychology Bulletin, 17*, 709–717. http://dx.doi.org/10.1177/0146167291176015

Caldwell, B. E. (2015). *Saving psychotherapy: How therapists can bring the talking cure back from the brink*. Los Angeles, CA: Benjamin Caldwell.

Cawley, J., & Meyerhoefer, C. (2012). The medical care costs of obesity: An instrumental variables approach. *Journal of Health Economics, 31*, 219–230. http://dx.doi.org/10.1016/j.jhealeco.2011.10.003

Ceci, S. J., Barnett, S. M., & Kanaya, T. (2003). Developing childhood proclivities into adult competencies: The overlooked multiplier effect. In R. J. Sternberg & E. L. Grigorenko (Eds.), *The psychology of abilities, competencies, and expertise* (pp. 70–92). New York, NY: Cambridge University Press. http://dx.doi.org/10.1017/CBO9780511615801.005

Chambless, D., Baker, M. J., Baucom, D. H., Beutler, L. E., Calhoun, K. S., Crits-Christoph, P., . . . Sheila, R. W. (1998). Update on empirically validated therapies II. *Clinical Psychologist, 51,* 3–16.

Chambless, D. L., & Hollon, S. D. (1998). Defining empirically supported therapies. *Journal of Consulting and Clinical Psychology, 66,* 7–18. http://dx.doi.org/10.1037/0022-006X.66.1.7

Chandler, A. (2019, July 20). Five myths about fast food [Opinion]. *The Washington Post.* Retrieved from https://www.newsday.com/opinion/commentary/fast-food-myths-chandler-1.33941915

Charness, N., Krampe, R., & Mayr, U. (1996). The role of practice and coaching in entrepreneurial skill domains: An international comparison of life-span chess skill acquisition. In K. A. Ericsson (Ed.), *The road to excellence: The acquisition of expert performance in the arts and sciences, sports, and games* (pp. 51–80). Mahwah, NJ: Erlbaum.

Charness, N., Tuffiash, M., Krampe, R., Reingold, E., & Vasyukova, E. (2005). The role of deliberate practice in chess expertise. *Applied Cognitive Psychology, 19,* 151–165. http://dx.doi.org/10.1002/acp.1106

Charney, N. (2017, July 14). Khaled Hosseini: How I write [Interview]. *The Daily Beast.* Retrieved from https://www.thedailybeast.com/khaled-hosseini-how-i-write

Cheng, V. (2016, May 27). *There's nothing wrong with finding out you're completely average.* Retrieved from https://www.elitedaily.com/life/why-its-ok-to-be-average/1504992

Cheung, T. (2006). *Element encyclopedia of the psychic world: The ultimate A–Z of spirits, mysteries and the paranormal* (1st ed.). New York, NY: HarperCollinsElement.

Chow, D. (2014a). *The study of supershrinks: Development and deliberate practices of highly effective psychotherapists.* (Doctoral dissertation, Curtin University, Australia). Retrieved from http://hdl.handle.net/20.500.11937/45

Chow, D. (2014b, April 22). Therapy learnings: A memorable practice [Blog post]. Retrieved from https://darylchow.com/frontiers/therapy-learnings/

Chow, D. (2016a, April 13). *"Angry Annie" difficult conversations in therapy project video #1* [Video file]. Retrieved from https://www.youtube.com/watch?v=pgJj288Xw_g&feature=youtu.be

Chow, D. (2016b, October 22). Scenius vs. genius [Blog post]. Retrieved from https://darylchow.com/frontiers/scenius-vs-genius/

Chow, D. (2017a, October 6). Develop your own wealth of learnings [Blog post]. Retrieved from https://darylchow.com/frontiers/develop-your-own-wealth-of-learnings/

Chow, D. (2017b, October 27). Develop first principles before the methods [Blog post]. Retrieved from https://darylchow.com/frontiers/develop-first-principles-before-the-methods/

Chow, D. (2017c, November 10). First principles: The 5-step process for deep and accelerated learning in therapy [Blog post]. Retrieved from https://darylchow.com/frontiers/first-principles-5-steps/

Chow, D. (2018a, March 26). Blackbox thinking for psychotherapists (part I of II) [Blog post]. Retrieved from https://darylchow.com/frontiers/blackbox-thinking-for-psychotherapists-part-i-of-ii/

Chow, D. (2018b). *The first kiss: Undoing the intake model and igniting first sessions in psychotherapy*. Perth, Australia: Correlate Press.

Chow, D. (2018c, October 9). Instead of the "10,000" hour rule, why not the "60" hour rule? [Blog post]. Retrieved from https://darylchow.com/frontiers/the-60-hour-rule/

Chow, D. (2018d). Reigniting clinical supervision: An in-depth online course. Retrieved from https://darylchow.com/courses

Chow, D., Lu, S., Miller, S. D., Kwek, T., Jones, A., & Tan, G. (2019). *Improving therapists' ability through deliberate practice: The difficult conversations in therapy (DCT) randomized clinical trial*. Manuscript in preparation.

Chow, D., & Miller, S. D. (2015). *Taxonomy of deliberate practice activities worksheets*. Chicago, IL: International Center for Clinical Excellence.

Chow, D. L., Miller, S. D., Seidel, J. A., Kane, R. T., Thornton, J. A., & Andrews, W. P. (2015). The role of deliberate practice in the development of highly effective psychotherapists. *Psychotherapy, 52,* 337–345. http://dx.doi.org/10.1037/pst0000015

Colvin, G. (2009). *Talent is overrated: What really separates world-class performers from everybody else*. New York, NY: Portfolio/Penguin.

Connolly Gibbons, M. B., Rothbard, A., Farris, K. D., Wiltsey Stirman, S., Thompson, S. M., Scott, K., . . . Crits-Christoph, P. (2011). Changes in psychotherapy utilization among consumers of services for major depressive disorder in the community mental health system. *Administration and Policy in Mental Health and Mental Health Services Research, 38,* 495–503. http://dx.doi.org/10.1007/s10488-011-0336-1

Constantino, M. J., Boswell, J. F., Coyne, A. E., Kraus, D. R., & Castonguay, L. G. (2017). Who works for whom and why? Integrating therapist effects analysis into psychotherapy outcome and process research. In L. G. Castonguay & C. E. Hill (Eds.), *How and why are some therapists better than others? Understanding therapist effects* (pp. 55–68). Washington, DC: American Psychological Association. http://dx.doi.org/10.1037/0000034-004

Cook, J. (2007). *The book of positive quotations* (2nd ed.). Minneapolis, MN: Fairview Press.

Corcoran, K., & Fischer, J. (2013). *Measures for clinical practice and research: A sourcebook* (5th ed.). Oxford, England: Oxford University Press.

Cornelius-White, J. H. D., Kanamori, Y., Murphy, D., & Tickle, E. (2018). Mutuality in psychotherapy: A meta-analysis and meta-synthesis. *Journal of Psychotherapy Integration, 28,* 489–504. http://dx.doi.org/10.1037/int0000134

Côté, J., Ericsson, K., & Law, M. P. (2005). Tracing the development of athletes using retrospective interview methods: A proposed interview and validation procedure for reported information. *Journal of Applied Sport Psychology, 17,* 1–19. http://dx.doi.org/10.1080/10413200590907531

Covey, S. R. (1990). *Principle-centered leadership*. New York, NY: Rosetta Books.

Coyle, D. (2009). *The talent code: Greatness isn't born, it's grown, here's how*. New York, NY: Bantam Books.

Coyne, A. E., Muir, H. A., Westra, H. A., Antony, M. M., & Constantino, M. J. (2018, November). *Uncovering trainable therapist effects*. Retrieved from https://www.societyforpsychotherapy.org/uncovering-trainable-therapist-effects-2

Curry, C. (2014, May 28). Maya Angelou's wisdom distilled in 10 of her best quotes. *ABCNews.* Retrieved from https://abcnews.go.com/Entertainment/maya-angelous-wisdom-distilled-10-best-quotes/story?id=23895284

Day is New Creative. (2015, March 2). Creativity is not just for artists [Blog post]. Retrieved from https://dayisnewcreative.com/creativity-not-just-artists/

Deakin, J., & Cobley, S. (2003). A search for deliberate practice: An examination of the practice environments in figure skating and volleyball. In J. L. Starkes & K. A. Ericsson (Eds.), *Expert performance in sports: Advances in research on sport expertise* (pp. 115–136). Champaign, IL: Human Kinetics.

DeAngelis, T. (2017, November). PTSD guideline ready for use. *Monitor on Psychology.* Retrieved from https://www.apa.org/monitor/2017/11/ptsd-guideline

DeJong, H., Broadbent, H., & Schmidt, U. (2012). A systematic review of dropout from treatment in outpatients with anorexia nervosa. *International Journal of Eating Disorders, 45,* 635–647. http://dx.doi.org/10.1002/eat.20956

Devlin, H. (2017, April 25). *"Granny style" is best way to take a basketball free throw, study shows.* Retrieved from https://www.theguardian.com/science/2017/apr/26/granny-style-is-best-way-to-take-a-basketball-free-throw-study-shows

Diamond, D. (2013, January 1). *Just 8% of people achieve their new year's resolutions. Here's how they do it.* Retrieved from https://www.forbes.com/sites/dandiamond/2013/01/01/just-8-of-people-achieve-their-new-years-resolutions-heres-how-they-did-it/#122467be596b

DiCarlo, R. C. (2018). Collaborative documentation: The impact of shared record keeping on therapeutic alliance. *Dissertation Abstracts International: B. Sciences and Engineering, 78*(10-B[E]).

Dick, P. K. (1995). *The shifting realities of Philip K. Dick: Selected literary and philosophical writings.* New York, NY: Vintage Books.

Diener, E., Oishi, S., & Tay, L. (2018). Advances in subjective well-being research. *Nature Human Behaviour, 2,* 253–260. http://dx.doi.org/10.1038/s41562-018-0307-6

Divinity school address by Ralph Waldo Emerson [Essay]. (n.d.). Retrieved from https://emersoncentral.com/texts/nature-addresses-lectures/addresses/divinity-school-address/

Doran, G. T. (1981). There's a S.M.A.R.T. way to write management's goals and objectives. *Management Review, 70*(11), 35–36.

Downar, J., Bhatt, M., & Montague, P. R. (2011). Neural correlates of effective learning in experienced medical decision-makers. *PLOS ONE, 6,* e27768. http://dx.doi.org/10.1371/journal.pone.0027768

Dragioti, E., Dimoliatis, I., Fountoulakis, K. N., & Evangelou, E. (2015). A systematic appraisal of allegiance effect in randomized controlled trials of psychotherapy. *Annals of General Psychiatry, 14,* Article 25. http://dx.doi.org/10.1186/s12991-015-0063-1

Drinane, J. M., Winderman, K., Roberts, T. S., Frierson Freeman, V., & Wang, Y. (2019). *Sexual identity disparities within therapist caseloads in a university counseling center.* Manuscript in preparation.

Duchon, D., & Burns, M. (2008). Organizational narcissism. *Organizational Dynamics, 37,* 354–364. http://dx.doi.org/10.1016/j.orgdyn.2008.07.004

Duckworth, E. (1964). Piaget rediscovered. *The Arithmetic Teacher, 11,* 496–499. Retrieved from https://www.jstor.org/stable/41186862

Duke, A. (2018). *Thinking in bets: Making smarter decisions when you don't have all the facts.* New York, NY: Penguin Random House.

Duncan, B. L., Hubble, M. A., & Miller, S. D. (1997). *Psychotherapy with "impossible" cases: The efficient treatment of therapy veterans.* New York, NY: Norton.

Duncan, B. L., & Miller, S. D. (2000). The client's theory of change: Consulting the client in the integrative process. *Journal of Psychotherapy Integration, 10,* 169–187. Retrieved from https://betteroutcomesnow.com/wp-content/uploads/2018/01/clients-theory-of-change.pdf

Duncan, B. L., Miller, S. D., & Sparks, J. A. (2004). *The heroic client: A revolutionary way to improve effectiveness through client-directed, outcome-informed therapy* (Rev. ed.). San Francisco, CA: Jossey-Bass.

Duncan, B. L., Miller, S. D., Wampold, B. E., & Hubble, M. A. (Eds.). (2010). *The heart and soul of change: Delivering what works in therapy* (2nd ed.). Washington, DC: American Psychological Association. http://dx.doi.org/10.1037/12075-000

Eco, U. (2007). *Foucault's pendulum* (W. Weaver, Trans.). New York, NY: Harcourt Books.

Ellentuck, M. (2017, November 4). *How Andre Drummond suddenly went from the NBA's worst free-throw shooter to a good one.* Retrieved from https://www.sbnation.com/2017/11/4/16606402/andre-drummond-free-throws-stats-how-is-he-making-them-now-lol

Ellick, A. B. (2001, March 1). Emil Zátopek, 1922–2000 [Obituary]. *Runner's World.* Retrieved from https://www.runnersworld.com/advanced/a20841849/emil-zatopek/

Elliott, R., Bohart, A. C., Watson, J. C., & Greenberg, L. S. (2011). Empathy. *Psychotherapy, 48,* 43–49. http://dx.doi.org/10.1037/a0022187

Elliott, R., Watson, J. C., Goldman, R. N., & Greenberg, L. S. (2004). *Learning emotion-focused therapy: The process-experiential approach to change.* Washington, DC: American Psychological Association.

Emerson, R. W. (1860). *The conduct of life.* Boston, MA: Osgood.

Eno, B. (2009). A press conference with the luminous Sydney festival curator, Brian Eno. Retrieved from http://www.moredarkthanshark.org/feature_luminous2.html

Erekson, D. M., Clayson, R., Park, S. Y., & Tass, S. (2018). Therapist effects on early change in psychotherapy in a naturalistic setting. *Psychotherapy Research, 14,* 1–11. http://dx.doi.org/10.1080/10503307.2018.1556824

Erekson, D. M., Lambert, M. J., & Eggett, D. L. (2015). The relationship between session frequency and psychotherapy outcome in a naturalistic setting. *Journal of Consulting and Clinical Psychology, 83,* 1097–1107. http://dx.doi.org/10.1037/a0039774

Ericsson, K. A. (1996). The acquisition of expert performance: An introduction to some of the issues. In K. A. Ericsson (Ed.), *The road to excellence: The acquisition of expert performance in the arts and sciences, sports, and games* (pp. 1–50). Mahwah, NJ: Erlbaum.

Ericsson, K. A. (2004). Deliberate practice and the acquisition and maintenance of expert performance in medicine and related domains. *Academic Medicine, 79,* S70–S81. Advance online publication. http://dx.doi.org/10.1097/00001888-200410001-00022

Ericsson, K. A. (2006). The influence of experience and deliberate practice on the development of superior expert performance. In K. A. Ericsson, N. Charness,

P. J. Feltovich, & R. R. Hoffman (Eds.), *The Cambridge handbook of expertise and expert performance* (pp. 683–704). Cambridge, England: Cambridge University Press. http://dx.doi.org/10.1017/CBO9780511816796.038

Ericsson, K. A. (2007). Toward a science of expert and exceptional performance in sport: A reply to the Commentaries. *International Journal of Sport Psychology, 38*(1), 109–123.

Ericsson, K. A. (2009). Enhancing the development of professional performance: Implications from the study of deliberate practice. In K. A. Ericsson (Ed.), *Development of professional expertise: Toward measurement of expert performance and design of optimal learning environments* (pp. 405–431). Cambridge, England: Cambridge University Press. http://dx.doi.org/10.1017/CBO9780511609817.022

Ericsson, K. A. (2014). Why expert performance is special and cannot be extrapolated from studies of performance in the general population: A response to criticisms. *Intelligence, 45,* 81–103. http://dx.doi.org/10.1016/j.intell.2013.12.001

Ericsson, K. A. (2016). Summing up hours of any type of practice versus identifying optimal practice activities: Commentary on Macnamara, Moreau, & Hambrick (2016). *Perspectives on Psychological Science, 11,* 351–354. http://dx.doi.org/10.1177/1745691616635600

Ericsson, K. A. (2018). The differential influence of experience, practice, and deliberate practice on the development of superior individual performance of experts. In K. A. Ericsson, R. R. Hoffman, A. Kozbelt, & A. M. Williams (Eds.), *The Cambridge handbook of expertise and expert performance* (2nd ed., pp. 745–769). Cambridge, England: Cambridge University Press. http://dx.doi.org/10.1017/9781316480748.038

Ericsson, K. A., & Charness, N. (1994). Expert performance: Its structure and acquisition. *American Psychologist, 49,* 725–747. http://dx.doi.org/10.1037/0003-066X.49.8.725

Ericsson, K. A., Charness, N., Feltovich, P. J., & Hoffman, R. R. (Eds.). (2006). *The Cambridge handbook of expertise and expert performance.* Cambridge, England: Cambridge University Press. http://dx.doi.org/10.1017/CBO9780511816796

Ericsson, K. A., Chase, W. G., & Faloon, S. (1980). Acquisition of a memory skill. *Science, 208,* 1181–1182. Retrieved from https://apps.dtic.mil/dtic/tr/fulltext/u2/a084754.pdf

Ericsson, K. A., Hoffman, R. R., Kozbelt, A., & Williams, A. M. (Eds.). (2018). *The Cambridge handbook of expertise and expert performance* (2nd ed.). Cambridge, England: Cambridge University Press. http://dx.doi.org/10.1017/9781316480748

Ericsson, K. A., Krampe, R. T., & Tesch-Römer, C. (1993). The role of deliberate practice in the acquisition of expert performance. *Psychological Review, 100,* 363–406. http://dx.doi.org/10.1037/0033-295X.100.3.363

Ericsson, K. A., & Lehmann, A. C. (1996). Expert and exceptional performance: Evidence of maximal adaptation to task constraints. *Annual Review of Psychology, 47,* 273–305. http://dx.doi.org/10.1146/annurev.psych.47.1.273

Ericsson, K. A., & Pool, R. (2016). *Peak: Secrets from the new science of expertise.* Boston, MA: Houghton Mifflin Harcourt.

Eubanks, C. F., Muran, J. C., & Safran, J. D. (2018). Alliance rupture repair: A meta-analysis. *Psychotherapy, 55,* 508–519. http://dx.doi.org/10.1037/pst0000185

Eugster, S. L., & Wampold, B. E. (1996). Systematic effects of participant role on evaluation of the psychotherapy session. *Journal of Consulting and Clinical Psychology, 64,* 1020–1028. http://dx.doi.org/10.1037/0022-006X.64.5.1020

Eysenck, H. J. (1952). The effects of psychotherapy: An evaluation. *Journal of Consulting Psychology, 16,* 319–324. http://dx.doi.org/10.1037/h0063633

Fancher, R. (1995). *Cultures of healing: Correcting the image of American health care.* New York, NY: Freeman.

Feifel, H., & Eells, J. (1963). Patients and therapists assess the same psychotherapy. *Journal of Consulting Psychology, 27,* 310–318. http://dx.doi.org/10.1037/h0046645

Feltovich, P. J., Prietula, M. J., & Ericsson, K. A. (2018). Studies of expertise from psychological perspectives: Historical foundations and recurrent themes. In K. A. Ericsson, R. R. Hoffman, A. Kozbelt, & A. M. Williams (Eds.), *The Cambridge handbook of expertise and expert performance* (2nd ed., pp. 59–83). Cambridge, England: Cambridge University Press. http://dx.doi.org/10.1017/9781316480748.006

Ferro, S. (2014, March 12). *Practice does not make perfect. Scientists debunk the myth that 10,000 hours of practice makes you an expert.* Retrieved from https://www.fastcompany.com/3027564/scientists-debunk-the-myth-that-10000-hours-of-practice-makes-you-an-expert

Fixsen, D. L., Blase, K. A., Naoom, S. F., & Wallace, F. (2009). Core implementation components. *Research on Social Work Practice, 19,* 531–540. http://dx.doi.org/10.1177/1049731509335549

Fleming, J. H., & Asplund, J. (2007). *Human sigma: Managing the employee-customer encounter.* New York, NY: Gallup Press.

Flor, J. A. (2016). De har i alle fall ikke blitt dårligere, har jeg trodd: en kvalitativ studieav psykologers perspektiv på forverring i terapi. [At least it's not gotten worse: A qualitative study of psychologists' perspectives on deterioration in psychotherapy.] (Unpublished master's thesis). Norwegian University of Science and Technology, Trondheim. Retrieved from https://ntnuopen.ntnu.no/ntnu-xmlui/bitstream/handle/11250/2401808/Flor,%20J%C3%B8rgen.pdf?sequence=1

Flückiger, C., Del Re, A. C., Horvath, A. O., Symonds, D., Ackert, M., & Wampold, B. E. (2013). Substance use disorders and racial/ethnic minorities matter: A meta-analytic examination of the relation between alliance and outcome. *Journal of Counseling Psychology, 60,* 610–616. http://dx.doi.org/10.1037/a0033161

Flückiger, C., Del Re, A. C., Wampold, B. E., & Horvath, A. O. (2018). The alliance in adult psychotherapy: A meta-analytic synthesis. *Psychotherapy, 55,* 316–340. http://dx.doi.org/10.1037/pst0000172

Foer, J. (2011). *Moonwalking with Einstein: The art and science of remembering everything.* London, England: Penguin Books.

Foster, K. R., & Kokko, H. (2008). The evolution of superstitious and superstition-like behaviour. *Proceedings of The Royal Society B: Biological Sciences, 276*(1654), 31–37. http://dx.doi.org/10.1098/rspb.2008.0981

Fractions of a second: An Olympic musical. (2010, February 26). *The New York Times.* Retrieved from https://archive.nytimes.com/www.nytimes.com/interactive/2010/02/26/sports/olympics/20100226-olysymphony.html?

Freud, S. (1953). Instincts and their vicissitudes. In E. Jones (Ed.), *Collected papers* (Vol. 4, pp. 60–83). London, England: Hogarth Press.

Froyd, J. E., Lambert, M. J., & Froyd, J. D. (1996). A review of practices of psychotherapy outcome measurement. *Journal of Mental Health, 5,* 11–16. http://dx.doi.org/10.1080/09638239650037144

Fuertes, J. N., Stracuzzi, T. I., Bennett, J., Scheinholz, J., Mislowack, A., Hersh, M., & Cheng, D. (2007). "Therapist multicultural competency: A study of therapy dyads": Correction. *Psychotherapy, 44,* 13. http://dx.doi.org/10.1037/0033-3204.44.1.13

Galili-Weinstock, L., Chen, R., Atzil-Slonim, D., Bar-Kalifa, E., Peri, T., & Rafaeli, E. (2018). The association between self-compassion and treatment outcomes: Session-level and treatment-level effects. *Journal of Clinical Psychology, 74,* 849–866. http://dx.doi.org/10.1002/jclp.22569

Gallimore, R., & Tharp, R. (2004). What a coach can teach a teacher, 1975–2004: Reflections and reanalysis of John Wooden's teaching practices. *Sport Psychologist, 18,* 119–137. http://dx.doi.org/10.1123/tsp.18.2.119

Gan, M., & Chen, S. (2017, February 13). *Being your actual or ideal self? What it means to feel authentic in a relationship. Personality and Social Psychology Bulletin, 43,* 465–478. http://dx.doi.org/10.1177/0146167216688211

Gardner, H. (1995). "Expert performance: Its structure and acquisition": Comment. *American Psychologist, 50,* 802–803. http://dx.doi.org/10.1037/0003-066X.50.9.802

Garfield, S. L. (1978). Research on client variables in psychotherapy. In S. L. Garfield & A. E. Bergin (Eds.), *Handbook of psychotherapy and behavior change* (2nd ed., pp. 191–232). New York, NY: Wiley.

Garfield, S. L. (1997). The therapist as a neglected variable in psychotherapy research. *Clinical Psychology: Science and Practice, 4,* 40–43. http://dx.doi.org/10.1111/j.1468-2850.1997.tb00097.x

Gates, B. (2013, May). *Teachers need real feedback* [Video file]. Retrieved from https://www.ted.com/talks/bill_gates_teachers_need_real_feedback

Geller, J. D., Norcross, J. C., & Orlinsky, D. E. (Eds.). (2005). *The psychotherapist's own psychotherapy: Patient and clinician perspectives.* Oxford, England: Oxford University Press.

Geneen, H. (1984). *Managing.* Garden City, NY: Doubleday.

Gibb, N. L. (2019, February 10). *5-point descent in diving.* Retrieved from https://www.thoughtco.com/five-point-descent-2963288

Gick, M. L., & Holyoak, K. J. (1983). Schema induction and analogical transfer. *Cognitive Psychology, 15,* 1–38. http://dx.doi.org/10.1016/0010-0285(83)90002-6

Gilovich, T. (1991). *How we know what isn't so: The fallibility of human reason in everyday life.* New York, NY: Simon & Schuster.

Gilovich, T., Griffin, D., & Kahneman, D. (2002). *Heuristics and biases: The psychology of intuitive judgment.* Cambridge, England: Cambridge University Press. http://dx.doi.org/10.1017/CBO9780511808098

Gingerich, W. J., & Eisengart, S. (2000). Solution-focused brief therapy: A review of the outcome research. *Family Process, 39,* 477–498. http://dx.doi.org/10.1111/j.1545-5300.2000.39408.x

Gladwell, M. (2008). *Outliers: The story of success.* New York, NY: Little, Brown.

Gobet, F., & Charness, N. (2018). Expertise in chess. In K. A. Ericsson, R. R. Hoffman, A. Kozbelt, & A. M. Williams (Eds.), *The Cambridge handbook of expertise and expert performance* (2nd ed., pp. 597–615). Cambridge, England: Cambridge University Press. http://dx.doi.org/10.1017/9781316480748.031

Goldberg, S. B., Babins-Wagner, R., Rousmaniere, T., Berzins, S., Hoyt, W. T., Whipple, J. L., . . . Wampold, B. E. (2016). Creating a climate for therapist improvement: A case study of an agency focused on outcomes and deliberate practice. *Psychotherapy, 53,* 367–375. http://dx.doi.org/10.1037/pst0000060

Goldberg, S. B., Hoyt, W. T., Nissen-Lie, H. A., Nielsen, S. L., & Wampold, B. E. (2018). Unpacking the therapist effect: Impact of treatment length differs for high- and low-performing therapists. *Psychotherapy Research, 28,* 532–544. http://dx.doi.org/10.1080/10503307.2016.1216625

Goldberg, S. B., Rousmaniere, T., Miller, S. D., Whipple, J., Nielsen, S. L., Hoyt, W. T., & Wampold, B. E. (2016). Do psychotherapists improve with time and experience? A longitudinal analysis of outcomes in a clinical setting. *Journal of Counseling Psychology, 63,* 1–11. http://dx.doi.org/10.1037/cou0000131

Goldman, R., & Papson, S. (1998). *NIKE culture: The sign of the swoosh.* London, England: Sage.

Gracián, G. (1904). *The art of worldly wisdom* (J. Jacobs, Trans.). New York, NY: Macmillan. (Original work published 1653)

Graham, B. A. (2013, March 6). Here are 16 things you probably don't know about Shaq, who turns 41 today. *Sports Illustrated.* Retrieved from https://www.si.com/extra-mustard/2013/03/06/here-are-16-things-you-probably-dont-know-about-shaq-who-turns-41-today

Graham, S., & Golan, S. (1991). Motivational influences on cognition: Task involvement, ego involvement, and depth of information processing. *Journal of Educational Psychology, 83,* 187–194. http://dx.doi.org/10.1037/0022-0663.83.2.187

Greenberg, L. S. (2002). *Emotion-focused therapy: Coaching clients to work through their feelings.* Washington, DC: American Psychological Association. http://dx.doi.org/10.1037/10447-000

Griffin, S. O., Regnier, E., Griffin, P. M., & Huntley, V. (2007). Effectiveness of fluoride in preventing caries in adults. *Journal of Dental Research, 86,* 410–415. http://dx.doi.org/10.1177/154405910708600504

Griffiths, J. (2018, January 2). Falling at the first hurdle: What are the most common New Year's resolutions and how long do people usually keep to them? *The Sun.* Retrieved from https://www.thesun.co.uk/fabulous/2489711/new-years-resolutions-2018-how-long-kept/

Griffiths, S., & Steen, S. (2013). Improving access to psychological therapies (IAPT) programme: Scrutinising IAPT cost estimates to support effective commissioning. *Journal of Psychological Therapies in Primary Care, 2,* 142–156.

Haley, A. (2014, December 9). *The 5 elements of a successful speed training program.* Retrieved from https://www.stack.com/a/speed-training-program

Hambrick, D. Z., Ferreira, F., & Henderson, J. M. (2014, September 28). Practice does not make perfect. *Slate.* Retrieved from https://slate.com/technology/2014/09/malcolm-gladwells-10000-hour-rule-for-deliberate-practice-is-wrong-genes-for-music-iq-drawing-ability-and-other-skills.html

Hannan, C., Lambert, M. J., Harmon, C., Nielsen, S. L., Smart, D. W., Shimokawa, K., & Sutton, S. W. (2005). A lab test and algorithms for identifying clients at risk for treatment failure. *Journal of Clinical Psychology, 61,* 155–163. http://dx.doi.org/10.1002/jclp.20108

Hansen, N. B., Lambert, M. J., & Forman, E. M. (2002). The psychotherapy dose-response effect and its implications for treatment delivery services. *Clinical Psychology: Science and Practice, 9,* 329–343. http://dx.doi.org/10.1093/clipsy.9.3.329

Hardwood and Hollywood Staff. (2018, April 12). *The unknown hobbies of top athletes.* Retrieved from https://www.hardwoodandhollywood.com/2018/04/12/unknown-hobbies-top-athletes/

Hatfield, D. R., & Ogles, B. M. (2004). The use of outcome measures by psychologists in clinical practice. *Professional Psychology: Research and Practice, 35,* 485–491. http://dx.doi.org/10.1037/0735-7028.35.5.485

Hayes, J. A., McAleavey, A. A., Castonguay, L. G., & Locke, B. D. (2016). Psychotherapists' outcomes with White and racial/ethnic minority clients: First, the good news. *Journal of Counseling Psychology, 63,* 261–268. http://dx.doi.org/10.1037/cou0000098

Hayes, J. A., Owen, J., & Bieschke, K. J. (2015). Therapist differences in symptom change with racial/ethnic minority clients. *Psychotherapy, 52,* 308–314. http://dx.doi.org/10.1037/a0037957

Hayes, J. A., Owen, J., & Nissen-Lie, H. A. (2017). The contributions of client culture to differential therapist effectiveness. In L. G. Castonguay & C. E. Hill (Eds.), *How and why are some therapists better than others? Understanding therapist effects* (pp. 159–174). Washington, DC: American Psychological Association. http://dx.doi.org/10.1037/0000034-010

Health Insurance Portability and Accountability Act of 1996, Pub. L. No. 104–191, 110 Stat. 1936 (1996).

Heisenberg, W. (1958). *Physics and philosophy: The revolution in modern science* [Lectures delivered at University of St. Andrews, Scotland, Winter 1955–56]. New York, NY: Harper and Row.

Helen Keller International. (n.d.). Careers: Impact. Access. Influence. Retrieved from https://www.hki.org/about-us/careers#.Xd7s9-hKiUm

Hiatt, D., & Hargrave, G. E. (1995). The characteristics of highly effective therapists in managed behavioral provider networks. *Behavioral Healthcare Tomorrow, 4,* 19–22.

Hill, C. E., & Castonguay, L. G. (2017). Therapist effects: Integration and conclusions (pp. 325–341). In L. G. Castonguay & C. E. Hill (Eds.), *How and why are some therapists better than others? Understanding therapist effects.* Washington, DC: American Psychological Association. http://dx.doi.org/10.1037/0000034-000

Hill, C. E., Knox, S., & Pinto-Coelho, K. G. (2018). Therapist self-disclosure and immediacy: A qualitative meta-analysis. *Psychotherapy, 55,* 445–460. http://dx.doi.org/10.1037/pst0000182

Hill, N. M., & Schneider, W. (2006). Brain changes in the development of expertise: Neuroanatomical and neurophysiological evidence about skill-based adaptations. In K. A. Ericsson, N. Charness, P. J. Feltovich, & R. R. Hoffman (Eds.), *The Cambridge handbook of expertise and expert performance* (pp. 653–682). Cambridge, England: Cambridge University Press. http://dx.doi.org/10.1017/CBO9780511816796.037

Hilmantel, R. (2016, May 12). 4 signs you have grit. *Time.* Retrieved from https://time.com/4327035/4-signs-you-have-grit/

Holt-Lunstad, J., Smith, T. B., Baker, M., Harris, T., & Stephenson, D. (2015). Loneliness and social isolation as risk factors for mortality: A meta-analytic review. *Perspectives on Psychological Science, 10,* 227–237. http://dx.doi.org/10.1177/1745691614568352

Holt-Lunstad, J., Smith, T. B., & Layton, J. B. (2010). Social relationships and mortality risk: A meta-analytic review. *PLOS Medicine, 7,* e1000316. http://dx.doi.org/10.1371/journal.pmed.1000316

Hubble, M. A., Duncan, B. L., & Miller, S. D. (Eds.). (1999). *The heart and soul of change: What works in therapy.* Washington, DC: American Psychological Association.

Hubble, M. A., Duncan, B. L., Miller, S. D., & Wampold, B. E. (2010). Introduction. In B. L. Duncan, S. D. Miller, B. E. Wampold, & M. A. Hubble (Eds.), *The heart and soul of change: Delivering what works in therapy* (2nd ed., pp. 23–46). Washington, DC: American Psychological Association. http://dx.doi.org/10.1037/12075-001

Hunt, E. (2006). Expertise, talent, and social encouragement. In K. A. Ericsson, N. Charness, P. J. Feltovich, & R. R. Hoffman (Eds.), *The Cambridge handbook of expertise and expert performance* (pp. 31–38). Cambridge, England: Cambridge University Press. http://dx.doi.org/10.1017/CBO9780511816796.003

Hysong, S. J. (2009). Meta-analysis: Audit and feedback features impact effectiveness on care quality. *Medical Care, 47*, 356–363. http://dx.doi.org/10.1097/MLR.0b013e3181893f6b

Imel, Z. E., Baldwin, S., Atkins, D. C., Owen, J., Baardseth, T., & Wampold, B. E. (2011). Racial/ethnic disparities in therapist effectiveness: A conceptualization and initial study of cultural competence. *Journal of Counseling Psychology, 58*, 290–298. http://dx.doi.org/10.1037/a0023284

Imel, Z. E., Sheng, E., Baldwin, S. A., & Atkins, D. C. (2015). Removing very low-performing therapists: A simulation of performance-based retention in psychotherapy. *Psychotherapy, 52*(3), 329–336. http://dx.doi.org/10.1037/pst0000023

Imel, Z. E., Wampold, B. E., Miller, S. D., & Fleming, R. R. (2008). Distinctions without a difference: Direct comparisons of psychotherapies for alcohol use disorders. *Psychology of Addictive Behaviors, 22*, 533–543. http://dx.doi.org/10.1037/a0013171

Ivers, N., Jamtvedt, G., Flottorp, S., Young, J. M., Odgaard-Jensen, J., French, S. D., . . . Oxman, A. D. (2012). Audit and feedback: Effects on professional practice and healthcare outcomes. *Cochrane Database of Systematic Reviews, 2012*(6), CD000259. http://dx.doi.org/10.1002/14651858.CD000259.pub3

Jacobson, N. S., Follette, W. C., & Revenstorf, D. (1984). Psychotherapy outcome research: Methods for reporting variability and evaluating clinical significance. *Behavior Therapy, 15*, 336–352. http://dx.doi.org/10.1016/S0005-7894(84)80002-7

Jacobson, N. S., & Truax, P. (1991). Clinical significance: A statistical approach to defining meaningful change in psychotherapy research. *Journal of Consulting and Clinical Psychology, 59*, 12–19. http://dx.doi.org/10.1037/0022-006X.59.1.12

Jevremovic, T. (2005). *Nuclear principles in engineering.* New York, NY: Springer.

Johns, R. G., Barkham, M., Kellett, S., & Saxon, D. (2019). A systematic review of therapist effects: A critical narrative update and refinement to Baldwin and Imel's (2013) review. *Clinical Psychology Review, 67*, 78–93. http://dx.doi.org/10.1016/j.cpr.2018.08.004

Johnson, S. (1751). *The rambler.* New York, NY: Argiope.

The joke. (n.d.). [Blog post.] Retrieved from https://www.carnegiehall.org/Blog/2016/04/The-Joke

Jones, M., & Silberzahn, P. (2016, March 15). Without an opinion, you're just another person with data. *Forbes.* Retrieved from https://www.forbes.com/sites/silberzahnjones/2016/03/15/without-an-opinion-youre-just-another-person-with-data/#3c202128699f

Joyce, J. (1946). *Ulysses.* New York, NY: Random House. (Original work published 1922)

Kahn, C., & Pike, K. M. (2001). In search of predictors of dropout from inpatient treatment for anorexia nervosa. *International Journal of Eating Disorders, 30*, 237–244.

Kahneman, D. (2011). *Thinking, fast and slow*. New York, NY: Farrar, Straus and Giroux.

Kalla, S. (2012, May 31). Keys to excellence (even Michael Jordan had to do it). *Forbes*. Retrieved from https://www.forbes.com/sites/susankalla/2012/05/31/six-keys-to-excellence-at-anything/#7f67457422f2

Kaslow, F. W., & Patterson, T. (Eds.). (2002). *Comprehensive handbook of psychotherapy: Cognitive-behavioral approaches* (Vol. 2). Hoboken, NJ: Wiley.

Kesebir, P. (2014). A quiet ego quiets death anxiety: Humility as an existential anxiety buffer. *Journal of Personality and Social Psychology, 106,* 610–623. http://dx.doi.org/10.1037/a0035814

Klaas, J. (1982). *The twelve steps to happiness: A handbook for all twelve steppers.* New York, NY: Ballentine Books.

Klein, G. (1998). *Sources of power: How people make decisions*. Cambridge, England: MIT Press.

Klein, G. (2013). *Seeing what others don't: The remarkable ways we gain insights.* New York, NY: PublicAffairs.

Kluger, A. N., & DeNisi, A. (1996). Effects of feedback intervention on performance: A historical review, a meta-analysis, and a preliminary feedback intervention theory. *Psychological Bulletin, 119,* 254–284. http://dx.doi.org/10.1037/0033-2909.119.2.254

Kolden, G. G., Wang, C. C., Austin, S. B., Chang, Y., & Klein, M. H. (2018). Congruence/genuineness: A meta-analysis. *Psychotherapy, 55,* 424–433. http://dx.doi.org/10.1037/pst0000162

Kopp, S. (1972). *If you meet the Buddha on the road, kill him! The pilgrimage of psychotherapy patients.* Palo Alto, CA: Science and Behavior Books.

Kostich, A. (2017, October 8). *10 elements of a perfect freestyle stroke*. Retrieved from https://www.active.com/triathlon/articles/10-elements-of-a-perfect-freestyle-stroke

Krampe, R. T., & Ericsson, K. A. (1996). Maintaining excellence: Deliberate practice and elite performance in young and older pianists. *Journal of Experimental Psychology: General, 125,* 331–359. http://dx.doi.org/10.1037/0096-3445.125.4.331

Kraus, D. R., Bentley, J. H., Alexander, P. C., Boswell, J. F., Constantino, M. J., Baxter, E. E., & Castonguay, L. G. (2016). Predicting therapist effectiveness from their own practice-based evidence. *Journal of Consulting and Clinical Psychology, 84,* 473–483. http://dx.doi.org/10.1037/ccp0000083

Kraus, D. R., Castonguay, L., Boswell, J. F., Nordberg, S. S., & Hayes, J. A. (2011). Therapist effectiveness: Implications for accountability and patient care. *Psychotherapy Research, 21,* 267–276. https://www.informaworld.com/10.1080/10503307.2011.563249. http://dx.doi.org/10.1080/10503307.2011.563249

Kruger, J. (1999). Lake Wobegon be gone! The "below-average effect" and the egocentric nature of comparative ability judgments. *Journal of Personality and Social Psychology, 77,* 221–232. http://dx.doi.org/10.1037/0022-3514.77.2.221

Lambert, M. J. (1979). *The effects of psychotherapy* (Vol. 1). Edinburgh, Scotland: Churchill Livingstone.

Lambert, M. J. (2010a). *Prevention of treatment failure: The use of measuring, monitoring, and feedback in clinical practice.* Washington, DC: American Psychological Association. http://dx.doi.org/10.1037/12141-000

Lambert, M. J. (2010b). Yes, it is time for clinicians to routinely monitor treatment outcome. In B. L. Duncan, S. D. Miller, B. E. Wampold, & M. A. Hubble (Eds.), *The heart and soul of change: Delivering what works in therapy* (2nd ed., pp. 239–266). Washington, DC: American Psychological Association. http://dx.doi.org/10.1037/12075-008

Lambert, M. J. (2012). Helping clinicians to use and learn from research-based systems: The OQ-Analyst. *Psychotherapy, 49,* 109–114. http://dx.doi.org/10.1037/a0027110

Lambert, M. J. (2013). Outcome in psychotherapy: The past and important advances. *Psychotherapy, 50,* 42–51. http://dx.doi.org/10.1037/a0030682

Lambert, M. J. (2017). Maximizing psychotherapy outcome beyond evidence-based medicine. *Psychotherapy and Psychosomatics, 86,* 80–89. http://dx.doi.org/10.1159/000455170

Lambert, M. J., & Barley, D. E. (2001). Research summary on the therapeutic relationship and psychotherapy outcome. *Psychotherapy: Theory, Research, Practice, Training, 38,* 357–361. http://dx.doi.org/10.1037/0033-3204.38.4.357

Lambert, M. J., & Barley, D. E. (2002). Research summary on the therapeutic relationship and psychotherapy outcome. In J. C. Norcross (Ed.), *Psychotherapy relationships that work: Therapist contributions and responsiveness to patients* (pp. 17–32). New York, NY: Oxford University Press.

Lambert, M. J., Harmon, C., Slade, K., Whipple, J. L., & Hawkins, E. J. (2005). Providing feedback to psychotherapists on their patients' progress: Clinical results and practice suggestions. *Journal of Clinical Psychology, 61,* 165–174. http://dx.doi.org/10.1002/jclp.20113

Lambert, M. J., Morton, J. J., Hatfield, D. R., Harmon, C., Hamilton, S., Reid, R. C., & Burlingame, G. M. (2004). *Administration and scoring manual for the OQ-45.2 (Outcome Questionnaire).* Orem, UT: American Professional Credentialing Services.

Lambert, M. J., Whipple, J. L., & Kleinstäuber, M. (2018). Collecting and delivering progress feedback: A meta-analysis of routine outcome monitoring. *Psychotherapy, 55,* 520–537. http://dx.doi.org/10.1037/pst0000167

Larrison, C. R., Schoppelrey, S. L., Hack-Ritzo, S., & Korr, W. S. (2011). Clinician factors related to outcome differences between black and white patients at CMHCs. *Psychiatric Services, 62,* 525–531. http://dx.doi.org/10.1176/ps.62.5.pss6205_0525

Larson, E. L., Patel, S. J., Evans, D., & Saiman, L. (2013). Feedback as a strategy to change behaviour: The devil is in the details. *Journal of Evaluation in Clinical Practice, 19,* 230–234. http://dx.doi.org/10.1111/j.1365-2753.2011.01801.x

Lasch, C. (1979). *The culture of narcissism: American life in an age of diminishing expectations.* New York, NY: Norton.

Lazar, E. (2017). *Client deterioration in individual psychotherapy: A systemic review* (Unpublished doctoral dissertation). Indiana University of Pennsylvania, Indiana.

Lee, B., & Little, J. (Ed.). (2000). *Striking thoughts: Bruce Lee's wisdom for daily living.* Rutland, VT: Tuttle.

Lehmann, A. C., Gruber, H., & Kopiez, R. (2018). Expertise in music. In K. A. Ericsson, R. R. Hoffman, A. Kozbelt, & A. M. Williams (Eds.), *The Cambridge handbook of expertise and expert performance* (2nd ed., pp. 535–549). Cambridge, England: Cambridge University Press. http://dx.doi.org/10.1017/9781316480748.028

Letters of Note. (2012, June 14). If I'm not a writer then I'm nothing [Blog post]. Retrieved from http://www.lettersofnote.com/2012/06/if-im-not-writer-then-im-nothing.html

Lipsey, M. W., & Wilson, D. B. (1993). The efficacy of psychological, educational, and behavioral treatment. Confirmation from meta-analysis. *American Psychologist, 48,* 1181–1209. http://dx.doi.org/10.1037/0003-066X.48.12.1181

Lloyd, V. (2016, August 8). *Turning data into insight*. Retrieved from https://www.thehrdirector.com/features/hr-in-business/turning-data-into-insight/

Loehr, J., & Schwartz, T. (2005). *The power of full engagement: Managing energy, not time, is the key to high performance and personal renewal*. New York, NY: Free Press.

Luborsky, L. (1954). A note on Eysenck's article "The effects of psychotherapy: An evaluation." *British Journal of Psychology, 45*, 129–131.

Luborsky, L., McLellan, A. T., Diguer, L., Woody, G., & Seligman, D. (1997). The psychotherapist matters: Comparison of outcomes across twenty-two therapists and seven patient samples. *Clinical Psychology: Science and Practice, 4*, 53–65. http://dx.doi.org/10.1111/j.1468-2850.1997.tb00099.x

Luborsky, L., McLellan, A. T., Woody, G. E., O'Brien, C. P., & Auerbach, A. (1985). Therapist success and its determinants. *Archives of General Psychiatry, 42*(6), 602–611. http://dx.doi.org/10.1001/archpsyc.1985.01790290084010

Luo, Y., Hawkley, L. C., Waite, L. J., & Cacioppo, J. T. (2012). Loneliness, health, and mortality in old age: A longitudinal study. *Social Science and Medicine, 74*, 907–914. http://dx.doi.org/10.1016/j.socscimed.2011.11.028

Lutz, W. (2014, December 11). *Practice-based evidence: Building an evidence-base from practice*. Paper presented at the Calgary Counseling Center Conference, Calgary, Canada. Retrieved from https://www.scottdmiller.com/wp-content/uploads/2016/09/Calgary-2014-Michael-Barkham.pdf

Macnamara, B. N., Hambrick, D. Z., & Oswald, F. L. (2014). Deliberate practice and performance in music, games, sports, education, and professions: A meta-analysis. *Psychological Science, 25*, 1608–1618. http://dx.doi.org/10.1177/0956797614535810 (Corrigendum published 2018), *Psychological Science, 29*, pp. 1202–1204. http://dx.doi.org/10.1177/0956797618769891

Maguire, E. A., Gadian, D. G., Johnsrude, I. S., Good, C. D., Ashburner, J., Frackowiak, R. S., & Frith, C. D. (2000). Navigation-related structural change in the hippocampi of taxi drivers. *Proceedings of the National Academy of Sciences, 97*, 4398–4403. http://dx.doi.org/10.1073/pnas.070039597

Maguire, E. A., Woollett, K., & Spiers, H. J. (2006). London taxi drivers and bus drivers: A structural MRI and neuropsychological analysis. *Hippocampus, 16*, 1091–1101. http://dx.doi.org/10.1002/hipo.20233

Malikiosi-Loizos, M. (2013). Personal therapy for future therapists: Reflections on a still debated issue. *European Journal of Counselling Psychology, 2*, 33–50. http://dx.doi.org/10.5964/ejcop.v2i1.4

Mamede, S., Schmidt, H. G., Rikers, R. M. J. P., Penaforte, J. C., & Coelho-Filho, J. M. (2007). Breaking down automaticity: Case ambiguity and the shift to reflective approaches in clinical reasoning. *Medical Education, 41*, 1185–1192. http://dx.doi.org/10.1111/j.1365-2923.2007.02921.x

Mantle, M., & Creamer, R. W. (1999). *The quality of courage: Heroes in and out of baseball*. Lincoln: University of Nebraska Press.

Marcus, G. (2012). *Guitar zero: The science of becoming musical at any age*. New York, NY: Penguin.

May, C. (2014, June 3). *A learning secret: Don't take notes with a laptop*. Retrieved from https://www.scientificamerican.com/article/a-learning-secret-don-t-take-notes-with-a-laptop/

Mayfield, W. A., Kardash, C. M., & Kivlighan, D. M. (1999). Differences in experienced and novice counselors' knowledge structures about clients: Implications for case conceptualization. *Journal of Counseling Psychology, 46,* 504–514. http://dx.doi.org/10.1037/0022-0167.46.4.504

McDaniel, M. A., Cahill, M. J., Robbins, M., & Wiener, C. (2014). Individual differences in learning and transfer: Stable tendencies for learning exemplars versus abstracting rules. *Journal of Experimental Psychology: General, 143,* 668–693. http://dx.doi.org/10.1037/a0032963

McLaney, E., Strathern, L., Johnson, S., & Allen-Ackley, D. (2010). An interprofessional education approach to teaching collaborative documentation practices: Exploring development, delivery and outcomes using the presage, process, product (3P) model. *Journal of Interprofessional Care, 24,* 466–469. http://dx.doi.org/10.3109/13561820903520377

Miller, S., Wampold, B., & Varhely, K. (2008). Direct comparisons of treatment modalities for youth disorders: A meta-analysis. *Psychotherapy Research, 18*(1), 5–14. http://dx.doi.org/10.1080/10503300701472131

Miller, S. D. (2011a, November 22). Cutting edge feedback [Blog post]. Retrieved from https://www.scottdmiller.com/cutting-edge-feedback/

Miller, S. D. (2011b). *Feedback-informed supervision* [Video file]. Hanover, MA: Microtraining Associates. Retrieved from https://search.alexanderstreet.com/preview/work/bibliographic_entity%7Cvideo_work%7C2462770

Miller, S. D. (2011c). *Feedback-informed treatment* [Video file]. Hanover, MA: Microtraining Associates. Retrieved from https://search.alexanderstreet.com/preview/work/bibliographic_entity%7Cvideo_work%7C1779390

Miller, S. D. (2014, December 11). Dinner with Paul McCartney (and others) [Blog post]. Retrieved from https://www.scottdmiller.com/1327/

Miller, S. D. (2017, January 7). *"Wow, I'm only helping half of my clients": Deliberate practice with Dr. Tony Rousmaniere* [Video file]. Retrieved from https://www.youtube.com/watch?v=4R7z0gz6J70

Miller, S. D. (2018a, May 24). I have some magic beans for sale . . . you want them? [Blog post]. Retrieved from https://www.scottdmiller.com/i-have-some-magic-beans-for-sale-you-want-them/

Miller, S. D. (2018b, November 2). What works in psychotherapy? Valuing "what works" rather than working with what we value [Blog post]. Retrieved from https://www.scottdmiller.com/what-works-in-psychotherapy-valuing-what-works-rather-than-working-with-what-we-value/

Miller, S. D., Chow, D., Wampold, B. E., Hubble, M. A., Del Re, A. C., Maeschalck, C., & Bargmann, S. (2018). To be or not to be (an expert)? Revisiting the role of deliberate practice in improving performance. *High Ability Studies.* Advance online publication. http://dx.doi.org/10.1080/13598139.2018.1519410

Miller, S. D., & Duncan, B. L. (2000). Paradigm lost: From model-driven to client-directed, outcome-informed clinical work. *Journal of Systemic Therapies, 19,* 20–34. http://dx.doi.org/10.1521/jsyt.2000.19.1.20

Miller, S. D., & Duncan, B. L. (2004). *The outcome and session rating scales: Administration and scoring manual.* Chicago, IL: Institute for the Study of Therapeutic Change.

Miller, S. D., Duncan, B. L., Brown, J., Sparks, J., & Claud, D. (2003). The outcome rating scale: A preliminary study of the reliability, validity, and feasibility of a brief visual analog measure. *Journal of Brief Therapy, 2,* 91–100.

Miller, S. D., Duncan, B. L., & Hubble, M. A. (1995). *Escape from Babel: Toward a unifying language for psychotherapy.* New York, NY: Norton.

Miller, S. D., Duncan, B. L., & Hubble, M. A. (2004). Beyond integration: The triumph of outcome over process in clinical practice. *Psychotherapy in Australia, 10*(2), 2–19.

Miller, S. D., Duncan, B. L., & Johnson, L. D. (2002). *The Session Rating Scale 3.0.* Chicago, IL: Author.

Miller, S. D., Duncan, B. L., Sorrell, R., & Brown, G. S. (2005). The Partners for Change Outcome Management System. *Journal of Clinical Psychology, 61,* 199–208. http://dx.doi.org/10.1002/jclp.20111

Miller, S. D., & Hubble, M. (2011). The road to mastery: What's missing from this picture? *Psychotherapy Networker, 35*(3), 22–31. Retrieved from https://www.psychotherapynetworker.org/magazine/article/328/the-road-to-mastery

Miller, S. D., & Hubble, M. (2017). How psychotherapy has lost its magick. *Psychotherapy Networker, 41,* 28–37, 60–61.

Miller, S. D., Hubble, M., & Chow, D. (2017). Professional development: An oxymoron? In T. Rousmaniere, R. K. Goodyear, S. D. Miller, & B. Wampold (Eds.), *The cycle of excellence: Using deliberate practice in supervision, training, and independent practice* (pp. 23–47). Hoboken, NJ: Wiley.

Miller, S. D., Hubble, M., & Chow, D. (2018). The question of expertise in psychotherapy. *Journal of Expertise, 1*(2), 1–8.

Miller, S. D., Hubble, M. A., Chow, D., & Seidel, J. (2015). Beyond measures and monitoring: Realizing the potential of feedback-informed treatment. *Psychotherapy, 52,* 449–457. http://dx.doi.org/10.1037/pst0000031

Miller, S. D., Hubble, M. A., Chow, D. L., & Seidel, J. A. (2013). The outcome of psychotherapy: Yesterday, today, and tomorrow. *Psychotherapy, 50,* 88–97. http://dx.doi.org/10.1037/a0031097

Miller, S. D., Hubble, M. A., & Duncan, B. L. (2007). Supershrinks: What's the secret of their success? *Psychotherapy Networker, 31*(6), 27–35, 56.

Minami, T., Wampold, B. E., Serlin, R. C., Hamilton, E. G., Brown, G. S., & Kircher, J. C. (2008). Benchmarking the effectiveness of psychotherapy treatment for adult depression in a managed care environment: A preliminary study. *Journal of Consulting and Clinical Psychology, 76,* 116–124. http://dx.doi.org/10.1037/0022-006X.76.1.116

Modoono, B. (1987, February 8). Free throws: Anyone can make 'em, so why doesn't everyone? *Chicago Tribune.* Retrieved from https://www.chicagotribune.com/news/ct-xpm-1987-02-08-8701100727-story.html

Mohl, R. (1995). Making the second ghetto in metropolitan Miami, 1940–1960. *Journal of Urban History, 21,* 395–427. http://dx.doi.org/10.1177/009614429502100305

Moore, M. (2010). Bedtime problems and night wakings: Treatment of behavioral insomnia of childhood. *Journal of Clinical Psychology, 66,* 1195–1204. http://dx.doi.org/10.1002/jclp.20731

Mueller, P. A., & Oppenheimer, D. M. (2014). The pen is mightier than the keyboard: Advantages of longhand over laptop note taking. *Psychological Science, 25,* 1159–1168. http://dx.doi.org/10.1177/0956797614524581 (Corrigendum published 2018, *Psychological Science, 29,* pp. 1565–1568. http://dx.doi.org/10.1177/0956797618781773)

Munder, T., Brütsch, O., Leonhart, R., Gerger, H., & Barth, J. (2013). Researcher allegiance in psychotherapy outcome research: An overview of reviews. *Clinical Psychology Review, 33,* 501–511. http://dx.doi.org/10.1016/j.cpr.2013.02.002

Murphy, D., Irfan, N., Barnett, H., Castledine, E., & Enescu, L. (2018). A systematic review and meta-synthesis of qualitative research into mandatory personal psychotherapy during training. *Counselling & Psychotherapy Research, 18,* 199–214. http://dx.doi.org/10.1002/capr.12162

Nehru, N. (1954). *Jawaharlal Nehru's speeches, 1949–1953.* Delhi, India: Publications Division, Ministry of Information and Broadcasting.

Neimeyer, G. J., Taylor, J. M., & Wear, D. M. (2009). Continuing education in psychology: Outcomes, evaluations, and mandates. *Professional Psychology: Research and Practice, 40,* 617–624. http://dx.doi.org/10.1037/a0016655

Neimeyer, G. J., Taylor, J. M., & Wear, D. M. (2011). Continuing education in professional psychology: Do ethics mandates matter? *Ethics & Behavior, 21,* 165–172. http://dx.doi.org/10.1080/10508422.2011.551472

Newport, C. (2016). *Deep work: Rules for focused success in a distracted world.* London, England: Piatkus.

Newport, C. (2019). *Digital minimalism: Choosing a focused life in a noisy world.* New York, NY: Penguin Random House.

Nienhuis, J. B., Owen, J., Valentine, J. C., Winkeljohn Black, S., Halford, T. C., Parazak, S. E., . . . Hilsenroth, M. (2018). Therapeutic alliance, empathy, and genuineness in individual adult psychotherapy: A meta-analytic review. *Psychotherapy Research, 28,* 593–605. http://dx.doi.org/10.1080/10503307.2016.1204023

Nilsen, P. (2015). Making sense of implementation theories, models and frameworks. *Implementation Science, 10,* 53, 1–13. http://dx.doi.org/10.1186/s13012-015-0242-0

Nisbett, R. E., & Ross, L. (1980). *Human inference: Strategies and shortcomings of social judgment.* Englewood Cliffs, NJ: Prentice Hall.

Nissen-Lie, H. A., Monsen, J. T., & Rønnestad, M. H. (2010). Therapist predictors of early patient-rated working alliance: A multilevel approach. *Psychotherapy Research, 20,* 627–646. http://dx.doi.org/10.1080/10503307.2010.497633

Nissen-Lie, H. A., Monsen, J. T., Ulleberg, P., & Rønnestad, M. H. (2013). Psychotherapists' self-reports of their interpersonal functioning and difficulties in practice as predictors of patient outcome. *Psychotherapy Research, 23,* 86–104. http://dx.doi.org/10.1080/10503307.2012.735775

Nissen-Lie, H. A., & Rønnestad, M. H. (2016). The empirical evidence for psychotherapist humility as a foundation for psychotherapist expertise. *Psychotherapy, 51*(2), 7–9.

Nissen-Lie, H. A., Rønnestad, M. H., Høglend, P. A., Havik, O. E., Solbakken, O. A., Stiles, T. C., & Monsen, J. T. (2017). Love yourself as a person, doubt yourself as a therapist? *Clinical Psychology & Psychotherapy, 24,* 48–60. http://dx.doi.org/10.1002/cpp.1977

Nobel Media. (2005, October 3). *The Nobel Prize in Physiology or Medicine 2005* [Press release]. Retrieved from https://www.nobelprize.org/prizes/medicine/2005/press-release/

Nolen, S. (1988). Reasons for studying: Motivational orientations and study strategies. *Cognition and Instruction, 5,* 269–287. http://dx.doi.org/10.1207/s1532690xci0504_2

Norcross, J. C. (2010). The therapeutic relationship. In B. L. Duncan, S. D. Miller, B. E. Wampold, & M. A. Hubble (Eds.), *The heart and soul of change: Delivering what works in therapy* (pp. 113–142). Washington, DC: American Psychological Association. http://dx.doi.org/10.1037/12075-004

Norcross, J. C. (Ed.). (2011). *Psychotherapy relationships that work* (2nd ed.). New York, NY: Oxford University Press. http://dx.doi.org/10.1093/acprof:oso/9780199737208.001.0001

Norcross, J. C., & Lambert, M. J. (2011). Psychotherapy relationships that work II. *Psychotherapy, 48,* 4–8. http://dx.doi.org/10.1037/a0022180

Norcross, J. C., Mrykalo, M. S., & Blagys, M. D. (2002). Auld lang syne: Success predictors, change processes, and self-reported outcomes of New Year's resolvers and nonresolvers. *Journal of Clinical Psychology, 58,* 397–405. http://dx.doi.org/10.1002/jclp.1151

Norcross, J. C., & Wampold, B. E. (2011a). Evidence-based therapy relationships: Research conclusions and clinical practices. *Psychotherapy, 48,* 98–102. http://dx.doi.org/10.1037/a0022161

Norcross, J. C., & Wampold, B. E. (2011b). What works for whom: Tailoring psychotherapy to the person. *Journal of Clinical Psychology, 67,* 127–132. http://dx.doi.org/10.1002/jclp.20764

Norman, G., Grierson, L., Sherbino, J., Hamstra, S., Schmidt, H., & Mamede, S. (2018). Expertise in medicine and surgery. In K. A. Ericsson, R. R. Hoffman, A. Kozbelt, & A. M. Williams (Eds.), *The Cambridge handbook of expertise and expert performance* (2nd ed., pp. 331–355). Cambridge, England: Cambridge University Press. http://dx.doi.org/10.1017/9781316480748.019

Ogles, B. M. (2013). Measuring change in psychotherapy research. In M. J. Lambert (Ed.), *Bergin and Garfield's handbook of psychotherapy and behavior change* (6th ed., pp. 134–166). New York, NY: Wiley.

Ogles, B. M., Lambert, M. J., & Masters, K. S. (1996). *Assessing outcome in clinical practice.* Boston, MA: Allyn & Bacon.

Okiishi, J. C., Lambert, M. J., Nielsen, S. L., & Ogles, B. M. (2003). Waiting for supershrink: An empirical analysis of therapist effects. *Clinical Psychology & Psychotherapy, 10,* 361–373. http://dx.doi.org/10.1002/cpp.383

Orlinsky, D. E., & Rønnestad, M. H. (2005). *How psychotherapists develop: A study of therapeutic work and professional growth.* Washington, DC: American Psychological Association. http://dx.doi.org/10.1037/11157-000

Østergård, O. K., Randa, H., & Hougaard, E. (2018). The effect of using the Partners for Change Outcome Management System as feedback tool in psychotherapy—A systematic review and meta-analysis. *Psychotherapy Research,* 1–18. Advance online publication. http://dx.doi.org/10.1080/10503307.2018.1517949

Owen Chamberlain banquet speech. (1959, December 10). Retrieved from https://www.nobelprize.org/prizes/physics/1959/chamberlain/speech/

Owen, J., Drinane, J. M., Kivlighan, M., III, Miller, S., Kopta, M., & Imel, Z. (2019). Are high-performing therapists both effective and consistent? A test of therapist expertise. *Journal of Consulting and Clinical Psychology, 87,* 1149–1156. http://dx.doi.org/10.1037/ccp0000437

Owen, J., Miller, S. D., Seidel, J., & Chow, D. (2016). The working alliance in treatment of military adolescents. *Journal of Consulting and Clinical Psychology, 84,* 200–210. http://dx.doi.org/10.1037/ccp0000035

Owen, J., Wampold, B. E., Kopta, M., Rousmaniere, T., & Miller, S. D. (2016). As good as it gets? Therapy outcomes of trainees over time. *Journal of Counseling Psychology, 63,* 12–19. http://dx.doi.org/10.1037/cou0000112

Owen, J., Wong, Y. J., & Rodolfa, E. (2009). Empirical search for psychotherapists' gender competence in psychotherapy. *Psychotherapy: Theory, Research, Practice, Training, 46,* 448–458. http://dx.doi.org/10.1037/a0017958

Owen, J. J., Adelson, J., Budge, S., Kopta, S. M., & Reese, R. J. (2016). Good-enough level and dose-effect models: Variation among outcomes and therapists. *Psychotherapy Research, 26,* 22–30. http://dx.doi.org/10.1080/1050 3307.2014.966346

Paris, B. (1996). *Audrey Hepburn.* New York, NY: Berkeley Books.

Paul, A. M. (2015, August 1). Researchers find that frequent tests can boast learning. *Scientific American.* Retrieved from https://www.scientificamerican.com/article/researchers-find-that-frequent-tests-can-boost-learning/

Pavot, W., & Diener, E. (2004). Findings on subjective well-being: Applications to public policy, clinical interventions, and education. In P. A. Linley & S. Joseph (Eds.), *Positive psychology in practice* (pp. 679–692). New York, NY: Wiley. http://dx.doi.org/10.1002/9780470939338.ch40

Pearson, K. (1900). Mathematical contributions to the theory of evolution: VII. On the correlation characteristics not quantitatively measurable. *Philosophical Transactions of the Royal Society of London, Series, A, 195,* 1–147.

Pinsof, W. M. (2017). The Systemic Therapy Inventory of Change—STIC: A multi-systemic and multi-dimensional system to integrate science into psychotherapeutic practice. In T. Tilden & B. Wampold (Eds.), *Routine outcome monitoring in couple and family therapy* (pp. 85–101). Cham, Switzerland: Springer.

Plimpton, G. (1958, Spring). Ernest Hemingway, the Art of Fiction No. 21 [Interview]. *The Paris Review.* Retrieved from https://www.theparisreview.org/interviews/4825/ernest-hemingway-the-art-of-fiction-no-21-ernest-hemingway

Pope, K. S., & Tabachnick, B. G. (1994). Therapists as patients: A national survey of psychologists' experiences, problems, and beliefs. *Professional Psychology: Research and Practice, 25,* 247–258. http://dx.doi.org/10.1037/0735-7028.25.3.247

Practice. (1976). In *Webster's new collegiate dictionary.* Springfield, MA: Merriam.

Prescott, D. S., Maeschalck, C. L., & Miller, S. D. (Eds.). (2017). *Feedback-informed treatment in clinical practice: Reaching for excellence.* Washington, DC: American Psychological Association.

Prochaska, J. O., Norcross, J. C., & Saul, S. F. (2019, November 25). Generating psychotherapy breakthroughs: Transtheoretical strategies from population health psychology. *American Psychologist.* Advance online publication. http://dx.doi.org/10.1037/amp0000568

Quotes [Blog post]. (n.d.). Retrieved from https://www.quotes.net/quote/59183

Richards, P. S., Baldwin, B. M., Frost, H. A., Clark-Sly, J. B., Berrett, M. E., & Hardman, R. K. (2000). What works for treating eating disorders? Conclusions of 28 outcome reviews. *Eating Disorders: The Journal of Treatment & Prevention, 8*(3), 189–206. http://dx.doi.org/10.1080/10640260008251227

Ricks, D. F. (1974). Supershrink: Methods of a therapist judged successful on the basis of adult outcomes of adolescent patients. In D. F. Ricks & M. Roff (Eds.), *Life history research in psychopathology* (pp. 275–297). Minneapolis: University of Minnesota Press.

Rieff, P. (1987). *The triumph of the therapeutic: Uses of faith after Freud.* Chicago, IL: University of Chicago Press.

Rogers, C. (1961). *On becoming a person.* New York, NY: Houghton Mifflin.

Rønnestad, M. H., Orlinsky, D. E., Schröder, T. A., Skovholt, T. M., & Willutzki, U. (2019). The professional development of counsellors and psychotherapists: Implications of empirical studies for supervision, training and practice.

Counselling & Psychotherapy Research, 19, 214–230. http://dx.doi.org/10.1002/capr.12198

Rosenthal, J. S. (2006). *Struck by lightning: The curious world of probabilities.* Washington, DC: Joseph Henry Press.

Rosenzweig, S. (1954). A transvaluation of psychotherapy; a reply to Hans Eysenck. *Journal of Abnormal and Social Psychology, 49,* 298–304. http://dx.doi.org/10.1037/h0061172

Roth, A., & Fonagy, P. (Eds.). (2013). *What works for whom: A critical review of psychotherapy research* (2nd ed.). New York, NY: Guilford Press.

Rousmaniere, T. (2009). *Why most therapists are just average (and how we can improve)* [Interview transcript]. Retrieved from https://www.psychotherapy.net/interview/scott-miller-interview

Rousmaniere, T. (2016). *Deliberate practice for psychotherapists: A guide to improving clinical effectiveness.* New York, NY: Routledge. http://dx.doi.org/10.4324/9781315472256

Rousmaniere, T., Goodyear, R. K., Miller, S. D., & Wampold, B. E. (Eds.). (2017). *The cycle of excellence: Using deliberate practice in supervision, training, and independent practice.* Hoboken, NJ: Wiley. http://dx.doi.org/10.1002/9781119165590

Rousmaniere, T. G., Swift, J. K., Babins-Wagner, R., Whipple, J. L., & Berzins, S. (2016). Supervisor variance in psychotherapy outcome in routine practice. *Psychotherapy Research, 26,* 196–205. http://dx.doi.org/10.1080/10503307.2014.963730

Sachs, M. B., Young, E. D., & Miller, M. I. (1983). Speech encoding in the auditory nerve: Implications for cochlear implants. *Annals of the New York Academy of Sciences, 405,* 94–113. http://dx.doi.org/10.1111/j.1749-6632.1983.tb31622.x

Safran, J., & Muran, C. (2000). *Negotiating the therapeutic alliance: A relational treatment guide.* New York, NY: Guilford Press.

Sahakian, B. J., & LaBuzetta, J. N. (2013). *Bad moves: How decision making goes wrong, and the ethics of smart drugs.* New York, NY: Oxford University Press.

Savitch, W. J. (1984). *Pascal: An introduction to the art and science of programming.* Menlo Park, CA: Benjamin Cummings.

Saxon, D., Ashley, K., Bishop-Edwards, L., Connell, J., Harrison, P., Ohlsen, S., . . . Barkham, M. (2017). A pragmatic randomised controlled trial assessing the non-inferiority of counselling for depression versus cognitive-behaviour therapy for patients in primary care meeting a diagnosis of moderate or severe depression (PRaCTICED): Study protocol for a randomised controlled trial. *Trials, 18*(1), 93. http://dx.doi.org/10.1186/s13063-017-1834-6

Saxon, D., & Barkham, M. (2012). Patterns of therapist variability: Therapist effects and the contribution of patient severity and risk. *Journal of Consulting and Clinical Psychology, 80,* 535–546. http://dx.doi.org/10.1037/a0028898

Saxon, D., Ricketts, T., & Heywood, J. (2010). Who drops-out? Do measures of risk to self and to others predict unplanned endings in primary care counselling? *Counselling & Psychotherapy Research, 10,* 13–21. http://dx.doi.org/10.1080/14733140902914604

Schafer, R. (1954). *Psychoanalytic interpretation in Rorschach testing.* New York, NY: Grune & Stratton.

Schmidt, H. G., & Rikers, R. M. J. P. (2007). How expertise develops in medicine: Knowledge encapsulation and illness script formation. *Medical Education, 41,* 1133–1139. http://dx.doi.org/10.1111/j.1365-2923.2007.02915.x

Schuckard, E., Miller, S. D., & Hubble, M. A. (2017). Feedback-informed treatment: Historical and empirical foundations. In D. S. Prescott, C. L. Maeschalck, & S. D. Miller, (Eds.), *Feedback-informed treatment in clinical practice: Reaching for excellence* (pp. 13–35). Washington, DC: American Psychological Association.

The score takes care of itself—Bill Walsh [List]. (n.d.). Retrieved from http://coachjacksonspages.com/The%20Score%20Takes%20Care.pdf

Sexton, A. (1962). *All my pretty ones.* Boston, MA: Houghton Mifflin.

Sherman, R. M., Sherman, R. B., & Rodgers, A. (1968). The roses of success [Lyrics]. Retrieved from https://www.allmusicals.com/lyrics/chittychittybangbang/therosesofsuccess.htm

Shermer, M. (2008, December). Patternicity [Blog post]. Retrieved from https://michaelshermer.com/2008/12/patternicity/

Silver, N. (2012). *The signal and the noise: Why most predictions fail but some do not.* New York, NY: Penguin Press.

Simpson, S. H., Eurich, D. T., Majumdar, S. R., Padwal, R. S., Tsuyuki, R. T., Varney, J., & Johnson, J. A. (2006). A meta-analysis of the association between adherence to drug therapy and mortality. *BMJ, 333,* 15. http://dx.doi.org/10.1136/bmj.38875.675486.55

Sims, P. (2010, July 15). Think like Chris Rock: Little bets [Blog post]. Retrieved from https://petersims.com/2010/07/15/think-chrisrock/

Singh Ospina, N., Phillips, K. A., Rodriguez-Gutierrez, R., Castaneda-Guarderas, A., Gionfriddo, M. R., Branda, M. E., & Montori, V. M. (2019). Eliciting the patient's agenda—Secondary analysis of recorded clinical encounters. *Journal of General Internal Medicine, 34,* 36–40. http://dx.doi.org/10.1007/s11606-018-4540-5

Sképseis. (2013, January 20). *The scientific method-Richard Feynman* [Video file]. Retrieved from https://www.youtube.com/watch?time_continue=1&v=OL6-x0modwY&feature=emb_logo

Smith, M. L., & Glass, G. V. (1977). Meta-analysis of psychotherapy outcome studies. *American Psychologist, 32,* 752–760. http://dx.doi.org/10.1037/0003-066X.32.9.752

Soderstrom, N. C., & Bjork, R. A. (2015). Learning versus performance: An integrative review. *Perspectives on Psychological Science, 10,* 176–199. http://dx.doi.org/10.1177/1745691615569000

Sommers-Spijkerman, M., Trompetter, H. Schreurs, K., & Bohlmeijer, E. (2018). Pathways to improving mental health in compassion-focused therapy: Self-reassurance, self-criticism and affect as mediators of change. *Frontiers in Psychology, 9*(2442), 1–6. https://dx.doi.org/10.3389/fpsyg.2018.02442

Sonnentag, S., & Kleine, B. M. (2000). Deliberate practice at work: A study with insurance agents. *Journal of Occupational and Organizational Psychology, 73,* 87–102. http://dx.doi.org/10.1348/096317900166895

Sonnentag, S., Niessen, C., & Volmer, J. (2006). Expertise in software design. In K. A. Ericsson, N. Charness, P. J. Feltovich, & R. R. Hoffman (Eds), *The Cambridge handbook of expertise and expert performance* (pp. 373–388). Cambridge, England: Cambridge University Press. http://dx.doi.org/10.1017/CBO9780511816796.021

Soper, T. (2013, January 30). Bill Gates' annual letter: How measurement can change the world. *GeekWire.* Retrieved from https://www.geekwire.com/2013/bill-gates-2013-annual-letter/

Spencer, J., Goode, J., Penix, E. A., Trusty, W., & Swift, J. K. (2019). Developing a collaborative relationship with clients during the initial sessions of psychotherapy. *Psychotherapy, 56*(1), 7–10. http://dx.doi.org/10.1037/pst0000208

Spielmans, G. I., Gatlin, E. T., & McFall, J. P. (2010). The efficacy of evidence-based psychotherapies versus usual care for youths: Controlling confounds in a meta-reanalysis. *Psychotherapy Research, 20,* 234–246. http://dx.doi.org/10.1080/10503300903311293

Spitzer, D. (1981). Education and development of the training professional: Problems and perspectives. *Performance Improvement, 20*(1), 18–32.

Springer, K. S., Levy, H. C., & Tolin, D. F. (2018). Remission in CBT for adult anxiety disorders: A meta-analysis. *Clinical Psychology Review, 61,* 1–8. http://dx.doi.org/10.1016/j.cpr.2018.03.002

Stanhope, V., Ingoglia, C., Schmelter, B., & Marcus, S. C. (2013). Impact of person-centered planning and collaborative documentation on treatment adherence. *Psychiatric Services, 64,* 76–79. http://dx.doi.org/10.1176/appi.ps.201100489

Starkes, J. L., Deakin, J. M., Allard, F., Hodges, N., & Hayes, A. (1996). Deliberate practice in sports: What is it anyway? In K. A. Ericsson (Ed.), *The road to excellence: The acquisition of expert performance in the arts and sciences, sports, and games* (pp. 81–106). Mahwah, NJ: Erlbaum.

Statista. (2015). Market share of leading brands in the United States fast food industry in 2015. Retrieved from https://www.statista.com/statistics/196611/market-share-of-fast-food-restaurant-corporations-in-the-us/

Statista. (2019). Revenue of McDonald's Corporation worldwide from 2005 to 2018 (in billion U.S. dollars). Retrieved from https://www.statista.com/statistics/208917/revenue-of-the-mcdonalds-corporation-since-2005/

Stephenson, N. (2008). *Anathem.* New York, NY: Harper.

Sternberg, R. J., & Lubart, T. I. (1996). Investing in creativity. *American Psychologist, 51,* 677–688. http://dx.doi.org/10.1177%2F1745691615569000. http://dx.doi.org/10.1037/0003-066X.51.7.677

Stigler, J. W., & Miller, K. F. (2018). Expertise and expert performance in teaching. In K. A. Ericsson, R. R. Hoffman, A. Kozbelt, & A. M. Williams (Eds.), *The Cambridge handbook of expertise and expert performance* (2nd ed., pp. 431–452). Cambridge, England: Cambridge University Press. http://dx.doi.org/10.1017/9781316480748.024

Stiles, W. B. (1988). Psychotherapy process-outcome correlations may be misleading. *Psychotherapy: Theory, Research, Practice, Training, 25,* 27–35.

Stiles, W. B. (2009). Responsiveness as an obstacle for psychotherapy outcome research: It's worse than you think. *Clinical Psychology: Science and Practice, 16,* 86–91. http://dx.doi.org/10.1111/j.1468-2850.2009.01148.x

Stiles, W. B., Barkham, M., Mellor-Clark, J., & Connell, J. (2008). Effectiveness of cognitive-behavioural, person-centred, and psychodynamic therapies in UK primary-care routine practice: Replication in a larger sample. *Psychological Medicine, 38,* 677–688. http://dx.doi.org/10.1017/S0033291707001511

Stiles, W. B., Barkham, M., & Wheeler, S. (2015). Duration of psychological therapy: Relation to recovery and improvement rates in UK routine practice. *British Journal of Psychiatry, 207,* 115–122. http://dx.doi.org/10.1192/bjp.bp.114.145565

Stiles, W. B., & Horvath, A. O. (2017). Appropriate responsiveness as a contribution to therapist effects. In L. G. Castonguay & C. E. Hill (Eds.), *How and why are some therapists better than others? Understanding therapist effects* (pp. 71–84). Washington, DC: American Psychological Association. http://dx.doi.org/10.1037/0000034-005

Strenze, T. (2007). Intelligence and socioeconomic success: A meta-analytic review of longitudinal research. *Intelligence, 35,* 401–426. http://dx.doi.org/10.1016/j.intell.2006.09.004

Strober, M., Freeman, R., & Morrell, W. (1997). The long-term course of severe anorexia nervosa in adolescents: Survival analysis of recovery, relapse, and outcome predictors over 10–15 years in a prospective study. *International Journal of Eating Disorders, 22,* 339–360. http://dx.doi.org/10.1002/(SICI)1098-108X(199712)22:4<339::AID-EAT1>3.0.CO;2-N

Swift, J. K., & Greenberg, R. P. (2012). Premature discontinuation in adult psychotherapy: A meta-analysis. *Journal of Consulting and Clinical Psychology, 80,* 547–559. http://dx.doi.org/10.1037/a0028226

Swift, J. K., & Greenberg, R. P. (2015). *Premature termination in psychotherapy: Strategies for engaging clients and improving outcomes.* Washington, DC: American Psychological Association. http://dx.doi.org/10.1037/14469-000

Swift, J. K., Greenberg, R. P., Tompkins, K. A., & Parkin, S. R. (2017). Treatment refusal and premature termination in psychotherapy, pharmacotherapy, and their combination: A meta-analysis of head-to-head comparisons. *Psychotherapy, 54,* 47–57. http://dx.doi.org/10.1037/pst0000104

Swindoll, C. (2000). *Day by day With Charles Swindoll.* Nashville, TN: Nelson.

Syed, M. (2015). *Black box thinking: Why most people never learn from their mistakes—But some do.* New York, NY: Penguin Random House LLC.

Taleb, N. N. (2004). *Fooled by randomness: The hidden role of chance in life and in the markets* (2nd ed.). New York, NY: Random House.

Talmon, M. (1990). *Single-session therapy: Maximizing the effect of the first (and often only) therapeutic encounter.* San Francisco, CA: Jossey-Bass.

Tappin, B. M., van der Leer, L., & McKay, R. T. (2017). The heart trumps the head: Desirability bias in political belief revision. *Journal of Experimental Psychology: General, 146,* 1143–1149. http://dx.doi.org/10.1037/xge0000298

Tasca, G. A., Sylvestre, J., Balfour, L., Chyurlia, L., Evans, J., Fortin-Langelier, B., . . . Wilson, B. (2014). What clinicians want: Findings from a psychotherapy practice research network survey. *Psychotherapy, 52,* 1–11. http://dx.doi.org/10.1037/a0038252

Theodore, N. (2017, June 7). We have data, let's look at data. *Medium.* Retrieved from https://casestudies.storetrials.com/we-have-data-lets-look-at-data-e8a06e2e3331

Thomas, J. (2013). Therapy: No improvement for 40 years. *The National Psychologist, 23,* 1.

Tilden, T., & Wampold, B. E. (Eds.). (2017). *Routine outcome monitoring in couple and family therapy: The empirically informed therapist.* Cham, Switzerland: Springer International. http://dx.doi.org/10.1007/978-3-319-50675-3

Tilley, C. (2015, January 12). *Eight things you might not know about black boxes.* Retrieved from https://www.abc.net.au/news/2014-03-26/black-box-flight-recorders/5343456

Tremonti, A. M. (Host). (2017, January 19). Soundclip (Jim Gaffigan) [Transcript]. *The Current.* Retrieved from https://www.cbc.ca/radio/thecurrent/the-current-for-january-19-2017-1.3941441/jan-19-2017-episode-transcript-1.3943608

Truscott, D. (2010). *Becoming an effective psychotherapist: Adopting a theory of psychotherapy that's right for you and your client.* Washington, DC: American Psychological Association. http://dx.doi.org/10.1037/12064-000

Tryon, G. S., & Winograd, G. (2011). Goal consensus and collaboration. *Psychotherapy, 48,* 50–57. http://dx.doi.org/10.1037/a0022061

Ullén, F., Hambrick, D. Z., & Mosing, M. A. (2016). Rethinking expertise: A multi-factorial gene–environment interaction model of expert performance. *Psychological Bulletin, 142,* 427–446. http://dx.doi.org/10.1037/bul0000033

van Os, J., Guloksuz, S., Vijn, T. W., Hafkenscheid, A., & Delespaul, P. (2019). The evidence-based group-level symptom-reduction model as the organizing principle for mental health care: Time for change? *World Psychiatry, 18,* 88–96. http://dx.doi.org/10.1002/wps.20609

Vygotsky, L. S. (1978). *Mind in society: The development of higher psychological processes.* Cambridge, MA: Harvard University Press.

Walfish, S., McAlister, B., O'Donnell, P., & Lambert, M. J. (2012). An investigation of self-assessment bias in mental health providers. *Psychological Reports, 110,* 639–644. http://dx.doi.org/10.2466/02.07.17.PR0.110.2.639-644

Wampold, B. E. (2001). *The great psychotherapy debate: Models, methods, and findings.* Mahwah, NJ: Erlbaum.

Wampold, B. E., & Brown, G. S. (2005). Estimating variability in outcomes attributable to therapists: A naturalistic study of outcomes in managed care. *Journal of Consulting and Clinical Psychology, 73,* 914–923. http://dx.doi.org/10.1037/0022-006X.73.5.914

Wampold, B. E., Budge, S. L., Laska, K. M., Del Re, A. C., Baardseth, T. P., Fluckiger, C., . . . Gunn, W. (2011). Evidence-based treatments for depression and anxiety versus treatment-as-usual: A meta-analysis of direct comparisons. *Clinical Psychology Review, 31,* 1304–1312. http://dx.doi.org/10.1016/j.cpr.2011.07.012

Wampold, B. E., Flückiger, C., Del Re, A. C., Yulish, N. E., Frost, N. D., Pace, B. T., . . . Hilsenroth, M. J. (2017). In pursuit of truth: A critical examination of meta-analyses of cognitive behavior therapy. *Psychotherapy Research, 27,* 14–32. http://dx.doi.org/10.1080/10503307.2016.1249433

Wampold, B. E., & Imel, Z. E. (2015). *The great psychotherapy debate: The evidence for what makes psychotherapy work* (2nd ed.). New York, NY: Routledge. http://dx.doi.org/10.4324/9780203582015

Washington Speakers Bureau. (n.d.). Gen. Colin Powell, USA (Ret.). Retrieved from https://www.wsb.com/speakers/gen-colin-powell-usa-ret/

Watkins, C. E., Jr. (2011). Does psychotherapy supervision contribute to patient outcomes? Considering thirty years of research. *Clinical Supervisor, 30,* 235–256. http://dx.doi.org/10.1080/07325223.2011.619417

Webb, C. A., DeRubeis, R. J., & Barber, J. P. (2010). Therapist adherence/competence and treatment outcome: A meta-analytic review. *Journal of Consulting and Clinical Psychology, 78,* 200–211. http://dx.doi.org/10.1037/a0018912

White, M. (Ed.). (2011). *In the words of E. B. White: Quotations from America's most companionable of writers.* Ithaca, NY: Cornell University Press.

The White House. (n.d.). White House Millennium Council 2000: National Millennium Time Capsule National Medal winner [Archived statement]. Retrieved from https://clintonwhitehouse4.archives.gov/Initiatives/Millennium/capsule/carter.html

Whitmore, D. (n.d.). Time study. Retrieved from https://www.managers-net.com/timestudy.html

Wiggins, G. (2012, September). Seven keys to effective feedback. *Educational Leadership, 70*(1), 10–16. Retrieved from https://blogs.svvsd.org/admininduction/wp-content/uploads/sites/8/2012/10/ASCD-Wiggins-Feedback-2012.pdf

Williams, A. M., Ford, P. R., Hodges, N. J., & Ward, P. (2018). Expertise in sport: Specificity, plasticity, and adaptability in high-performance athletes. In K. A.

Ericsson, R. R. Hoffman, A. Kozbelt, & A. M. Williams (Eds.), *The Cambridge handbook of expertise and expert performance* (2nd ed.; pp. 653–676). Cambridge, England: Cambridge University Press. http://dx.doi.org/10.1017/9781316480748.034

Williams, R. L. (2013). Overview of the Flynn effect. *Intelligence, 41,* 753–764. http://dx.doi.org/10.1016/j.intell.2013.04.010

Winerman, L. (2016). The debt trap. *Monitor on Psychology, 47,* 44.

Wooden, J., & Jamison, S. (1997). *Wooden: A lifetime of observations and reflections on and off the court.* New York, NY: McGraw-Hill.

Woollaston, V. (2014, October 8). *How often do you look at your phone? The average user now picks up their device more than 1,500 times a week.* Retrieved from https://www.dailymail.co.uk/sciencetech/article-2783677/How-YOU-look-phone-The-average-user-picks-device-1-500-times-day.html

Woollett, K., & Maguire, E. A. (2011). Acquiring "the knowledge" of London's layout drives structural brain changes. *Current Biology, 21,* 2109–2114. http://dx.doi.org/10.1016/j.cub.2011.11.018

World Health Organization. (1946). Constitution. https://www.who.int/about/who-we-are/constitution

World Health Organization. (1988). *WHO psychiatric Disability Assessment Schedule (WHO/DAS) with a guide to its use.* Geneva, Switzerland: Author. Retrieved from https://apps.who.int/iris/bitstream/handle/10665/40429/9241561114.pdf

Worthington, R. L., Mobley, M., Franks, R. P., & Tan, J. A. (2000). Multicultural counseling competencies: Verbal content, counselor attributions, and social desirability. *Journal of Counseling Psychology, 47,* 460–468. http://dx.doi.org/10.1037/0022-0167.47.4.460

Wray, J. (2004, Summer). Haruki Murakami, the Art of Fiction No. 182 [Interview]. *The Paris Review.* Retrieved from https://www.theparisreview.org/interviews/2/haruki-murakami-the-art-of-fiction-no-182-haruki-murakami

'You can't be brave if you've only had wonderful things happen to you': Mary Tyler Moore's best quotes. (2017, January 26). *The Telegraph.* Retrieved from https://www.telegraph.co.uk/women/life/cant-brave-had-wonderful-things-happen-mary-tyler-moores-best/take-chances-make-mistakes-grow-pain-nourishes-courage-have/

Zaentz, S. (Producer), & Forman, M. (Director). (1984). *Amadeus* [Motion picture]. United States: Orion Pictures.

Zeig, J. (2017). The history of the first evolution conference. *The Milton H. Erickson Newsletter, 37*(2), page 4.

Zimmerman, B. J. (2006). Development and adaptation of expertise: The role of self-regulatory processes and beliefs. In K. A. Ericsson, N. Charness, P. J. Feltovich, & R. R. Hoffman (Eds.), *The Cambridge handbook of expertise and expert performance* (pp. 705–722). Cambridge, England: Cambridge University Press. http://dx.doi.org/10.1017/CBO9780511816796.039

INDEX

ABOUT THE AUTHORS

Scott D. Miller, PhD, is the founder of the International Center for Clinical Excellence, an international consortium of clinicians, researchers, and educators dedicated to promoting excellence in behavioral health services. Scott conducts workshops and training in the United States and abroad, helping hundreds of agencies and organizations, both public and private, to achieve superior results. He is the author, coauthor, and coeditor of 14 books and many professional articles on the curative factors of psychotherapy and the development of expertise performance. His work on routine outcome measurement led to the development of feedback-informed treatment vetted and approved by the Substance Abuse and Mental Health Services Administration's National Registry of Evidence-Based Programs and Practice.

Mark A. Hubble, PhD, is a founding member and senior advisor at the International Center for Clinical Excellence. He is the coauthor and coeditor of many professional papers and several books, including the award-winning first edition of *The Heart and Soul of Change: What Works in Therapy* (1999). Mark is a graduate of the prestigious postdoctoral fellowship in clinical psychology at the Menninger Clinic and formerly served on the editorial review board for the *Journal of Systemic Therapies*. In years past, he founded and directed the Brief Therapy Clinic at the University of Missouri–Kansas City and was a contributing editor for what then was *The Family Therapy Networker.* With Scott Miller, Mark has focused his most recent work on expert performance, deliberate practice, and the history and role of "magick" in psychotherapy. Mark is also a professional bass player.

Daryl Chow, PhD, is a senior associate of the International Center for Clinical Excellence. He conducts research and workshops on the development of expertise and highly effective psychotherapists, and ways in which practitioners can accelerate learning. In 2015, his research on the role of deliberate practice in cultivating superior performance in psychotherapy was nominated the "Most Valuable Paper" by the American Psychological Association. Daryl is the author of *The First Kiss: Undoing the Intake Model and Igniting First Sessions in Psychotherapy* (2018), the coauthor of many articles, and coeditor and contributing author of *The Write to Recovery: Personal Stories and Lessons About Recovery From Mental Health Concerns* (2011). Currently, he maintains a private practice at Henry Street Centre, Western Australia, and continues to serve as a senior psychologist at the Institute of Mental Health in Singapore.

Please visit http://www.betterresultsbook.com for more information.

promoting many small ingroups to reduce the perception of Other as intrinsically different/threatening

promoting the identification of "shared fate of mankind"/identification of many smaller "ingroups"

the more communities one is part of, the less that are available to view as a threat.